Horsesnoe Bay

An Autobiography

A Legacy of Loss and Laughter

To Sheila

best wishes

Win

Winifred Rowland

with

Wendy J. Woodcock

Cover photograph of Winifred Rowland by Frederick Rowland,
Guernsey, circa 1960.

Cover photograph of Port Soif, Guernsey,
(Horseshoe Bay) © Mike Bonsall Gallery of Guernsey landscapes
at https://www.mikebonsallphotography.com/

Illustration photo of a sunset at Port Soif, Guernsey (Horseshoe
Bay) © Tim Sebire
Gallery of Guernsey landscapes and seascapes
at https://www.timsebire.co.uk/

For fun, each chapter has a song title which suggests what lies
ahead. You will find the referenced song list and a selection of
my cherished photographs at the end of this book.

Paperback Edition 2 – July 2020
ISBN 978-1-9163169-2-8

Table of Contents

Preface

Expect laughter and sadness when together, we explore episodes in my long life. I became an accidental author, with no intention of writing a memoir. One gloomy winter, I planned to preserve vivid moments and half-forgotten fragments for my family, before they slipped through my mind like seawater in the sand.

When persuaded to celebrate my 90th birthday, it jolted me to register the significance of my grand age. Inside, I still felt 36, vibrant, optimistic, and eager for new experiences. So, I wrote feverishly, as if my time was running out. Like *Scheherazade of the 1001 Nights*, every morning for months, my subconscious branched out and touched those long-forgotten relatives and friends who clamoured to be recorded.

To my surprise, the creativity of writing became all-consuming, a genuine joy, but the process came to a standstill, when, as I raked through my life, I experienced mixed emotions. *Should my innermost thoughts be exposed for other people to pick over?* I overcame my qualms and became philosophical - *This is not a fiction novel; this is my life!*

Memories can contain love and delight, while others are sad, still painful but honest. I longed to evoke a whiff of nostalgia and for readers to enjoy my recollections which offer a glimpse into a different era and, hopefully, a glimmer of inspiration.

I grew up in a deprived grey industrial city in the shadow of war but had a warm and loving family. Evacuation to the countryside became a life-enhancing experience; this verdant landscape became my benchmark.

As I strived to gain an education, it became evident I needed help to progress. The kindness and inspiration from family, friends and strangers made all the difference in my struggle.

My memory is good, but not remarkable, my early background was sketched in using family legends; and my clearest memories start from the age of three. With little distraction, only donated books and newspapers, we enjoyed our own entertainment of songs and recitations. I was raised within a family with live-in grandmothers and aunts who discussed everything and everyone; hence these stories are remembered and passed on.

Years ago, an astrologer analysed my natal chart and said, 'I wonder what you did in your last life, that they gave you such an interesting one in this?' Not a tangible present tied with a ribbon, but a gift of incomparable people, and I will take you to meet them.

Chapter 1 - Living For The City

(Stevie Wonder)

I was born in the rented front room of a three-storey brick house in Red Bank, Manchester, a dirty, rain-soaked and smoke-filled industrial city in the North of England. Our rooms were cramped, too small for a growing family, but despite the chipped paint, damp, and disrepair, my parents, Betsy and Billy Briggs, were grateful to have a roof over their heads.

They called me Winifred, "Winnie", and I was their second daughter, born in March 1927, two years after Elsie, and inherited Mum's fair complexion, grey eyes and glossy blonde hair.

There was an atmosphere of oppressive, sultry stillness on this narrow strip of land, crammed with dark crumbling buildings, which lay between Strangeways Prison and the River Irwell, under a mile from Manchester's city centre.

Perched on the edge of these little backstreets was our house, where languorous, lazy cats stretched out and rolled about on sooty windowsills. It fronted a narrow cobbled street with pavements, edged along one side with iron railings which overlooked the rippling river. There was no rubbish in or around the waterway, and the pungent, pleasant odour of damp soil banks always evoked nostalgia from my first five years.

In Victorian times, Red Bank was a small housing settlement built at the bottom of Cheetham Hill Road, and before the houses became rentals, the middle-class with servants lived pampered lives in the area.

The area declined as the industrialists, bankers, and merchants in cotton and textiles moved away. They had rapidly earned money from a growing Manchester, and wanted homes away from the smoke, grime, and absolute poverty of the centre but close enough to keep an eye on their factories.

This overpopulated slum provided a place of settlement for poor Eastern European Jewish immigrants and others who had fallen on hard times and worked towards improving their lot.

Even in poverty, there were standards; landlords in our road only took in clean, respectable tenants. Mum and Dad were considered decent, a working couple, married with two tiny girls, but they might have been looked upon differently if the owners knew their well-timed history. I can tell you how things *really* began for them, both aged 20, in love and engaged.

In 1924, on the shortest day, the bitter Manchester city afternoon was already gloomy, matching the mood of the young couple as they entered Ardwick's red-brick church, with its musty whiff of stacked hymn books and bibles.

Betsy Rowlands was a tall, wiry girl with perfect teeth and blonde pin curls which skimmed the collar of her green, handmade woollen coat. She hid behind her stocky, round-faced beau, Billy Briggs, as he explained their dilemma to the church minister.

'We have a baby on the way and need you to marry us quickly,' Billy said. He glanced over at Betsy, who blushed, head bowed, too embarrassed to respond.

Unmarried girls tried to hide their pregnancies, were shunned, called sluts and slags, and their families suffered humiliation at the hands of gossips. Boys often denied culpability, which suggested the girl was promiscuous. Hasty shotgun weddings were arranged with no way the culprits could wriggle out of it. Mum and Dad's only recourse was to seek help from the church.

The elderly, chubby priest, Arthur F. Fryer, nodded and pointed to the three oak chairs tucked around his battered vestry table. He joined them and arranged his long, black robes across his knees so they wouldn't crease. The rim of his white dog collar irritated him, hot and tinged with sweat from his long day's work.

He placed his steel-rimmed glasses in front of a well-thumbed Bible, and looked intently at the forlorn couple, 'How far along are you?'

Betsy couldn't look him in the eye and studied where his balding silver hair met his craggy face. Her gaze lowered to the lines around his mouth, gained from years of being inscrutable and kindly disposed of towards his parishioners.

'I've missed one month,' she croaked, as tears trickled down her pale face and she fingered and turned her engagement ring through her woollen gloves.

3

Billy turned to her, dabbed at her cheeks with his folded handkerchief, and rested his stubby, calloused workman's hand on her shoulder. They sat upright in front of this thoughtful cleric, as he took time to ponder, and they waited for a miracle.

Rev. Fryer hated the prospect of this distraught, pretty young woman suffering the horrible, bloody fate of other young parishioners, who sneaked off to illegal backstreet abortionists. Some lost their lives when ignorant, but well-meaning relatives intervened. They recommended drinking a bottle of gin in a boiling-hot bath, falling downstairs, or worse, poking about with a bent, steel knitting-needle.

Billy didn't know then that his sister, Grace, survived the ministrations of a backstreet abortionist and suffered lasting consequences. Her loss of blood resulted in permanent pernicious anaemia, and she required daily medication to function. In her kitchen cupboard, she hid the tins of Pepsac, a powder derived from desiccated hog's stomachs, which she took for the rest of her life.

Looking at the scared young couple through his owlish glasses, the vicar repeated, 'Only one month. That's good. I'll marry you as soon as I can, and no-one needs to know about your predicament.'

The sorry pair perked up, but the cleric shook his head. 'Oh dear, it's Christmas next week, the busiest time in the church calendar.'

Crestfallen, Billy clasped Betsy's hand as they stared at his red, round face, willing him to find a solution.

After a few heartrending moments, the Reverend leant forward, triumphant, 'I'll marry you next week. On Christmas Day.' Betsy wept again, this time with relief and joy.

There's nothing like the shared sense of despair to get things going. Betsy didn't want to get married. She didn't even want to socialise with rough boys like Billy. She felt obliged to go out with him when she heard he had won the right to court her after beating his rival in a punch-up for her affections.

Sex was *the* big secret; sheltered and naïve, she believed only bad girls indulged, but she fell for Billy's persuasive charms, his mysterious green eyes, and sense of mischievousness, which led them to this sorry state.

He adored Betsy, who was worth fighting for, the prize on the block, a real stunner. Although not so sure about him, Billy might turn out to be a diamond in the rough.

Early on Christmas morning, just before the festive service, the small wedding party attended the brief ceremony in a side room in St Silas' Church. Bells rang, and the choir, dressed in their crisp white robes, sang carols softly as the congregation started to fill the pews. The bride and groom signed the register in front of their two witnesses, Betsy's brother, Tom, and his fiancée Elizabeth.

The wedding breakfast was the usual traditional family Christmas lunch. Billy's sister, the slight, fair-haired Grace, had

5

not attended the nuptials. Instead, she'd stayed behind to prepare the festivities; the turkey and trimmings bought cheaply off the market the previous evening. She had enough pennies left over to decorate the living room table with candles and holly. Neighbours loaned her a few chairs to seat the extended family for this token feast of celebration.

That afternoon, Betsy and Billy were thrilled to move into the rented room in Red Bank next to Grace and her young son, George, to start married life and prepare secretly for their baby.

Even though Manchester was a booming textile city, the poorer, working-class, just got on with doing whatever they could to scratch out a living and survive.

Betsy, a pregnant clothes machinist in a factory, was slim, pretty and chosen to model samples of clothes for the occasional wholesale buyers.

It was company policy; expectant mothers left work when they showed the slightest sign of pregnancy. Her bump wasn't evident for months, and she needed to work for as long as possible to pay for a layette, furniture, and rent. She was a hard-working and helpful girl, so the staff turned a blind eye and ignored her bulge for weeks. When she became too large, the management and staff colluded and asked her to stop modelling but stay hidden to work as a machinist.

Their first child, Elsie Briggs, was born in July 1925, within an acceptable gestation period, eight months. No-one questioned the early arrival; they were too busy cooing over the bonny summer baby, with its blonde curls, rosy cheeks, and big blue eyes, who soon became the centre of attention.

They were humble and optimistic, even though surrounded by squalor. Both suffered traumatic setbacks in their schooldays, and as a young married couple, they soon experienced their share of sorrows, which pushed them sideways but didn't knock them down.

Billy's bricklayer wages were low, but they kept their precious rent book up to date with a little left on which to live. They threw nothing away; cut up old towels for nappies, face cloths, and sanitary items. Their families, also with little to spare, helped with household essentials whenever they could.

His pensioner parents, Helena and Albert, lived in a terraced house in a sweep of identical red-bricked homes which stretched to the top of Cheetham Hill. They lived two buses away, on the other side of Manchester, so even though they wanted to, it was impractical to babysit or help with any daily domestic arrangements.

The overwhelming, blackened, industrial landscape rose from the brickfield and had the desolate gloom and foggy air from smoking chimneys, reminiscent of Lowry paintings. Part of this vast area belonged to Billy's family years ago as a thriving brickmaking business. His father lost the company when their bookkeeper stole the profits and jailed for embezzlement.

With no money left, no legal aid, no advice, or other expertise, Billy's family became destitute and forced to rent a small Victorian terraced house, which overlooked the brickfield once owned by them. It must have been heart-breaking, but he was a feisty, cheerful lad, trained as a specialist bricklayer and tiler, and always found enough work.

Betsy's story was no less devastating. Born in Crewe in 1904, she lived a settled life, but it too was destroyed. Her mother, Felicitous Johnson (Cissy), was blonde, with grey eyes and straight white teeth, who worked hard as a seamstress to keep the family together. She married George Rowlands, and at 25, they had Violet May, who died aged two. During the following eight years, three further children were born.

Their family unit was fractured when Cissy received the biggest shock of her life when her eldest daughter, Annie, then 17, breathless from her bicycle ride, announced, 'I've just seen Dad with his other family.'

She was livid but determined to find out the truth. Was her husband leading a double life? She discovered, to her horror, for many years, he'd kept another woman and their children in Nantwich, the adjacent town. It was unbelievable, a secret family just a few miles apart.

Instead of confronting him, as their love had withered long ago, her impulse was to cut and run, but Cissy watched his every move for several months, gathered funds, and put together an escape plan. She couldn't have sued George for bigamy, as he hadn't married again, but she was sick of the pack of lies, glad never to see her philandering husband again.

It was 1917, and the First World War was raging. Most young men were serving in the forces, so plenty of work was available when Cissy, aged 43, moved to Liverpool, to be near her auntie.

Betsy was only 13, not old enough to leave school, but it didn't seem worth enrolling in a new one for just six months. It was more practical that she worked in the club to supplement the family income.

So, from comfortable beginnings, Billy and Betsy had level peggings in the misery stakes. Fateful changes during their youth hadn't embittered them, just made them more resilient and hopeful.

My earliest memory in Red Bank was watching Mum struggle to keep us, and the rooms clean without any hot water on tap or electricity. Each evening, we sat in the living room lit by oil lamps and warmed ourselves beside the shiny black coal stacked on the open fire grate, and in the mornings, Mum disposed of the dusty cinders in the yard. The city boasted Victorian drains, so I imagine there was a toilet outside.

A wave of Jewish immigrant shopkeepers plied their trades or performed menial jobs to survive while they became established.

Mrs Pass (the name suggests a truncated version of Eastern European origin) owned our house. Mum's voice lowered, and face softened whenever she mentioned her name, so I assumed she treated them with kindness.

Mr Putinski owned the bakery next door. 'Putt,' to those who knew him, was a smiley Jewish refugee. When Dad was laid off work because of bad weather, he helped in the bakery on special occasions and during religious feasts. His prowess proved useful and sparked off a love of cooking that in time inspired his children.

The yeasty aroma from the warm bakehouse bread seeped out and couldn't fail to entice passers-by into the shop. To me, a child with an unpolluted palate, the bagels tasted delicious with their smooth, golden crusts and soft, semi-sweet centres.

Throughout my life, I always hoped to find bagels of this quality. The recipe was such a performance; too much fuss in rising and boiling the dough. One mistake, and you gnawed on a hard quoit or a miniature lavatory seat.

I enjoyed the vibrancy of our produce market, and Mum held my hand as we marched to the myriad of stalls within walking distance. The lanes echoed with vendors who shouted and hawked their wares. Ingenious tenants in the tenements ate like kings. At closing time, they lined up and purchased perishable food for a token few pence, rather than let the stallholders throw it away.

I stood mesmerised as marketers purveyed their local fresh fruit and vegetables piled high on wooden trestle tables. A row of butcher's shops flanked them and on the pavement outside, displayed caged hens, dead or alive, and boxes of cheeping day-old chicks who peeped out.

The large pub with an entrance, tiled in vivid green, sold the tastiest ham and lentil soup. In the street, we joined customers and stall keepers and drank the broth from old mugs with one hand free to dunk and chew on fresh crusty bread.

In our smoky ghetto, the corner shop provided everyday necessities and ethnic food. Wooden barrels hampered the doorway, and I was never tall enough to peer inside to see the rollmops, (rolled pickled herrings), but the strong odour of fish in brine permeated the air and always made me hungry.

Moss Side, another inner Manchester slum, was a violent Dickensian nightmare, plagued with disease and crime – "hell on earth", the place you wanted to escape. Redbank was different; these religious people courted a quiet life and worked hard to improve their lives. As a teenager, Red Bank became a dirty word; no-one wanted the stigma of originating from that area of rundown buildings and dismal poverty.

When recent research unearthed black and white photographs depicting the soot-covered enclave of tall, dark, overpowering buildings, it increased my admiration for those warm-hearted and long-suffering tenants. They rose above deprivation and those brutal living conditions.

Decades later, a permanent exhibition was installed at the Manchester Jewish Museum to commemorate the one square mile of Red Bank and the persecuted Jews and ethnics who settled there.

Even though I lived there, my childhood memories differ from those pictures. I remember a peaceful haven with no heavy drinking, noise, or rowdiness. My parents had done an excellent job of sheltering me from the sordid reality of destitution and filth.

Where the outside steps rose to join the house, there was a dark corner where I was well hidden from passersby. One day, as I kneeled and played with my doll, a lady sidled up to me, 'Rats have been seen here, you should move.' I didn't know what a rat was, but it was obviously to be avoided, and I never played there again.

Not a blade of grass or leaf existed amid this grim concrete jungle and greyness, but Mum's mum, Granny Rowlands, told me I created my first makeshift garden there at four years old. With few toys, I played in the streets and one day was thrilled when I found treasure, a discarded biscuit tin lid in the corner of a lock-up shed. I never dared wipe anything on my starched white cotton pinafore, so I removed the soot and grime using the hem of my dark dress.

With one last rub with my sleeve, I peered wide-eyed like a barn owl into the shiny tin lid and could see my out-of-focus reflection; straight blonde hair with the wobbly fringe which bounced off the rim of my round, tortoiseshell glasses.

I wore spectacles because I broke a finger when a heavy door slammed on it at nursery school. The shock left me with an awful squint in my left eye. A flesh-coloured eye patch worn over the stronger eye stimulated the weaker eye muscles to correct the squint. Whenever alone, I was mischievous and lifted the shade to marvel at picture books with both eyes.

Glasses were expensive, so I took extra care not to break mine. For low-income families like ours, living in a city, free healthcare treatment came from the council. In 1931, before the National Health Service started in 1948, progressive eyewear to keep pace with my growth failed dismally. In my two childhood photographs, my specs were oversized when I first wore them, and too small for my face when ready for renewal.

One Sunday, I sat with my prized tin lid on my lap, my legs stretched out onto the dusty grey cobblestones in front of the padlocked row of bicycle lock-ups. Behind one cracked door with peeling green paint was a handcart, that during the week was pushed around the streets to collect old clothes and rags. They exchanged anything for jam jars filled with water and live goldfish. String handles were tied around the rim so children could carry them inside. I never received a goldfish, as we had nothing to throw away.

I scavenged around the street for things to place in my new tin lid and plucked the velvet green moss from the cracks in the pavements and arranged it around the sides. Fragments of jagged stone made a path edged with two pipe cleaners, and shards of red brick led to a make-believe pond, the shiny lid of a cocoa tin. A bench fashioned from a cut cork found in the gutter completed the miniature moss scene.

Mum came to look for me when it got dark and carefully carried my tin lid garden home. For weeks, I kept the moss dampened and nurtured it.

This enjoyment of garden creation has never left me. I still rejoice at the first signs of bulbs and seedlings poking their heads through the earth and the success of cuttings sliced from favourite plants.

Chapter 2 - In The Ghetto

(Elvis Presley)

Dad, a strong swimmer, often waded into the murky, inky-black Irwell River and rescued adventurous, stranded cats from the riverbanks which emerged during dry summers. I saw a film on floods which featured cats swimming and learned they are as proficient as dogs in the water but hated getting their well-groomed fur wet. Perhaps Dad interrupted and rescued them when they were content to be there, basking on the warm sandbanks, feasting on rats. If so, it was ironic the RSPCA awarded him a solid gold medal in a presentation box. In it, we placed the newspaper cutting of the story with his photograph. We thought Mum deserved the medal for washing his wet, dirty, stinking clothes afterwards.

In July 1928, Elsie, their firstborn, tragically died aged three, which I will cover later in this story. In November, my sister Annie was born, (who subsequently wished to be called 'Nan') and two years after, Grace came long. In keeping with the family traits, they were both blonde and named after Mum and Dad's sisters.

Nan had curly hair until I took her underneath the table which I'd turned into a beauty salon and snipped off all her curls. Mum didn't scold me; she was just relieved I hadn't cut Nan or myself with her sharp tailoring scissors. She said, 'It's only hair. It will grow back.' It did, but it grew back straight and was never curly again. Nan never forgave me.

Our family leapt out of abject poverty when they moved from the crowded rented rooms to a rented terrace house in Lyon Street, Ardwick. Granny Rowlands and her sister, my Auntie Annie, already lived there and procured a home for us, a favour from their rent collector. Mum locked away her precious rent book, which recorded our life in Red Bank, and started on a new one for Ardwick.

Mum was still under 30 and stayed at home to raise Nan, Grace, and me. She relished her newfound freedom in her improved living conditions. In Red Bank, washing up was performed in a bowl on the table with water from a kettle hung over the open fire. She shared cooking arrangements with the other lodgers in the dingy rooming house. Here, in Ardwick, Mum had a kitchen to herself, with a flagged stone floor, a cold water tap over a long red shallow pottery sink (slop stone), long enough to take a bowl, and a crockery drainer.

On dry days, to wash our clothes, Mum filled a galvanised dolly tub with lots of soap powder and cold water from the tap in the yard. She inserted the dolly, which comprised a wooden handle, and pole mounted on a round, three-legged stool, which she used to rub the clothes backwards and forwards against the uneven washboard indentations, dislodging the dirt. On rainy days, the kitchen was dank from the washing hung on the kitchen's clothes airer, a pulley with wooden slats, suspended from the ceiling which raised and lowered the laundry. On the rough brick yard wall hung a tin bath on a long nail, a mangle to squeeze the water out of the clothes, and the dolly tub, proud testament to Mum's high standards.

In the far corner of the yard stood a brick-built water closet which housed a porcelain toilet bowl and an incongruous white pottery, pull-flush, that triggered the flow of water from a wooden overhead tank. For toilet paper, we used newspaper scrounged from other people, which we cut into squares and hung on a nail in the lavatory.

In the freezing winter months, we played a game where we waited until the last moment and jumped up and down clutching ourselves rather than face the cold dash to the outside lav. We ignored the old coat and umbrella hung behind the door, and on icy days as we ran past, we rattled the frozen sheets hung on the line.

The other water game took place on Friday nights. We formed a queue in the living room/kitchen and watched as Dad filled the tin bath using pans of hot water. When bathed, we moved into the parlour onto the three-seater sofa and warmed our feet in front of the roaring fire, swathed in large towels with smaller ones wrapped around our heads.

One time, Dad came in and surveyed us, three girls seated in a row. He smiled at Mum, 'Beautiful snow maidens,' he said, and carefully carried the bath out of the kitchen, tipped the grey, lukewarm water into the yard drain, and hung it back on the wall.

17

Dad was a big murder-mystery reader. Agatha Christie's mysteries and detective stories were all the rage in the '30s. So how did Dad know the Russian folktale about snow maidens? Had seeing us in white turbans rekindled his image of the childless woodcutter and his wife, who created their much wanted, living daughter out of snow?

Our cul-de-sac in Ardwick was at the start of a busy, arterial road, a mile away from the city centre. On the right was a terrace of five houses, Granny Rowlands and Auntie Annie occupied the end terrace house. In the house between us lived an older couple with a canary that squawked incessantly through the paper-thin walls. In warmer weather, they sat on their shiny steps with the canary in a cage and viewed the action in the street.

Tenants scrubbed clean their terraced house steps each day and or whitened using pipe-clay or lime donkey stone - an arduous and time-consuming task (and particularly unpleasant on cold days), but often seen as an essential chore.

There was nothing very much for sale in the corner shop that faced our street and the main road. A few bicycle pumps and some utilitarian replacement items were laid in the window, as I remember they provided a breakdown and repair service. It was an odd job sort of place where they charged up our radio batteries.

On the garment factory windows opposite, a thick layer of city grime-covered sheets of thin steel mesh. With little natural light, those workers inside must have resembled troglodytes in the gloom.

At the end of our street was a substantial Victorian junior school, Bank Meadow, from where we could look down a steep incline to the railway sidings and resting trains below. At night, when the noise from the traffic on the road subsided, it left a faint waxing and waning of staccato clatter from the railway wagons shunting together like supermarket trolleys.

Real life was hard; you witnessed daily misery and wretchedness, nothing as stylish or jovial as the *Coronation Street* TV series. It was filthy; no running hot water or electricity was available.

We created thick rugs by punching holes in the sacking and knotting strips of wool from old clothes through it. With constant use, the warm rugs became grimy. So, when Granny Rowlands complained and stopped bashing them with a carpet beater over the clothesline in the yard, we sat around a new piece of sacking and made another rug.

Even though we lived with no money and just enough food to stave off hunger, everyone had time to stop and talk to you. The men seemed jollier in those days, smiled and whistled popular tunes as they went about their chores.

In winter, at school playtime, Granny Rowlands sneaked us hot toast and cocoa, and in summer, cooling lemon drinks. She handed the pottery mugs through the railings to us as if we were jailbirds; my first taste of preferential treatment, to the envy of the other kids.

Every year, during Whit Week, my sisters and I became excited to participate in our local church's Walk of Witness. This procession of Sunday school scholars originated from 1821 to commemorate the coronation of George IV. The walk took place on Whitsunday, 'White Sunday,' as white clothes were worn by the newly baptised on that day. According to the Bible's New Testament, the annual Christian festival commemorated the descent of the Holy Spirit upon the disciples of Jesus Christ.

Our starting place for the walk was the parish church, and we strutted about, dressed to the nines in our new, home-made, long, pale satin dresses and matching white satin shoes. The city congregations were large, and each church allocated two men to hold aloft its woven banner depicting the church's name. The order of the procession began with these banner holders, followed by a brass band, then the Sunday school pupils, and finally, the congregation.

We stately marched from Ardwick to Manchester's city centre, which took about an hour. Buses brought those who lived outside the city so youngsters could participate in the walk, and when they tired, their parents carried them.

When held during scorching summer days, the tarmac melted. We arrived home, horrified to see black pitch covered our white satin shoes and stained the hems of the long dresses. The unsightly damage didn't faze Mum. She threw away the cheap shoes, cut off the blackened hems and shortened the skirts, and we wore them time and time again to the summer Sunday school.

The sooty, crumbling old Dickensian terraces earmarked to be demolished and swept away during the slum clearance, meant we would be in line for a rented council house with a garden. But Mum noticed the slum removal hardly moved, and she didn't want to live there as her children grew, with no hope for a better home in the immediate future.

Motivated and with renewed vigour, she started on the next bout in their fight for a better life. Most people treated rent books with the reverence afforded to passports today. This book held Mum's 'visa', stamped and ready to escape from the decaying backstreets. A pristine rental record was vital to improve your accommodation. Mum ensured she always stayed in the black. A row of red figures showed you were in arrears and disqualified you from applying for a rented house.

Mum felt empowered; she held two record books and possessed a full postal address, not just a room number. With her rental history and steely determination, she was strong enough to stake her claim for somewhere better to live. She lobbied the council housing department but was not eligible, so she contacted various institutions, but they only dealt with the homeless.

For months she kept going to the housing department, and one day a clerk said, 'I can't help you, Mrs Briggs, but these people might.' He scribbled Sutton Housing Trust's contact details on a piece of paper and, by way of introduction, gave her his business card with her name written on the reverse.

Without delay, she visited Suttons and showed the precious card. They completed the application form for her as Mum explained she never learned to write. To have dyslexia and continually show her lack of education must have been a humiliating ordeal.

Later that week, Mum and Dad were astounded and thrilled when a letter arrived from Suttons with a request to visit their office on an estate in Gorton.

Local folklore says Gorton derives its name from Gore Town, from the battles that ensued between the Saxons and Danes around AD890 to 910. The stream which cut through the deep gorge ran red with blood following these skirmishes, now known as Gore Brook. It widened to form a lake and carried onto Reddish, so-called after another battle, where blood left 'reddish' stains.

The office clerk took them to view a semi-detached house with a modest garden. 'This is Forber Crescent. It's only got two bedrooms,' he explained, 'But for you, with all girls, it'll do just fine.' They returned to the office, unable to believe their good fortune.

The clerk handed Mum her two prized rent books and said, 'You won't need these anymore. You pop the rent into us every Friday. Any payment problems just come here.' He smiled, shook hands, and they left the building clutching their now-defunct rent books.

He gave them a copy of their strict rules and informed them that Sutton Trust carried out maintenance and free decoration. They would provide wallpaper samples and colour cards in plenty of time, and the tenants were responsible for the upkeep of the garden and to clip the privet hedges to a specific height.

Sutton Housing Trust, a benevolent organisation, established housing reform. It started in London and expanded to other cities. My family was part of a social experiment in the Manchester area. *I took this reformation for granted, but years later, I hoped they had erected a statue or some recognition given to Mr Sutton, the commendable reformer and philanthropist, but I found nothing. They are still active today, lobbying for the underprivileged.*

In the garden outside the Sutton Trust office, Mum and Dad approached two men.

'Do you live on a Sutton estate?' Dad asked.

One looked up, 'Yes. Are you moving here?'

Dad nodded. 'Forber Crescent. We have three girls and outgrown our old place.' This wasn't strictly true; they desperately wanted to leave the slums.

'Oh, the crescent is safe for kids, in the centre, away from traffic. Gorton Mount School's only ten minutes away, and you can swap houses within the Trust when anything changes.'

It was surreal to Mum and Dad, who, for all their misfortunes and demons, were also proud and intelligent people. They wanted for nothing, took time to settle and enjoy the space and tranquillity of their Utopia.

I returned decades later to Ardwick, and the avalanche of slum clearance hadn't even started. How fortunate for us that Mum was proactive and enterprising and didn't wait.

Finally, they had their own home with a precious patch of green lawn and mature trees. The move transformed our family life; we got dogs and threw balls in the playing field and around the square in the middle of the crescent.

Nan and I, fascinated with greenery, planted our first seeds in cardboard egg boxes. We watered and watched over them, mesmerised when the leggy seedlings grew into healthy specimens which we transplanted into Dad's garden borders. This early start in horticulture, creating something living, tangible, always changing shape, left us both with a lasting love of gardening.

Soon we were joined on our estate by Mum's brother, Uncle Tom, with Auntie Elizabeth, 'Lizzie', and their two sons. Our house was quieter, away from the main road, but it was more convenient for them to be near the shops and the children's playground. Mum thought the free-spirited Lizzie was slightly rough because she frequented the local pubs.

Uncle Tom worked in a brewery and to curtail any thieving; they gave the workers a beer allowance. For extra cash, most of them sold their supplies, but Uncle Tom regularly drank his, which led him down the slippery slope of alcoholism and he died young. This explained why Mum frowned upon anyone who indulged in alcohol.

Chapter 3 - We Are Family

(Sister Sledge)

Grace, the smallest of us, was skinny and fragile, which added to her attraction - an adorable child, whose quiet gentleness charmed everyone. I appointed myself as her guardian, and she revelled in this. Nan, strong and feisty, was not to be bossed by me. One evening, in the kitchen, I ate something of hers, which infuriated her. She rushed at me and, with a lucky punch, knocked me on the jaw and sent me reeling. Dazed, I grabbed the roller towel to save myself from falling. Therefore, from an early age, our sibling hierarchy was established, which left me free to focus on defenceless Grace.

One day, I dislodged a few papers, and an envelope fell out containing three large, individual, black and white professional pictures of Nan, Grace, and me.

My sisters looked cute; Grace had a sweet, heart-shaped face, her light eyes framed by wispy blonde hair, and Nan, a jolly, chubby child with a round face. Mine was shocking, the odd-one-out. I was not wearing glasses, and my squint with the pupil lodged in the corner of my left eye dominated the photograph.

Mum heard me sobbing, grabbed the photos, flung them in the fire, and hugged me. Complexes are rooted in scenarios like this. My assumption was I was ugly-looking without glasses, and just ordinary when wearing them. The saying, *"Boys don't make passes at girls who wear glasses"* was my limiting belief. That attitude was sensible, and I cultivated a *"just get on with it, do your best"* kind of outlook. I expected no one to look twice at me, so diverted my activities towards sewing, swimming, hiking, dancing, and talking.

Childhood traumas are sometimes the peg on which our memories hang. As much as I tried, I couldn't shield my sisters from everything.

Mum and I raced into the kitchen when we heard Grace screaming. In the sink, a disgusting mess of pink plaster floated in the water with a bobbing, decapitated doll's head. Mum sifted for anything substantial in the flotsam and angrily whispered to me, 'The body was papier mâché. What a cheat.'

I wrapped my arms around Grace to stop her crying, while Mum performed the funeral rites, a visit to the dustbin. From then on, whenever she bought other china dolls, she ensured the bodies were also porcelain.

Dad found us moulded, life-sized, shiny celluloid dolls. They were solid but beautiful, just like actual babies with painted hair, pink cheeks and blue eyes. We dressed them in handmade hand-me-down clothes outgrown by the newborn babies. Celluloid was not the perfect material for toys; hard, flammable and deteriorates if exposed to moisture. It's also prone to cracking and yellowing, nowadays forbidden for manufacturing dolls.

Traffic was sparse; we only encountered the clip, clop of horses and carts that delivered sacks of coal, and the clinking of glass milk bottles from the milkman on his electric float who stopped by before breakfast.

The big boys arranged rounders, rode bikes and roller skates, while the girls played hopscotch and skipping. I begged the boys to teach me roller skating. We set off, one lad on each side, holding me up by my arms. I travelled a short distance before I lost control of my legs, did the splits which tripped the boys up, and we ended in a tangled mess in the middle of the road. This mayhem caused hoots of laughter but never any bullying or nastiness.

In the slums, we had cats, but such capricious creatures often moved to more desirable, quieter residences with tastier morsels. Toddler Grace was inseparable from the new tin pram that Dad had found. He hammered it into shape and gave it a new wheel. It didn't matter to her that it didn't match. He offered to do it up, even though paint was costly, and she didn't notice the inexpensive sludge colour he painted the battered bodywork. To engage with her, kindly passersby would peep inside the pram and automatically say, 'What a pretty dolly'. They jumped back when our latest cat stared up at them and blinked. The pram was only eighteen inches high, so Grace soon outgrew it.

As soon as we moved to a house with a garden, Dad bought us a handsome white and brown collie, who suited the name, Patch. I have enjoyed several pets in my long life; fewer things have given me greater pleasure.

One Saturday morning, when about seven years old, I stood on the back doorstep and let the spring sunshine warm my face. I noticed the sparkling blanket of droplets on the lawn and smiled. No school today.

Mum came up behind me. 'Your Dad will be pleased with this heavy dew on his plot,' she said, looking across the lawn to our veg patch before returning inside. 'Your toast is ready. Auntie Grace sent another jar of her marmalade.'

I plastered my warm toast half an inch deep with this homemade gold while she looked on and shook her head with disapproval at such greed.

Dad had already left the house as he started work at dawn. The overtime paid for a start on the stockpile of dried and tinned food, stored on top shelves in the pantry for the wintertime when wet weather stopped construction work, and he didn't get paid. Coal was bagged up and hidden behind the shed. Here is where we learned self-control and restraint. For Mum, wartime rationing was a joke; with no money, she had been on rations all her life.

Mum handed me a sixpenny bit and the homemade sacking shopping bag. 'Dad left this for you to buy a bottle of pop for a picnic.' I dropped the polished silver coin into my little purse and ran off, hoping to surprise the other two if I got back before they woke.

Patch always accompanied me when I went out walking, and I turned to ensure he was scampering behind. In that brief, dizzying moment, a squeal of brakes shattered my young life.

29

I glanced at the car, slewed across the road, and watched the driver tumble out in haste. The impact had thrown Patch into the street. I darted across as my stomach churned, too shocked to speak, as I helped to pick him up. He lay unconscious, warm and heavy, as we carried him onto the pavement. I sat on the flags, legs outstretched, and they draped him across my knees, but nothing moved. His tongue lolled out of his mouth; he lay silent, like a broken dolly.

I flinched at the tiny pool of blood left on my lap, when Mrs Kilgour, our neighbour, helped scoop him onto a blanket and tenderly placed him on the car's back seat.

She said to the stunned driver, 'I was just behind and saw him race across. You couldn't have stopped in time.' The driver was blameless, and I whimpered when I heard him mention the word *vet*.

The driver scribbled down my address, and Mrs Kilgour waved her arm toward our crescent. He drove off with Patch cradled in the blanket.

Mrs Kilgour pulled me to my feet, and half carried me, sobbing, around the corner to my home.

An hour later, the driver came to the house with Patch's collar. Mum answered the door, 'I'm so sorry,' he said, looking guilt-ridden and glum. 'How's your little girl?'

In the hallway, I heard his words, 'Three broken legs, no hope of a full recovery.' I dashed and locked myself in the lavatory to weep; the one place in the house where privacy was guaranteed.

I sobbed longer and harder than I'd ever done before and only agreed to unlock the door when Mum whispered, 'Nan and Grace are very upset too. Do come out, they need you. It wasn't your fault.'

I splashed my burning, red face with cold water and stepped out.

'Why don't you take your sisters to the shop to buy the pop,' Mum suggested, draping her arm around my neck.

Still in shock, wrung out with red sore eyes, I trudged with them to the corner shop. The warmth had left the sun.

What followed was a blur. Over dinner, as everyone sat in morose silence, my parents exchanged pained glances across the table.

'No more dogs,' Mum shouted, shattering the silence, 'We can't go through this again.'

Poor Mum - not only had she lost a delightful and much-adored pet but had witnessed her beloved children have their first taste of death. Later in life, she told me, 'You get used to it.' She was so wrong.

A few weeks later, after tea, Auntie Grace, she of the marmalade and delicious coconut cake, walked in, wearing her big black coat. A strange time to come, we thought.

'Your Mum said I could bring you this,' she said, her eyes sparkling. She resembled a conjurer pulling a rabbit out of a hat, as she lifted a small black puppy from her deep pocket and placed it in my hands.

31

Mum and Dad stood behind her to watch our happy faces and Dad produced the box the fluffy little creature came in.

'My old jumper can be his bed,' Grace offered and ran upstairs two at a time. She returned with a moth-eaten woolly and smoothed it around the box. 'He has such shiny eyes and silky black fur.'

Dad said, 'That's his name then, Blacky.'

Losing Patch, the way we did, cast a shadow over us and I thought my heart would never mend, but when I saw Blacky's warm, soulful, brown eyes, I melted and fell in love again. I also learned a hard, heart-breaking lesson: no dog ever left our house without being on a lead.

I received another unexpected gift that would open a world of storytelling. My junior schoolteacher supplied me with a coveted library card that started my lifelong book obsession. We owned a few dog-eared classic books, received as presents or Sunday School prizes. With a library card, I now had hundreds of books at my disposal, just half an hour away from home, a bottomless wonderland at my fingertips.

It was of the utmost importance to Mum that I learned to read and write. I hadn't appreciated Mum had dyslexia; I thought she just couldn't write very well because she had missed out on an education. The teachers must have known I had to write my sick notes on Mum's behalf.

One day, I came home from school to find Blacky had chewed my library book to shreds. I was inconsolable, wept, and wailed. My life was all but over.

Mum gathered the soggy pieces, waved the brown paper bag, and said, 'Put your coat on, we're going to the library to explain.'

In the library entrance, my hands sweated, and my knees knocked. It took a real act of courage to step inside.

Before we reached the counter, the librarian must have summed up the scene; the abject fear on my tear-stained face and a concerned Mum who carried the bag of remnants.

In her heartiest voice, the lady boomed, 'Had a little accident with your book, have we?'

I peered over my glasses in utter shame.

She smiled, 'I've got another copy if you haven't finished it. We can't let a little thing like a broken book stop you from reading, can we?' With a flourish, she stamped the inner cover of the duplicate and handed it to Mum.

'When you go to senior school, you'll have two tickets,' she promised. I brightened up and imagined myself with a stack of books and dreamt of other worlds.

Mum handed me the paper bag which held the precious replacement, and I couldn't get out of there fast enough.

At home, as Dad took our coats, I held out the new book and relayed our story. 'I was so scared to go in, but the lady at the library wasn't angry and stamped me a new one. She told me I get two library tickets at senior school.'

He nodded, looked down at me and said, 'Come on, lass, wash your face, and make your Mum a nice cuppa tea.'

Nan and I often made up stories and acted out plays where Grace was the heroine, but we were set up for life when I got my library ticket. We often did our chores with a book propped up somewhere convenient, such as when we washed dishes, the book balanced on the windowsill at eye level.

My favourite books were Little Women and Pride and Prejudice, and they had the most influence on me growing up. I loved the cosiness and family-oriented stories and the lessons learned by each character.

At the Victorian-style junior school, Nan and I passed the 11-plus exam. It meant nothing to us at the time as we were poor and nobody from our estate expected to go to Grammar school. We knew our parents didn't have any money for the Grammar uniform or tennis racket, so we looked forward to starting at our local senior school, Spurley Hey, with its vast playing fields and glass-walled classrooms.

I had two favourite teachers there, one, plain and dumpy but a marvellous classical pianist. She would play dreamy, romantic music such as Schubert, Chopin and Schuman as we assembled in the hall each morning. The other, a beautiful redhead with green eyes, taught art and gave us free rein to explore our artistic ideas on whatever subject she set. Once more, I experienced heaven while gaining knowledge, which added to the enjoyment of my schooldays.

Christmas was simple in our household. A cooked family dinner, of course, but not a grand affair. We were unaware of any poverty, as we got involved in fun things leading up to the big day. We created endless lengths of twisted paper chain decorations with coloured paper strips stuck together with a paste, mixed from flour and water.

Nan often beat me at games like draughts and cards, and Mum kept us busy in the dreary winter months as we cut out, pasted, and crayoned Christmas cards to hand around the family. Dad knocked nails into the mantlepiece, and we were always thrilled to find three stockings hanging there, each stuffed with an apple, orange, and nuts.

I wasn't often naughty, but on Christmas Eve, encouraged by my sisters, we waited until Mum and Dad went out to grab the last-minute bargains of turkey and trimmings before the markets closed.

I clambered onto a sturdy kitchen chair and perched on the wringer's tabletop. From the kitchen's top shelf, I pulled the line of "hidden" presents towards me and remembered the exact layout as I handed each one down to Nan.

Mum had saved up for months for dolls, drawing and colouring books, crayons and games. Our main present was a book, a large annual edition of our favourite comic, and she let us choose which one we wanted each year. She wrapped individual items in smoothed-out brown paper or old Christmas wrapping, saved and ironed from earlier gifts.

We carefully undid the string bows and wrapping paper and decided between us which items we wanted. Grace always wanted the doll, Nan, the colouring book and crayons, and of course, I chose the reading books. After we agreed on our selection, we re-wrapped each gift, and I replaced the packages into their exact spot on the shelf.

It always amazed our parents that on Christmas Day, we took one glance at our gifts and immediately started to swap. We always had a happy day, and everyone was thrilled with their Christmas presents.

We were lucky with our neighbours. Laura Chilton lived opposite and became my best friend in junior school. Mousy and easily frightened a contrast to her sophisticated, beautiful sister, eight years older than us. She seemed to have an enthralling, glamorous life and was happy to let us sit and watch her apply make-up, set her hair in the latest fashion and twirl around in her various evening dresses ready to go out to the dance hall.

The mysterious adult world fascinated me; so, Laura and I set out to find more information on babies after Mum told us she was growing yet another.

Mum said to us, 'When it's ready, it'll know the time and pop out.'

I asked Granny Rowlands how it came out. 'It comes out the way it got in,' she explained which puzzled us even more. Laura and I explored our stomachs. Problem solved; it uses the belly button.

In the classroom, those already in the know giggled and gave furtive glances. A classmate whispered, 'It's all about the penis.'

We dashed home to the unhelpful ancient dictionary. It informed us, '*Penis: the male member, the sexual organ.*'

Laura stared at me and said, 'Sounds to me like someone in the choir.' We shrieked with laughter and closed the book. We lived such sheltered lives, but that was about to change.

It took a lot for me to relive and write the details of the following incident because, until now, it was my shameful secret.

Gorton had a recreational area, a stretch of parkland maintained by the Council. There were two vast, clean water-storage reservoirs in acres of open land, locally known as 'The Rezzers.' In summer, I swam there in the warm shallows with our dog, Blacky, while other family groups picnicked.

One afternoon, I held hands with Nan and Grace as we stumbled over the deserted scrubland to where we saw a middle-aged man fishing. We plonked ourselves beside him, and dangled our legs over the concrete edging, keen to check if he'd caught anything. He slipped his hand into his pocket and offered me toffees. Alarm bells rang. I distinctly heard Mum's voice saying, 'Never take sweets from a stranger.'

There was something creepy about him as he breathed heavily and widened his shark-like grin. He pointed to his lap, and I peered over, stunned and disgusted to see him holding up his penis. It was the first time I had seen an adult one, fully erect.

I looked away and stood frozen for a moment, knowing I needed to run, and blot this terrible predator from my memory. Horrified, I stayed calm, so my sisters were unaware of anything awkward.

'Better get going now. We're late,' I mumbled, grabbed my sisters' hands, and hurried them away.

His hollow laughter followed us. I can still hear it.

I was only eight, so never told Mum what I'd seen for fear of upsetting her and having our walks in the park curtailed. That experience made me cautious of strangers, a mother tiger guarding her cubs.

Shame is a powerful thing. I hid this dirty, guilty secret for decades. It made me weep long after, to know this sick, perverted flasher got his kicks by upsetting me and distorting my innocence. The sordid memory of this prowling pervert, exposing himself to children, still bothers me. For a time, it made me wary of men, and whenever a man tried to get close to me, I stiffened, flinched, and willed him to go away.

In January 1936, it was a sombre time. King George V's health had deteriorated, and people sat around the radio and listened for news. Solemn music played all day long, and every hour they gave a short bulletin on his health. He died on 20th January, and King Edward VIII ascended the throne. He caused a constitutional crisis when he proposed to his lover, Wallis Simpson, the American divorcée, and abdicated later that year, succeeded by his younger brother, George VI.

Government changes or royal accession made no real difference in our lives, but our huddled household was looking forward to happy news. My two sisters and I danced around our cramped bedroom with excitement, eager to cuddle the new baby when it arrived. A midwife dressed in a blue uniform chatted with Mum downstairs. Dad, not at work, fussed around the home in a palpable air of expectation. He promised to wake us when the baby was born. We were still chatting in bed when he bounded up the creaky stairs.

Dad was over the moon. 'It's a boy!' he shouted, unable to contain his excitement. 'We've called him William. You can see him and Mum first thing tomorrow.' The firstborn son often took the father's name, so no surprises there.

In the morning, as soon as we heard the baby's cry, we stumbled downstairs. In the living room, we peered at baby William, who resembled a doll lying in a drawer, the makeshift crib. After a few days, Mum and Dad took him to the hospital, and every day for a week, they visited him. When we asked about him, there were furtive glances between them, but it was a shock to us all when they brought him back, dead. They cosseted him in a shoebox-sized casket, adorned with white satin frills and lace. His tiny body lay in state, incongruous on the lounge sideboard, surrounded by pale flowers.

Our neighbours came to view him, lying in his miniature coffin, and cry. We explained he was born with a defective heart, destined for a miserable life if he lived. When they heard this, they understood and stopped sobbing.

On one rare occasion, I ate my tea alone, and my eyes strayed across the table to my image reflected in the mirror over the mantlepiece. Superimposed was the scene my mind still refuses to bury. Behind me, my baby brother lay in his open coffin. Startled, I turned away from the mirror, but I still smelt the cloying, heady perfume of lilies that wafted across the room. It was the first time I sat so around the sickly-sweet smell of death. That shocking image of my baby brother in his tiny funeral casket has stayed with me, seared in my memory, for over 80 years.

Most of our relatives are not aware that above Sunny Brow Park, in the churchyard, is the headstone for William Briggs, aged two weeks, whom I never got to hold or cuddle.

In those days, children seldom attended funerals, and a kindly neighbour looked after us for the afternoon. When I returned home, I found Dad alone in the living room, crying, terrible, racking sobs which shook his shoulders. It shocked me, as I believed men were strong and unbreakable. He had kept a stiff upper lip at the funeral to support Mum and let it all out when he reached home. With anxiety and fear on my face, Granny

Rowlands, a calming presence, explained that men always wept when they lost a baby son.

Mum had already lost one child, Elsie, and even though William was unplanned, and they could ill afford it, as the baby grew inside, her maternal instincts kicked in. But when he died, she was stoical and, being a busy working mother, with three young children, had to push it aside and get on with everyday life.

Chapter 4 - School's Out

(Alice Cooper)

Whenever Auntie Grace took us out for the day, we always had fun. We got off the bus at the busy Cheetham shopping centre, bought sweets, and she called into her pub to say "hello" and for just "one glass". They didn't allow children inside, so we played in another impressive green-tiled doorway. The pub was busiest during lunchtime, and we were overjoyed when occasional customers sneaked out chocolate for us as they left. Sometimes other children joined us, and we played hopping on and off the step.

Mum would have been furious if she had known Auntie Grace had abandoned us on a public house step for an hour, and I had the good sense not to tell her.

After the foray to the pub, we walked to her flat for lunch and a slice of her delicious home-made coconut cake.

On our way to the bus home, we joined other families in a queue outside the Crumpsall Biscuit Works, owned by the Co-op. White-coated workers came out and for a shilling, gave us a stiff brown paper bag with hundreds of the day's freshly baked biscuits. We waited for our bus and nibbled at the few broken ones, while the other joyful groups carried their precious haul home.

When our bus arrived, Auntie Grace spoke to the bus driver, and we crammed ourselves into the front seat behind him. Nan held the biscuits with care, and I warmed Grace's cold hands.

Our dinner was ready for us when we got back, and we fell into bed, our stomachs full of biscuits. Nan slept in a single bed, and as Grace always felt the cold, even in summer, I shared the double to keep her warm. Throughout the winter, Dad spoilt us by placing hot water bottles in our beds before we retired. We hugged them until they turned cold, then we threw them out onto the wooden floor, and nodded off, warm and snug.

While I was fascinated by the nearby grown-up world, Nan and Grace loved going off on adventures. It was usual for them, young girls of eight and six, to play outside with the other kids on our street or wander off on their own, in any weather. On the estate, everyone knew where each child lived, and naturally looked after each other's wellbeing. We had grown up together, attended the same school, and the neighbourhood was safe to walk without your parents, play in the park or go shopping.

I usually accompanied my sisters, but because it was cold, damp, and snowing, I preferred to stay in to help Mum with her sewing. It was a treat to have Mum to myself.

By six o'clock, they had still not returned for their tea. Mum had left the sitting room curtains open and peered out of the window into the dark grey gloom. The relentless snowfall had stopped at last.

She paced the room, her drained face as white as the path outside. 'Where are they?' she said, her eyes wide with concern.

Seeing her upset and curtain-twitching, Dad reassured her from the sofa. 'They can't be very far. Nan's stomach will bring them home.'

I was optimistic as Nan seemed to be a sensible child and could cope in most situations and expected them to walk in at any minute, with her asking for food. Mum bustled about trying to settle, frustrated.

No-one had telephones, and there was no point in searching on such a large estate. On the brink of tears, Mum's voice cracked, 'They could be anywhere.'

Dad, also now worried, tried to be hearty and reassuring as he got up, and tied the laces of his heavy, black working boots. Mum fumbled in the hallway and brought us our warmest coats and gloves.

We left the back door unlocked, hall light on, and curtains open. Smiling wanly, Dad grabbed my hand and assured me, 'We're going to Belle Vue Police Station. They'll know what to do.'

We slithered along the path and followed the line of lamplights reflected in the wet pavement. The snow shimmered in the light, and I deliberately breathed out heavily to watch my trail of white steam evaporate in the iciness.

Half an hour later, in the warm police station waiting room, Mum and Dad sat staring into mugs of scolding tea while I gnawed on a shortbread biscuit.

As the minutes passed, Mum, pale and silent, wrung her hands and wondered if she'd ever see her kids again. Dad sat beside her, intense and gloomy. Through their bravado, their fear still transmitted to me. My heart raced as my mind whizzed into overdrive. I thought they might be outside, lying abandoned, frozen solid in the snow, and panic set in. I whimpered, and Dad put his arm around me.

'Don't worry, lass. They'll be found soon enough.' After an hour which seemed like an eternity, a policeman burst in, eager to tell us the cheerful news.

'Tucked up in bed they are,' he said, breaking into a smile. 'My colleague at Cheetham peeped in at them. Mrs Briggs will bring them back when the weather clears. It gave her a right shock, I can tell you, when she opened the door to a bobby. She presumed you knew where they were. Little monkeys.'

They had dropped in on Dad's sister, Auntie Grace, a two bus-ride away, but when the snow worsened, she decided to keep them indoors, safe and warm. This bus journey was not out of the ordinary for Nan and Grace as they'd done it several times with me.

Dad, relieved, turned down the offer of a lift home in the police van as the bobbies had been helpful enough. A successful

45

search is the rewarding side of police work, and we left the two policemen smiling at a job well done.

On the way back, we hardly spoke as we shuffled along the craggy, icy path. It was a quicker journey back as Dad decided the snow reflected enough light to illuminate the shortcut by the railway track.

'Snowballs tomorrow,' croaked Mum, who had suddenly found her voice.

'Hot cocoa and an early night,' Dad announced, as he locked the doors and drew the curtains.

I fell into my bed, alone, but eager to relate my adventure to the truants the following morning.

Mum distrusted Uncle Charlie because she had heard he was a boozer with a past. We girls loved him; a tall, bluff and hearty, a Father Christmas-type figure. If he had hidden a dodgy background, nobody discovered it. He 'took up' with Dad's sister, Auntie Grace and when 'they could,' they married, to enable her to draw a widow's pension. We found this marriage amusing, as they seemed old to us children. It turned out to be a good investment since she outlived him by decades.

I knew her as a middle-aged lady, petite, blonde, with pink cheeks and unusual green eyes resembling Dad's. She was something of a wild spirit and, as a young girl, she had got in with the wrong crowd, married a black sailor who left her and their infant child, George, and returned to life at sea. 'At least he married her,' they'd said.

Mum told me Auntie Grace's story as a cautionary tale - the difficulties and stigma facing a woman with an illegitimate mixed-race child in severe and hostile 1920s Britain.

There are few secrets these days. While researching our family tree, George's birth certificate was requested; it listed no father, just his mother's maiden name. No marriage had taken place. The clan kept that secret for years, to avoid the double shame of the boy, labelled in those days, "a black bastard".

George inherited the best traits from both races. With small delicate facial features and warm caramel skin, he resembled a dark version of my Dad. I remember, years later, when I sat on George's knee and ran my fingers through his hair, the texture of his black, tight curls, a complete contrast to my fine, straight, blonde hair. As a goal-scoring footballer, he was popular, lovable, with a throaty, infectious laugh. Even as the only mixed-race boy in his school, he never experienced being bullied.

His employers observed his long-standing affinity with animals and employed him as a carter for the railway. Magnificent brown Shire horses pulled the carts and wagons and delivered goods from the railway to the factory premises. He treated the horses as if they were his children, and in his spare time, he took me to the stables under the arches, to tend to them. I always kept out of their way at the rear of the yard as they towered menacingly over me. They were gentle heavy-looking beasts with glossy brown coats and a wealth of hair which formed their manes. In contrast, they had white "feathers", horsehair that splayed out and swamped their hooves which shimmied as they walked. Pungent horse manure still reminds me of my dear cousin George.

When he retired, they gave him a fitting leaving present of a large fine-china Beswick Shire horse. It remains with us; we appreciate the perfect detailing, its sentiment, and hold it as an heirloom for the next generations.

George never married, despite longstanding liaisons. Auntie Grace wanted to confide in someone, and told me of a mystery, on pain of death if I ever told another soul. She had discovered, hidden in his bedroom drawer, a black-and-white photograph which showed a dark-skinned toddler who looked very much like George at the same age. She presumed it was his and craved to be part of this child's life. It was a shame he never mentioned his secret lovechild, and neither did we.

Everyone loved Auntie Grace. At her funeral, the black hearse made a detour past two pubs. Her friends came out and stood on the pavement and raised their glasses to a sparky old lady.

After junior school lessons, I often took Nan to play in Sunnybrow Park in Gorton. It was a picturesque clearing surrounded by mature trees. The hilly landscape ruled it unsuitable for housing but a perfect location for a park. The steep path to the lake quickened my pace to the brick-built bridge that spanned the stream which dropped to a trickle in summer.

Nan, who took a different steeper slope, slid down the damp, slippery grass on her bum. I glanced to my right, in time as she veered towards a sheer drop, a cut-away made for a new summerhouse. She took avoiding action, slithered, toppled over, and broke her arm. Mum never blamed me. She knew it was just Nan's adventurous spirit and rotten luck.

Mum had a busy life and ran an efficient household. She kept the rooms clean, shopped on a tight budget, cooked and cared for three young children, and even found moments to be attentive to Dad, who worked most of the time. A natural diplomat, she was the only person I knew who cut a cake at the dining table, and measured slices using a school ruler, to avoid unrest and mumbling.

One afternoon, Mum sent me to buy an emollient for her chapped lips. After brushing the paths, she automatically applied the stick to the edges of her lips and came inside. We shrieked and fell about with laughter; she had outlined her mouth in bright red, looking like a grotesque clown. I'd accidentally bought lipstick, not Lipsyl.

Mum hung her head and slunk away, ashamed we would treat her like that. She worked so hard and thought we were disrespectful to mock her. It was punishment enough for us that we had upset her with our selfish behaviour.

As a female-dominated household, Mum taught us to use the treadle sewing machine at a young age before we'd even learnt to read and write. At home, we created a toy post office and acted as postmasters. I fashioned imitation postage stamps by running the unthreaded needle up, down, and across pieces of paper to make perforations.

Dad cultivated my interest and passion for gardening. On days off, Dad loved nothing more than tending our small swathe of greenery and the plot crammed with rows of a variety of vegetables. Not one for planting daffodil or tulip bulbs, marigolds, or potting on flowers and shrubs, the tiny greenhouse lay empty until summer when he grew his prized tomato plants up strings. It was such a fuss for nothing because you could buy cheap tomatoes on the market. His crops were so proliferous; he always managed to exchange them for his evening pint at the local pub, The Haxby, trading a jar of home-grown pickled shallots or whatever veg was plentiful.

Auntie Annie made huge top-quality industrial tents, and we spent month-long seaside holidays in Blackpool in one of them when our two families camped together during August. We enjoyed the anticipation and organisation for these memorable excursions as much as going on them. A week beforehand, a train transported our cabin trunks of provisions, pots, pans, and camping essentials. We didn't own duplicates of anything, and it was fun to make do at home with odd assortments of cups and utensils in the week leading to our trip.

When we arrived at Squiresgate campsite, miles outside Blackpool, a massive bale of prickly straw was waiting for us to fill our mattresses. We had sewn enormous bags together from old cotton sheets, which were filled and rolled up during the day to provide seating. We threw rugs over them to stop our legs from being pricked by the sharp straw.

Eight of us shared the tent, sleeping head to toe, and Dad joined us at weekends when he had time off work. Each morning, the smell of bacon wafted over the campsite. We salivated while waiting for our breakfast of fried eggs and crispy bacon, cooked outside on the primus stove, a welcome change from cereal or toast we had at home. We spent weeks enjoying beach activities, swimming in the freezing sea, running up and down sand dunes. It seemed like our school holidays were always sunny and lasted forever.

Chapter 5 - What A Wonderful World

(Louis Armstrong)

How many people can pinpoint a pivotal moment in their life, however fleeting, that made the most impact on their outlook, choices and ambitions? For me, it was 31st August 1939, and I was eleven years old when Mum and Dad called Nan and me into our sitting room.

'Your school is being evacuated tomorrow. You're taking a train to the countryside and living with another family.'

'Ooh, great. How long for?' I asked and smiled at Nan. We weren't clingy children who worried about separation, we loved anything out of the norm and revelled in an adventure. Mum had brought us up to be inquisitive, robust, resilient and independent.

Mum continued, 'No-one knows how long, but treat it like one of our Squiresgate camping holidays. We're staying behind to take care of things and will visit as often as we can.'

I wasn't concerned, we'd been apart before and always enjoyed it, so why would this be any different? As part of a larger family, there was a continuous interchange between our cousins, and we often stayed over at each other's houses.

At school, we had heard rumblings and rumours about an impending war, how Hitler had invaded Poland and could be heading our way. As a child, Europe seemed so far away, and we had no concept of how or whether it would impact our lives. It turned out this World War II would transform our lives for six years and beyond.

We got caught up in "Operation Pied Piper", the largest and most concentrated mass movement of people in Britain's history. They temporarily evacuated certain civilians and children to safer places in the countryside from densely populated cities or areas at a high risk of bombing or invasion.

That evening we visited our sister Grace, who, at only eight years old, was quarantined in hospital, with an infectious virus, scarlatina. At the isolation unit, we placed our hands over hers through the glass screen as we said, 'Goodbye, for now, and see you soon.'

All that mattered for us was that she was over the worst of her illness. They delayed her evacuation and, as pioneer, protective sisters, we were excited and ready to pave the way for her to join us.

The following morning, Mum and Dad walked with us to the school and watched as they herded us into our classes. I don't remember being upset, sad, or noted anyone who displayed histrionics as we left our parents. I'm sure there must have been some heart-wrenching moments, but nothing registered with me. I'm surprised, we treated it so lightly as the war was imminent, and this could have been the last time we were to be together as a family. No doubt, they kept a stiff upper lip for our benefit, until out of sight.

They evacuated the whole school, including teachers, and we were taken by bus to London Road Station (now Piccadilly) where we boarded the 40-minute train to Macclesfield, a busy factory town.

Our evacuation train left the station, crammed with silent schoolkids carrying small suitcases, and a cardboard box strung across their bodies that contained a gas mask in case of chemical attacks. The Ministry of Health leaflet had shown Mum what we needed to pack: a change of underwear, nightclothes, house shoes or plimsolls, spare socks, a toothbrush, comb, towel, soap, and face washcloth. Instructions issued each child to wear a warm coat with handkerchiefs in the pockets, a name label with school and evacuation authority pinned to our lapels and to carry a packed lunch.

With such precise military organisation, the children in our group looked nervously at each other, anxious, a little scared but secure, in this mass exodus.

It must have been traumatic for thousands of families up and down the country who had undertaken voluntary separation from their loved ones. Mum and Dad had a nervous wait to find out where the authorities had relocated us. A few days later, they received relief in the form of a postcard notification.

Government ministers used private billets rather than create evacuation camps. It was an epic logistical challenge, with thousands of volunteers all over England who provided practical assistance and snacks at train stations and cared for those exhausted, scared or tearful children.

Sutton's Village Church was a small, Victorian, gothic-style building perched on a hill in the rural suburbs. Nan and I treated it as a voyage of discovery, as we sat on the front wooden pew in the half-empty hall and waited for our prospective foster parents to claim us.

We giggled as we assessed the people who arrived to collect their new charges and rather fancied a jolly farmer, but he was not for us. I started to become anxious when we were the only ones left. What would happen if we weren't collected?

Our fleeting worries disappeared when a dark-haired, good-looking man in a suit smiled as he approached us. In a breathless and deep cultured voice with a slight Canadian accent, he introduced himself, 'Phew! I'm Douglas Curphey, and I apologise for my delay.' He looked at me with kind hooded eyes and enquired 'Winnie?' and turned to Nan, 'And you must be Annie?'

We nodded, and he scooped up our little suitcases and led us to his Austin 8 motorcar. As we strode over, I looked over at Nan and gave her a reassuring delighted smile and took her hand. I realised we were lucky to have such a welcoming, protective guardian, and obediently we hopped onto the polished leather back seats. It was a special treat to be driven, as working-class people didn't own cars and only rode in taxis for special events, like weddings or funerals.

At our new home-away-from-home, the younger Mrs Mary Curphey waited for us. She was an attractive, caring, elementary school teacher with curly brown hair, subtle makeup, in a smart woollen suit. Her fragrance of sweet floral perfume wafted about as she greeted us.

Their two-storey house, Gaw End House, Lyme Green, had been built for them, on a hill on the corner of one of her mother's fields. It was modern but had a doll's house quaintness.

Mr Curphey told us he worked for the Education Committee, visiting headmasters. We found out later he held a prestigious School Attendance Officer, hence the car and petrol allowance.

Mrs Curphey showed us to our room, apologetic we were sharing. It was a bright, first-class billet, a welcoming, snug room with floral wallpaper and two single wrought-iron beds piled with cosy throws and cushions, like nothing I'd ever seen before. We didn't mention we slept three abreast in our bedroom at home and pushed the single and double bed together to make room to walk around.

I dashed over to the large picture window, and gazed, in awe at the unspoilt, quiet stretch of green open meadows, dotted with brown grazing cows. Mrs Curphey was pleased with our reaction and showed us into their third bedroom, used for storage. She pulled open a drawer, stockpiled to the brim with large slabs of dark chocolate, her insurance against food shortages. We told her we knew about rationing, and during our stay, we were never tempted; her chocolate was sacrosanct against starvation.

Chocolate was worth stockpiling because it lasted years. After the Great War, they found secret stocks of edible chocolate and tinned fish. I can imagine revellers tucking into feasts of chocolate and sardines on Armistice Day, 1918?

One morning, from the kitchen window, I noticed next door's cows were creating havoc. They had broken the fence and stampeded into our garden. I shouted, 'Cows in the garden!' I grabbed Nan, and we raced outside. Being a city child, afraid of cows, I was no help. He never swore, but as Mr Curphey rounded them up, we were shocked when he shouted, 'Those bloody cows are eating my cabbages.'

I stood at a distance, in admiration, as Nan got stuck in. Without fear, she slapped the cow rumps and vigorously shoved them towards the field.

Nan was incorrigibly adventurous, one afternoon, she scrambled out of the bedroom window onto the roof of the adjacent porch. In the kitchen, the Curpheys heard clay roof tiles crashing onto the pathway. They hurried upstairs just in time to see me pull Nan back through the window. To my amazement, they didn't wallop her.

'You mustn't do that again,' they gently scolded her. 'Imagine if I had to tell your parents you'd been killed.' That hit home, Nan realised her impulsive actions had consequences.

Most weekends, Mum and Dad came to join us for afternoon tea. Poor Mum, dressed in her finest, was nervous and overawed by this middle-class affluence of soft furnishings and decorative trinkets. Sensing her discomfort, the Curpheys, were always sweet and kind and tried to put her at ease.

Nan confessed to Dad she had climbed onto the roof and, as she scrambled about, might have broken some tiles. He asked Mr Curphey for a ladder to examine the porch for damage and discovered the entire house roof had loose tiles; none nailed to the struts.

He told Mr Curphey, 'Leave it to me.' On his next visit, he brought some tools, replaced some tiles and ensured the rest of the roof was secure. After that, they received VIP treatment, and Mum relaxed, the favour repaid, she no longer felt like the poor relation.

Many years later, I came to understand why adoption agencies fought to keep families together. It was important for shared experiences and bonding, knowledge of family traits, for familiarity and mental security.

We had missed Grace and were glad she had recovered from the virus. She joined us a few weeks later, she wasn't living with us but billeted in the farm next door with Mrs Curphey's mother, Mrs Slack and her brother, Alfred. One morning, as I visited Grace, he offered to show me how to milk cows. I didn't want to offend him and tried hard to hide my fear, so, with bravado, I straddled the low stool and rested my head against their flanks. He pulled off his beret, plonked it on my head, laughed and pointed to the cows, 'They would know if you weren't suitably dressed.' With trepidation, I squeezed the teats and was successful in splashing a few squirts into the bucket, but I fell backwards off the stool when the cow ambled forward. At least I had tried but would never have become a proficient milkmaid.

Every day was exciting for my sisters and me. Green-fingered, we ran wild and explored the surrounding countryside. In the autumnal, sun-swept meadows, which led to the dappled woods, we discovered endless hours of freedom to roam and pick berries. We ate breakfast and lunch at the kitchen table and never tired of the magnificent view of rolling hills and pastures which sloped to the distant Macclesfield Forest.

Every fortnight for three months, a letter arrived with few lines from Auntie Annie, which enclosed a postal order for sixpence, which to us was a small fortune. We had such enjoyment planning which sweets would last the longest until her next gift arrived. Fascinated with our exciting, new environment, we soon adapted, and the postal orders were reminders of another distant world.

Nan was a devil, an expert in delayed gratification. She watched us swiftly demolish our goodies, then brought out her stash to chew deliberately and noisily, which she knew would hold our attention like a drooling dog to the last mouthful.

Our formal education was sketchy. We attended the small village school in Sutton, Macclesfield, during the evacuation. I was protective towards Nan, and as we queued outside the school, a much older girl said, 'Hurry up, you,' to Nan, and poked her with an umbrella.

59

Nan glanced back at me, hurt and alarmed. I grabbed the umbrella and pretended to break it across my knee. To my surprise, it snapped, and I handed it back in two pieces with a deadpan face. No further trouble occurred during the time we shared the school. The street phrase, *"Don't mess with our kid"* seemed appropriate.

The local school pupils had morning sessions in the classrooms, while the evacuees took the afternoon slot. This arrangement reversed the following week. The rest of the time, we played games in the hall, in the schoolyard or surrounding fields. Occasionally, two small classes had to share a room, and if we got bored with our subject, we earwigged into the other group. We played haphazard hockey in a field behind the school, careful to avoid the crusty mounds of cow dung.

We didn't know how long we would be displaced, but it felt like we were marking time to get back to our real lives. The four months passed so swiftly we never had time to tire of the arrangements, it was like an extended holiday. Of course, the autumn weather was favourable, so I reflect happily on this time of long sunny days in the country.

Nan and I were fortunate in our placement. Mrs Curphey was a competent cook and made delicious individual mousses or fruit blancmanges, which we had each day for dessert, lunch, or dinner, no doubt made with the fresh milk from their cows. It was harvest time, so she filled bowls overflowing with freshly picked apples, pears, and blackberries for snacks.

As the three of us discovered more country secrets, the journey to and from school took longer. In the evenings, Nan and I enjoyed our homework and excelled with the luxury of personal tuition from our two teachers, Mr and Mrs Curphey. Everything was different living with them, all our needs effortlessly catered for, and we were blissfully happy and settled.

The Government made it compulsory for homes to take in assigned evacuees, and host families were paid ten shillings and sixpence (the equivalent of £26 today) for the first unaccompanied child, and eight shillings and sixpence for any subsequent children.

Three and a half months into the 'Phoney War', Hitler was not ready for a full-scale attack on Britain, and there was a false sense of safety. Nothing dramatic happened, no invasion or air raids, so children trickled back home.

Mrs Curphey's mother and uncle adored Grace and begged my parents to let them adopt her. Dad just said politely, 'Sorry, she can't be spared.'

After the war years, some children who had lost their families in the bombing stayed permanently. The farmer across the road legally adopted his charges. Adoption often happened to childless couples who discovered the joyous mayhem of parenthood. I was not envious of the adopted evacuees, because my real home life entailed being with Mum, Dad, and my sisters.

Later, it emerged, our rapid return was because of Mrs Curphey's pregnancy and her suffering morning sickness. We sent thank-you letters to them and made one token, stilted visit. It never crossed our minds to keep in contact; we lived in such vastly different worlds.

During our three month evacuation, Nan and I glimpsed green "heaven". We had watched trees and wide-open fields change colour from summer as it ventured into autumn. The dramatic landscape and enormous living spaces changed and influenced us forever. We had been grabbed by the shoulders and given a good shake out of our everyday existence. A generation of youth reshaped, some not so fortunate, but I happened to be one of the lucky ones.

I had finished junior school at Gorton Mount and was due to start at senior school, Spurley Hey, in September 1939, but because of evacuation, the war stole a year of my formal education, and I didn't go there until 1940.

After my short evacuation, I had no choice but to return to Gorton Mount in December 1939, run by a skeleton staff. Textbooks and homework were available to those eager to continue their learning. A handful of pupils took advantage of this, including me. Lessons were sporadic, and children's whereabouts still scattered. It taught us reality, self-discipline, and a valuable lesson: our education was in our own hands.

The progressive Labour council wanted children to have the facilities afforded to grammar schools. It transpired I lived on an architectural model estate and also attended an educational model school. After two grim Victorian granite schools, Spurley Hey was a revelation, all shimmering white walls, and glass. Bungalow buildings built in an E-shape had inward-facing windows which overlooked the two playgrounds, one for the girls and the other for the boys. They segregated the boys for most of the lessons, nurtured them as future artisans, which was progressive for the time, and they attended a day-release system in a brand-new school, with a lot to prove.

Acres of playing fields were on one side of the road and the council cricket and football fields on the other. We enjoyed the open spaces with the distant Pennine views, the "backbone of England", from the outward-facing classroom windows.

The thrill of starting at the new school disappeared as the war continued. The teachers stuck a sizeable coloured world map to the classroom wall, and we learned geography as we pinned a flag to the areas which designated the war-time posting location of our relatives and friends. My cousin George, Aunt Grace's son, was stationed in Burma, an exciting place to pinpoint being so far away from England. As the war progressed, sadly the teachers discreetly removed flags without undue ceremony.

They turned the street lights off and teachers instilled into us how city lights were beacons to German enemy bombers, and blackouts essential. Householders replaced their curtains to be dense enough, so no chinks of light shone onto the street. Windows without curtains, such as shops, had to be painted with blackout paint and customers had to leave and enter without any light escaping. Smaller panes of glass were covered with thick paper and tacked in place with drawing pins. Each street took blackout seriously, and fines introduced for non-compliance. In September 1939, cars drove with sidelights only until accidents with fatalities on the roads almost doubled in one month.

We never complained about shortages of goods or food rationing; we took it for granted and soldiered on at home; we had fun beating the system. Old clothes were unearthed and worn with glee, no matter how inappropriate or threadbare.

For two academic years, my new senior-school friend, Peggy Bradshaw and I followed a curriculum based on arts, music, drama, and domestic sciences, where we enjoyed the subjects without exam restraints. Peggy, had been transferred from another junior school, had a thick brown bob and tall like a beanpole, the polar opposite to me. We hit it off right away, and after lessons, I would often go for tea at her house, opposite Levenshulme Library, where we had the luxury of listening to classical music on her parent's gramophone. I made sure to get home before any blackout times or sirens.

Dad carried on work as a builder but eventually called up for service in the army. They chose men in age order, and because at 38, he was an older soldier, the war had been on for two years before he left us in 1942. He hoped the conflict would end soon so he wouldn't have to go. We enjoyed his company at home, where we played cards, or darts using his homemade dartboard that hung on the living room door.

He was still with us when the first of the warning sirens sounded in our area. We donned our fluffy, pink, all-in-one siren suits and marched to the Anderson shelter in the back garden. The local authorities half sunk the corrugated iron bunker into the ground, and Dad had made it homely. He had lined it, secured it with a door and built bunk beds, so it resembled a caravan, cramped but warm. Outside, the roof was rounded and covered in soil to match the rest of the garden, and he planted vegetables on it, so the leaves gave camouflage from our kitchen window.

On the first bombing wave, the Luftwaffe dropped incendiaries, to highlight the cities and start small fires in difficult to reach areas, such as rooftops. Mum and Dad took it in turns with the neighbours to patrol the area for these incendiary bombs. They carried large buckets of water and a stirrup pump, but thankfully never used them. With the targets highlighted, the second wave of bombers followed carrying high explosive bombs.

On the nearby fields at Mellands, our men fired the massive anti-aircraft guns stationed there, which shook the whole neighbourhood with a deafening boom. Someone assured us these guns were for our protection, so in bed, we ignored any vibrations. Afterwards, we realised it was because of them we could have been sitting ducks. Fortunately, our neighbourhood escaped the bombing, as the enemy's primary objective was to avoid these guns and drop bombs on strategic targets such as transport and munitions.

The army stationed Dad on an anti-aircraft gun emplacement near Brighton in the south of England. We wrote often and eagerly awaited his colourful and humorous letters. Mum was encouraged to read and write to keep in contact with him. We never saw her notes, which, considering her dyslexia, must have been a laborious few lines, but undoubtedly tender and heartfelt.

In our household telepathy was common, and to appease my anxiety concerning Dad, Mum told me that in the last letter she received, he was fine and enjoying a quiet time. A day later, he walked in, on sick leave. His "quiet time" had been spent in hospital with severe infections in both feet, caused by damp boots. I was comforted when he had nothing more serious.

Regulations stipulated that pupils from secondary schools left education at the end of the term in which their 14th birthdays occurred. As my birthday fell in March, I finished school at Easter in 1941, crushed and angry to leave my formal education. I enjoyed those few years of schooling with sporadic teaching during the evacuation, and I lost a further term, forced to go before the summer holiday. Nobody took exams that year; it was unfortunate timing, and I cried on my way home. I wanted to stay there forever, and I vowed somehow to get a proper education.

Enforced termination of schooling by birth date ensured a steady stream of school-leavers entered the workforce throughout the year rather than flood the employment market. Youths then enlisted in droves for the armed forces, which provided the chance for them to choose the service they wanted, rather than wait for the call-up.

I often escaped from the hectic clamour of wartime living and found tranquillity in music concerts and walking the wild moors. As a teenager, I hiked in spring and autumn, but only in dry weather. Belle Vue station was on the line to Edale in the Pennine moors. On Sunday mornings, at the crack of dawn, the designated train was crammed full. Young men stood at intervals on the Edale platform and directed us according to our walking knowledge. Experienced youth leaders led groups, up to a dozen in each, to an appropriate hiking trail.

I never made friends on these outings, as I found it arduous to keep pace on the hard slog of the moor's rough, hazardous terrain, in stark contrast to the smooth pavements in the streets, several miles below shrouded in the city smoke.

We were too puffed out and exhausted to chat. The buzz of bees and bird song broke the countryside stillness whenever we stopped for a rest and refreshments.

Out of strength, but uplifted by the ramble in the crisp, chilly air, we arrived at the station for our return journey. Volunteers shepherded us to our carriages, earmarked for designated stops. An eerie atmosphere pervaded the gloomy carriage as blackout demanded dimmed lights. Most of us lolled on each other, and, as ours was the last stop, we slept for the half-hour trip. Stumbling off the train in the dark, we followed the torch carrier as we picked our way along the rutted path by the side of the railway, the perilous shortcut to our estate.

After my hike if Dad was home, as a precaution, he oiled and pummelled my calves. The following day, after the hike, I'm sure a few of the youngsters were stiff, but thanks to Dad, I wasn't one.

As he massaged my feet, I asked, 'Where did you learn this?'

'Football,' he said and told me a secret.

He told me that as a youngster living amidst the slums, to fit in, he joined a gang of opportunist thieves who broke into houses. On his first outing with the gang, the police arrested them, and he received the same punishment, lashes with a birch meted in proportion to the crime's severity.

The experience was so physically painful, and the prospects of being locked up in prison terrified him and would mess up his life. When he was escorted to the police station and onto court proceedings, it taught him a lasting lesson. He did nothing illegal again, kept his nose clean, and concentrated his energy on kicking a ball around "the red recs", a red gravel recreational area, and hence became an excellent football player.

Lancashire, a booming county, with cotton and textile mills, ensured sewing was in the blood and became our creative outlet. Most houses contained precision-engineered, treadle-operated sewing machines, handed down through the generations.

As a girl, Mum trained as a tailoress and created evening dress trousers and could create or alter anything to fit any shape. She did 'outdoor work,' not in a factory, but from home, using her sewing machine. During inclement winters, when Dad couldn't work, it provided the essential income to keep us well fed and warm. Mum was astute, stockpiling coal and squirrelling away tinned food in the summer to prepare for these harder winter times.

The factory owner delivered bundles of garments to our house, cut out and ready to sew. Work Mum had promised would be completed was given the dreaded term, "dead horse". On collection, she was paid and given another selection of work. She always met her deadlines, ate force-fed meals at her machine, desperate to fill her quota. We girls worked efficiently as a team, helped her turn collars and cuffs inside out and snipped cotton ends. To keep household spirits up, we chatted, listened to the wireless, and enjoyed the intimacy with our Mum.

During the Second World War, women on the home front were encouraged to contribute to the war effort by knitting for the troops, promoted as a public duty. Advertising at the time stated: "England expects – knit your bit". Many free knitting patterns and wool were sent to schools so children could knit gloves, scarves and balaclava helmets for the forces.

In my spare time, I knitted gloves with fingers, but my ultimate disaster was a crochet bra. It sat on top of my C cups like pan lids, useless in the support department.

'The under-endowed could pad it,' was suggested by sympathetic sisters. I suspect they showed my creation to mum who must have rolled about laughing.

The Co-op Society was our guardian angel. Mum paid in a fixed amount from her wages, and as it accrued every month, we spent it on items unable to be made at home, such as shoes.

Young Bet, my cousin, on my Mum's side, was the star, a sample hand. She worked with the dress designers on prototype garments. They circulated samples to buyers who often sold huge numbers worldwide. During the war, they forced her to waste her sewing talents in a munition factory, making guns. She would have been more suited to making uniforms, but it was already covered.

Mum's ambition was for us to work in a clean office and wear smart clothes. Grace had other ideas, and her goal was to become a nurse. In retrospect, she would have made an ideal candidate for the caring profession, but I forcefully talked her out of that nonsense. I didn't think she would enjoy pools of blood and disinfectant.

Grace was a poor student, attributed to me because I read to her so much. We didn't know then, but she had dyslexia, like Mum. She left school and started work in a factory sewing ladies coats. Not long after, she was removed from the factory line and installed in the office; perceived to be too refined and not suitable for the rough and tumble of the dirty factory floor. The management adored her, and when she protested she couldn't read very well, they found her a suitable clerical position, in which she stayed for years.

Grace must have done some sewing there, as once she came home with marked-down samples of woollen car coats in pillar-box red, grass green, canary yellow, and sky blue. If any of us sisters wanted to reserve a specific colour to wear the following day, we would hide it from the others the evening before. As these coats were samples, Mum didn't have to use her precious clothing coupons.

I wanted to be a dress designer, a career that Mum knew a little about, but she soon put me straight; they couldn't afford for me to go to college and I would need a degree from art school in such a competitive field.

So, we three girls took the easy route and fulfilled our Mum's wishes and worked in offices. Our first salaries just about matched the price of our stockings. It made no difference if we didn't cover our share of the rent, as Mum had a steady income and continued to complete her 'dead horse' in time.

Chapter 6 - Work To Do

(Average White Band)

Girls left education at 14 and entered work with no formal training. Those school years gave me a longing to read novels, listen to classical music, and go to the theatre to escape and dream, and I lived in Manchester, the right city for all that culture.

Fate intervened with a lucky contact. My schoolfriend, Peggy, had a career path mapped out, as her father had a senior position at the Post Office in the telegraphy department. We found fill-in jobs for a year before eligible to work there at 15. The local employment exchange gave me a simple examination to assess my capabilities and registered me for clerical work.

The helpful employment officer who handled my case found me a position, a trainee wages clerk, at the munition factory which manufactured large anti-aircraft guns. It was ideal, a short bus ride from home, and being a wage clerk had good career prospects for me, a keen and bright girl if I failed to enter my first choice, the Post Office.

Petrol rationing forced everyone to cycle, ride buses or take trams. From the bus into work, I enjoyed the comical sight of the pantomime of bowler-hatted city gents who rode bicycles, upright, metal ankle clips strapped across their striped trousers. During the war, they manufactured bicycles for the forces, but not for public use, so there was no opportunity for me buy one, which is why I ended up with a large policeman's bike with a crossbar. I dismounted by leaning and toppling off, unladylike, onto the pavement.

Three months later, the employment exchange secured me a job at the Post Office's telephone department. It was a separate entity to the telegraphy section where I intended to join Peggy. I never knew why she never joined me at the Post Office, as I never saw her again as she lived on the other side of Gorton and may have taken another job arranged by her father, during that gap year. Hers was one of the first of many female losses I would encounter.

The Post Office permanent position was a welcome surprise, and I jumped at the opportunity of working in the vibrant city centre.

The vast building housed two separate telephone exchanges, which stretched the full length along the block. Hundreds of girls worked at walls covered in boards faced with lights and holes for plugs. We wore headsets and sat shoulder to shoulder, plugging cables into the flashing lights.

One exchange dealt with the local tolls, and I was lucky again and trained for the country-wide trunk calls. We received these from telephone boxes in the streets and inside designated buildings. The caller picked up the phone; the signal came to me, where I inserted the plug into one socket. They gave me a telephone number, and when answered and accepted, I plugged in the second line to connect them.

When it involved other district operators, we worked in tandem, I announced the price for three minutes according to the distance, and the caller deposited coins in the box. When the three minutes ended, a light flashed on my board, and I interrupted by saying in an authoritative voice, 'Caller, your time is up. Will you have further time?' We withdrew the plug on a negative response, and I turned to the next flashing light. They replicated the banks of lights throughout the boards, so no-one waited very long.

Work shifts and holidays were interchangeable, which allowed us to have a vibrant social life. In small groups, we went to the pictures, swimming, dancing, walking, or shopping, depending on our spare cash, which remained after paying for food and board. We were shoals of fish, shifting, and changing companions with the tides.

A group of older girls invited me to join them. They were friendly with the generous American soldiers stationed in the suburbs, who plied them with cigarettes, gifts of stockings, perfumes, and cosmetics. Photographs of them having parties convinced me to think about tagging along, but when I saw these GIs were black this put me off, I made excuses and didn't join them. I was not racist, having George, my mixed-race cousin, but my parents indoctrinated me with shocking stories of pregnant girls, who had black American babies. Single mothers were considered sluts and fell into lives of interminable poverty and hardship.

74

At 15, the Post Office transferred me as a probationer to the telegraph and counter clerk section for a year. The uniform was leaf-green, silky cotton, full-length overalls, crossed at the front and tied at the back, and we hung our day clothes in the lockers. This provision meant no differentiation between those who had the means to buy working clothes or not. It gave breathing space and time to accumulate suitable office attire.

Here I met Marjorie Wilkinson, and we developed a long-standing friendship. She was a smart and attractive brunette, confident and sophisticated. They gave us clerical positions, and, at 16, with probation over, we entered 'Telegraph School' for a few months. We learned to type on a teleprinter with an integral keyboard comprising capital letters and numerals, and we used an adapted typewriter.

Customers used call boxes to request telegrams and inserted their coins and told us the address and message. We became ingenious at adapting messages to fit the number of words for customers' payments. Greetings telegrams were special, twice the size and embellished with flowers, with their message printed on it, not to be confused with the stark, brown telegram that sometimes brought devastating news. Boys delivered them within a few hours, and we knew stock phrases for every occasion. When we read the message back, typed on the caller's behalf; they gasped with pride and delight, 'Did I really say that?'

We worked for only two hours on various activities to stem boredom and keep us efficient. They designated one teleprinter to a specific area in the countryside, and one of us typed while the other gummed up the tapes which spewed out of the machine's side. Proficient typists carried out long conversations with each other as they sent the telegrams, without missing a single letter.

In the rush hour, during the day, the noise level was deafening when the clattering teleprinters joined with the chattering of teenage girls. With 24-hour service, the men preferred to work the evening shifts as they worked longer hours but had more time off the following week with their families. They worked Sundays, Bank Holidays, including Christmas Day, for overtime money. I only worked two night shifts, and the men took pity on me and let me sleep, curled up, between the teleprinters.

A year later, Marjorie and I enrolled at the Post Office Counter school. We were swots and revelled in education and excelled in the short hours and classroom environment. I was popular with the Post Office counter staff, but not with the postmistresses. They accused me of being opinionated and a rabble-rouser, which was probably right, as Dad had influenced me, being pro-union. He had grown up with and enjoyed the improvements brought by the unions for the exploited down-trodden workers. But I soon learned to be anti-establishment got me nowhere. In various city-centre offices, I practised diplomacy and sycophancy towards the postmistresses. They chose me to be the peripatetic substitute for holidays and sick leave.

Marjorie became a counter clerk but had become addicted to her classroom activities. She left and qualified to become a teacher and met her future husband at the Sheffield Teacher Training College. I saw her for the last time when she became my bridesmaid, another female loss I had no control over.

Nan left school and joined the Post Office as a telephonist in the toll section. She loved the lifestyle and shift work and stayed until she married.

I enjoyed the stimulus of working in the heart of Manchester. The irony of the name, Spring Gardens, was not lost on me, as a complex of multi-storey department stores surrounded the office block. There wasn't a leaf or a speck of green within a ten-mile radius, apart from the sparse Piccadilly Gardens.

While on leave, Dad heard over the radio that in north Manchester, a stray landmine had hit the row of modern estate houses where his brother, Harold, his wife, and their two children lived.

When Dad was sure the threat of danger had passed, on that clear and bright afternoon, we travelled by two buses to the district, with Mum and Dad worried sick, unaware of what we might find.

We arrived at dusk as the lingering smoke shrouded the town; a dark giant cloud blotted out the sunset. A German bomber, on escape, had jettisoned an enormous landmine which flattened several dozen homes and gardens, leaving a pile of smoking rubble and ash.

An acrid smell filled the air, the equivalent to a million bonfires. I scanned the burn-out lot where tidy rows of homes once stood and wondered how such a small space accommodated so many houses.

The bomb site was teeming with anxious, hopeful relatives who frantically searched the displaced community. Officials milled around the destruction and directed them to the church hall, by this time, filled with groups of distressed and frantic residents.

Over the deafening clamour of voices, we were relieved to hear a shout, 'Billy, over here.'

We eased ourselves through the crush of people to Dad's brother and his family, eager to connect and give us details of their ordeal.

Harold, though, in shock, was cheery and delighted to see us. 'We were here, in the shelter, when we heard a tremendous crash which shook the ground. When the all-clear siren sounded, we hurried outside. We expected it to be a shocking scene, but it was much worse. Our house is gone. We've lost everything.'

He acknowledged they were "the lucky ones, despite everything". Typical of the British spirit, they surveyed the devastation, had lost their home, their community, and every single thing they owned, but jubilant everyone survived.

In wartime, it was possible to have victory over red tape. With the power to requisition empty houses, the council swiftly rehoused Uncle Harold and his family. Ironically, replacements for clothes and furniture were often of far superior quality to those lost. Standards of living improved when they allocated unoccupied homes away from council estates. Council scouts found empty properties, stuck a label on the door, and they informed the owners and landlords they had requisitioned it. Sometimes these properties were held by people away in the war or working in a different area. The lucky recipients of the tenancy sometimes had fully furnished accommodation.

On some wintry Sunday afternoons, I attended the rehearsals of the world-famous Halle Orchestra, held in the sports arena in Belle Vue Stadium, rather than the main concert hall in the city centre. In contrast, the evening before, wrestling took place to a packed audience.

It was a real concert even though a full rehearsal, and we paid a pittance to attend, one and sixpence. The whole arena was available for seating, but we gathered in comforting groups.

Barbirolli conducted the guest performers in a relaxed atmosphere, without pomp, with the orchestra dressed in day suits. The acoustics were not ideal, as the stadium had a flimsy roof and aircraft engines or thunderstorms drowned out the orchestral musicians. The audience cheered when the conductor smiled and pretended to conduct any extraneous noise.

In 1944, the army transferred Dad from one end of the UK to the other, from Brighton up to Scapa Flow in the Orkneys,

Scotland. Again, he worked on the anti-aircraft batteries, in a location selected as the leading British naval base because of its earlier successful and strategic position in the first World War.

He learned to tat and crochet during those long, bitter, winter nights. On leave, he brought home his runners and tray cloths that we used and admired for years. How he managed such delicate needlework with his stubby, broad, builder's hands remains a mystery.

City dwellers found it particularly challenging to supplement rations. Like most of our neighbours, we grew vegetables, and there was space for a hen run next to the Anderson air-raid shelter. Mum brought home from the market, a box of day-old chicks, sexed, only females for egg-laying. An old drawer on the hearth kept them warm and amused us for hours.

Chicks have a rapid rate of growth. They changed from fluffy yellow balls to gangly creatures, that sprouted uneven tufts of shimmery feathers. At this ugly stage, we transferred them to an outside pen in the back garden. The sex selector made one mistake; one turned out to be a rooster.

From the first week, he acted differently, head and shoulders above the others. His alpha-male demeanour meant he strutted around the pen and dominated the females. He became so obnoxious, I named him Lefty, after a notorious American gangster of the day. When we entered the chicken run, he charged at us, even though we brought his food.

We became scared to go into the hen run, so Mum became intrepid and tackled him. She held the bucket of food in one hand and brandished a hand brush in the other and wailed like a banshee as she fended him off.

The hen food was an original mix of leftover kitchen scraps, prepared potato peelings, bran, grit, and Parrish's Chemical Food. They fed racing pigeons and poultry this tinned traditional iron supplement to maintain strength and appetite. The pigeons thrived as it was essential for red-blood-cell formation to ensure maximum oxygen uptake for top racing performance.

It amazed me when an elderly lady mentioned that in her infancy, she took Parrish's Chemical Food, a foul-tasting, red medicine, as a prescription for her anaemia. I didn't know humans consumed it, and she was unaware it was a supplement given to racing birds.

At Christmas, we celebrated by cooking and eating Lefty. All his shortened life, he had been a bad-tempered, wicked old rooster. At the table, a young wag suggested it may be a useful idea if we disposed of all our nasty relatives by cooking and eating them.

In domestic science classes, I couldn't learn how to bake cakes because there was nothing spare from the family food rations of sugar, butter, or eggs. However, unlimited flour, grains, yeast, lard, and margarine allowed us to bake bread and pies to a high standard.

We had endured six years of shortages and conserving everything possible, which became a way of life. With more access to food, daily living was more comfortable in the country than in the city.

Mrs Kilgour, our dear next-door neighbour, became terminally ill. They brought her bed downstairs, so her husband could nurse her, helped by Mum. Sometimes I sat at her bedside and brought her up-to-date with the local gossip.

One evening, I showed her the new dress I'd made. She praised my handiwork and said, 'Win, take off your glasses.'

'Oh, no, I can't,' I replied, alarmed, 'I never take them off.'

'You can manage without them, can't you?'

'Yes, but they cover up and correct my squint.'

'They're a little severe. Let me see your face.' As I stood there, self-conscious and exposed, she studied me. 'You're fine, no squint now. It's gone. Look.'

She handed me a mirror from her bedside cabinet. I moved my head from side to side and tried to trick my eyes into squinting.

'You're right,' I said, surprised and pleased.

Wise old Mrs Kilgour coaxed me out from behind my specs, and someone else I trusted, would later boost my confidence.

Devastation, doom, and drama befell our Mum once again. One night after tea, I overheard her confide to her sister, Annie, 'When Billy came home, we had no protection, and he couldn't wait. I've missed twice.'

The baby would be Mum's sixth, and she treated Dad like a disgraced whipped dog during the months when he came home on leave.

When Mum's pregnancy sickness subsided, and the happy hormones kicked in, we started the tribal knitting. In June 1944, Dad notified Sutton's housing office that our circumstances had changed; they now had a boy, Alan, who altered the household dynamics. We became eligible to have a larger house, and they found one for us in Fremantle Avenue, with three bedrooms and a double-sized garden.

The Trust had enough petrol to allow one trip that week for the removal van to move our heavy furniture. Dad was still away in the army, so, the removers were amiable seeing a household of women and a newborn baby and carried the cumbersome pieces of furniture into the new house.

We borrowed a hand cart for the smaller items and devised a system. Nan loaded the cart in the crescent; Grace unloaded it in the avenue, while I assumed the role of carter. With the bits and pieces stuffed into suitcases and wooden crates, it was easy for me to push the handcart a few times around the corner.

I always dressed for the part and wore my "dirty jobs" gear, a tailored-to-fit, second-hand khaki army uniform and sported fashionable bright lipstick with my hair pinned up. I must have resembled the ubiquitous war-time poster girl.

Dad arrived days later, awarded compassionate leave on account of the new baby. He found us already living at the top end corner of Fremantle Avenue. It astounded him we had moved and installed the furniture without his help. The spacious garden backed onto a clearing in front of a single-storey factory, but no noise or dirt disturbed us.

Life became more comfortable and less of a struggle for Mum. She rested in the sunshine with their light blonde curly-haired baby boy. Elated, Dad gloated on his son and planned the new garden.

I was 16 when the threat of bombing passed. My cousin, George, who missed his horses, was still stationed in Burma. It was a strategic holding pattern in the war, and his battles were about survival against tropical disease and the searing heat of a humid jungle.

On the home front, we won minor skirmishes in the form of food rationing and shortages of household goods. The earliest fake tan turned up in shops, a purple surgical bottled lotion which turned brown on the skin. My sisters and I took turns sitting in this bath of diluted permanganate of potash, which resulted in colouring our nether regions a brown oak, which lasted the summer. With a ruler and eyebrow pencil, we drew a line down the centre back of each calf to simulate seamed stockings. Hair grips and combs held our hair in rolls on top of our heads, and we paraded like film stars ready to entertain the troops.

In my teens, I dyed Auntie Grace's old lace curtains black to make a dance dress. To me, it evoked pure glamour. The dye didn't take well, but in the dance hall's dim light, any pulls and snags on the faded grey lace were invisible.

I had just turned eighteen, when on 8th May 1945, they declared victory for the Allies in Europe, V.E. Day. It was a long glorious summer day, because of double summer-time and celebrations seemed to last days not hours.

Every street had long makeshift tables covered with pristine bedsheets, decorated with vases of garden flowers. So much food on display was overwhelming. Nan and I, along with the other youngsters, visited other streets, eating giggling and flirting. Gramophones were brought out later and provided a musical backdrop to the merriment, with the singing of Vera Lynn songs, of course.

On 15th August 1945, the Allies - that is Britain, the US and other countries who were fighting together, marked a victory over Japan, V.J. Day. They announced news of the surrender to the world, which sparked spontaneous celebrations over the end of World War II. This announcement passed me by; we had already returned to austerity and stagnation.

As we know, teenagers live from minute to minute, birthday to birthday engrossed in their battles of growing up. Long gone was the danger to our lives from bombs, and my Dad and my cousin were safely home. Even with austerity still in the city, girls turned up to the offices, smartly dressed in mismatched, home-made outfits.

The monarchy changes did not affect working-class lives; it was the Government that made differences. The returning Forces elected the Labour government, but everyone became disenchanted with continued rationing and a black market. As is the way of politicians, they hadn't fulfilled their promises.

When the Tory party came into power in 1951, we noted a significant change. They lifted the rationing; clothes, chocolate, and furniture appeared in the shops.

Chapter 7 - Call Me Irresponsible

(Frank Sinatra)

The summer after I turned 17, I became pretty, and boys noticed me. They swooned around and often complimented me on my billowing bosom and wasp waist. They were the erogenous zone of the war years, as the chaste films of that period bear out. My friends thought, through narrowed eyes, with my wavy blonde bob and ruby-red lipstick, I looked like the Hollywood movie star and wartime pin-up Betty Grable.

The male opening gambits did not delude us; my work friends and I had heard them all. Telegraphists worked shift hours, and on alternate days, we finished at two or three in the afternoon. In winter, we swam at the municipal baths with heated pools. We changed in the office and emerged as butterflies in the afternoon light.

More often, we danced at the Ritz Ballroom, the best one in the city. A live band with a professional singer played strict tempo dance music several afternoons a week. The management scrutinised us when we paid our entrance fee, spied on us during the matinee dances, and frowned upon any sign of sluttish or working-girl activity.

A scented haven with soft lights, a secret sanctuary, gave the uniformed men dressed in various colours, a few hours escape from the war.

Throughout my teens, I wondered if my scant education was noticeable and, if discovered, would I be shunned or dumped? My choice of boyfriends became older than me, and, in my youthful insecurity yearning for their approval, I wanted to impress them with my intelligence. They played along with this and provided me with in-depth discussions on books and music to keep me sweet.

One of my partners, a well-dressed local, was plain and dumpy but surefooted. When dancing, he captured my attention when he referred to a group of people near the bar as "Pure Manet; almost Renoir".

Glancing over his shoulder when we turned, impressed, I agreed. I fell for the "come up and see my etchings" classic line. We took a taxi to his one-bed flat, where he showed me his sketches and large art books. We played classical records, while he cooked me a meal of eggs and bacon.

After dinner, he ordered another taxi and accompanied me back to the bus terminal. We parted with a peck on the cheek. 'See you soon.' It was over, was I intrigued, or was I hooked?

We met a few weeks later, chatted and danced before we ventured back to his flat. This time he played it differently. He draped his arms around my neck and leant lightly against me. 'May I?' he asked, touching the zip of my dress. 'I'll take precautions.' He was so careful, with his creams, sheaths, and douches, that I felt nothing physically or emotionally. It was the quickest, most unsexy performance I ever experienced.

Afterwards, he said, 'Do you mind if I sketch you?'

He draped a small scarf across my naked body and handed me a glass of cider to sip. His charcoal scratched across the parchment, as I lay seductively, dreaming of another plate of rationed eggs and bacon.

After ten minutes, he left me soaking in a fragrant bath while he fixed up the meal. Easy-listening records provided the soundtrack to our evening. Then we flicked through his art books until my taxi arrived.

In my mind, a dalliance with an artist, a portrait painted for eggs and bacon was sheer sophistication. Not interested in the mechanics of sex, my attitude toward it was very matter of fact. Mum instilled the idea that copulation being a duty, to be avoided at all costs or get it over with as fast as possible. I thought sexual intercourse was just going through the motions, and apart from a couple more sessions with him, I came to no harm. Once again, I dodged a bullet, no pregnancy or criminal involvement.

We met once more at the Ritz. 'Win, I've got something for you,' the artist called and beckoned me into an alcove and handed me a square brown-paper parcel.

I unfastened the package with clumsy trembling hands. When I saw the portrait, it was a relief, not a bawdy, titillating picture, but a graceful girl, shy and almost virginal, reclining in a classic pose on the dark green plush sofa. One arm along the back, the other holding the end of a blue silk scarf draped across her thigh and tumbling to the carpet.

'It's superb,' I said, running my hand over the ridges in the paint. It was heart-breaking to tell him this elegant, finished portrait was unsuitable.

'I'm so sorry. I can't take it home. My Mum would be too shocked that I'd posed in the nude.' I handed the picture back to him and noticed his crestfallen face as he reluctantly took it from me.

'It's beautifully painted,' I said, trying to console him. 'But, honestly, my friends would brand me a tart, a scarlet woman.'

He acknowledged my appreciation of his artistic talent. As a bright afterthought, I added, 'It's such a flattering portrait of my body, overpaint it with a different head, and it'll do for another girlfriend.'

He kissed me and said, 'You're so funny, Win,' and we parted in gales of laughter. It was a fun diversion with a competent artist and companion, but a decidedly lousy lover. Deep down, I knew I wouldn't see him again.

A vacancy arose in the Counter Clerk school, so no more shift work for me, and I never revisited the Ritz. Instead, I danced at the local Palais at the weekend with my sisters, at the precise time engineered by fate.

Chapter 8 - What Are You Doing The Rest Of Your Life?

(Frank Sinatra)

I was 19 in 1946 and still living at home with my sisters when Mum fell pregnant for the final time. Linda, our new-born sister, was a week-old when Nan and Grace tried to persuade me to go to the Saturday dance at our local Palais. The regular five-piece band comprised professional male and female singers and played a strict tempo swing music. I didn't really want to go and made an excuse about having nothing to wear.

'You can have my new skirt,' Nan offered. I tried on her noble sacrifice, but it wasn't a style of my choosing. The heavy brown figure cotton hugged the waist and flared out towards the hem, with a swinging skirt perfect for dancing and swirling. To please her, I wore her creation and joined them.

What a good job I went; that night changed my life.

The Palais on Saturday nights was the highlight of the week. The dancehall was the social scene heart. Inside, beating vibrantly, beneath its vaulted Art Deco ceilings, dreams fizzed with electricity and excitement. Eager young men and women showed up to dance to the rhythm of the music in skirt-swinging and knee-jerking explosion. Groups of girls who wished to dance stood and chatted on the large carpeted area on the dance floor's perimeter. When the lights dimmed, and music started, the boys rushed up to the girls they had already picked out.

A tall young man, Fred, strode over and asked me to dance. It was etiquette after the first dance to return their original group. When the music started again, Grace saw him hurry over. She stood back and pushed me forward. Girls chose on the second tentative approach, whether they wanted another dance. In Fred's case, I had no choice; he'd laid claim. He scooped me up and whisked me away, ready to be the first for the ecstatic sweep across the empty dance floor.

I clasped him, which sent static electricity through my arms. An excellent dancer, masterful, and muscular, I could feel his strength as he pushed me around the dancefloor. I assumed a suitable blasé expression but churned inside. I melted in his firm, toned arms and wanted this dance to last forever.

In the break, when the lights came on, I took a discreet appraisal of my suitor. Even without my glasses, I noticed he was rugged, well over six-foot-tall, with short dark-brown curly hair, a long upper lip, and a cleft chin, like the film star Fred McMurray. For the first time in my life, someone made me feel like a delicate doll and could lift me without effort.

My sisters in the distance gazed at our performance and agreed, 'That's that then. She's taken.'

Over a coffee break, Fred told me the RAF had demobbed him. He stared at me with his soulful dark-brown eyes, 'I suppose everyone tells you how photogenic you are.'

I tried to look unfazed, but thought, *Clever. What a good line;* I had heard quite a few.

He told me that during a lull, known as the 'phoney war,' members of the armed forces were encouraged to take classes or other meaningful activities. Fred took a photography course at Guildford College and was now a proficient photographer.

The almost empty shops held no further stocks of photographic film because of the war, but there were plenty of plate cameras on tripods. Fred said he learned to view subjects reversed and reused the resurfaced plates. Since it was expensive to have professional photographs taken, he explained that only the rich commissioned portraits and studio ones reserved for special occasions.

After midnight, he escorted me home alone since my sisters had already left. We walked for 40 minutes, right to the door. After knee-shaking kisses, I forced myself to feign indifference.

'Are you free tomorrow night?' he asked.

'No,' I lied, 'But I am free the next day.'

The following day, Grace couldn't contain herself and told Mum, 'Win found somebody interesting last night, but he's got to leave for Germany soon… a new government position.'

'This war is taking all the good ones away,' Mum observed.

'Yes, it's a shame as they were getting on so well.'

After dinner, as we gathered around the kitchen table, a loud knock on the front door made us jump. We weren't expecting anyone. I peeked around the curtains and saw Fred on our doorstep. Even though I had said I wasn't available that evening, he still came to the house - typical Fred, eccentric, with tunnel vision.

'Sorry to come without warning,' he said, as he stood on our doorstep. 'I thought you ought to know I'm not going to Germany after all.'

'But why?' I spluttered, 'It's such a good opportunity. What's happened?'

'I've decided to stay here and marry you.'

If this happened nowadays, a stranger you'd only known for a few hours appeared on your doorstep and announced he's going marry you, you'd immediately call the police.

Mum stuck her head around the half-open door. 'In that case, come in for a cup of tea,' she said. 'We're in a mess as I had a baby last week, and my bed's still down here.'

She made a disorganised tidy up on her way to the kitchen and selected the best of the unmatched crockery. Fred politely viewed the baby in the cot. Nan and Grace entered from the kitchen, and we babbled while Fred sat with a broad smile.

Grace seemed to adore him and adopted him as her older brother. Nan, jealous, said, 'He's too soppy, looking at our Win all the time.'

'Nice chap,' Dad said, 'Good footballer.' Alan, aged three, tried to kick him in the shins.

I'm glad he felt so at home and comfortable, given the hundreds of lunchtime hours he would later spend in that room. I watched him, flushed, as he chatted away with confidence and worldliness, and already in love. This man blew into my life with hurricane swiftness and, in an instant, changed everything.

As he talked about his military life and travels, he told us the British Control Commission forwarded his name to the air force. He passed the exam, and they offered him an Officer's post in Germany, with office hours, which provided him with a promising future.

'At the last minute,' he said, catching my eyes across the room, 'I refused the offer because I'd met Win, and if I'd gone overseas, I'm sure she would've taken up with somebody else, and I wasn't taking any chances.'

I'd only known him 24 hours, but with his wit and dashing good looks, Fred captured my heart, and I dropped the other two of my aspiring suiters.

We discovered a few things in common; his father, like mine, was called William, (but never Billy), and born on the 2nd May. I'm surprised we never met, because, for ten years, we lived only half a mile away from each other in Gorton. We both attended Spurley Hey Senior School, but six years apart. He assumed I was a pupil at the local grammar school. A few days later, after Fred had declared his honourable intentions, I confessed I had not had further education at the grammar school, and I placed my glasses on my nose for his reaction.

He nodded, smiling adoringly. 'They suit you,' was all he said.

I inwardly thanked God - I can marry him. He now knows the worst things about me; I wear glasses and my lack of education.

Fred said his schooldays at Spurley were short-lived, involved in two incidents where they labelled him a troublemaker. In one episode, he defended a bullied boy. Fred stretched his arm out to stop the perpetrator who tripped, fell down the stairs, and broke his arm. Another time, while waiting for the teacher, he showed the other pupils how to carry a chair in self-defence. A teacher strode in as Fred charged around with the chair on his head, emulating a raging bull. The teacher said the action appeared too aggressive, that Fred had attacked him, and once more, they marched him to the headmaster.

The maths teacher, who had already recognised Fred's potential, stepped in and stopped his expulsion. They organised an entrance exam for a grammar school scholarship, which he passed. As Fred was a poor boy, the council bought the uniform, books, and other school essentials.

For years he cycled the return journey to the school of several miles, never missing a day. His parents never attended the prize-giving days. His school was another world to them, two buses away. He brought home his trophies and made light of any wins.

His class treated football goal scorers like royalty. When Fred won athletic events, he often exchanged the silver, first-place cups for the substantial and useful second or third prizes, sports shoes, or equipment. Posh kids usually owned doubles of sports equipment, and with nothing of his own, Fred won several tennis tournaments with borrowed rackets. He loved this breezy middle-class life and sports world and only returned home to sleep.

When he won a hurdle event, they awarded him an expensive, ornate nine-carat rose-and-yellow gold, shield-shaped medal. The second prize was a coveted bicycle. Unsuccessful in his swap, he returned home disenchanted, threw the pendant on the kitchen table, and marched off. His father thought it an honour to win such a prize and took it to Woolworth's for engraving with Fred's initials, FB. We still wear this decorative medal as an unusual, fancy pendant on a chain.

Fred didn't think he was special, believed anyone could achieve anything with the help of a book and perseverance, failing that, find an inspiring teacher. He was single-minded in his studies, and at grammar school, he ensured he excelled at typing and shorthand and on leaving aspired to become a newspaper reporter because this job also gave him a motorbike!

There was always more to learn, and he never boasted of his accomplishments. Those who met him found him to be a jolly good bloke, if somewhat eccentric.

Fred took an insurance clerical position, usually reserved for sons of the executives. They took him on, not only for his business acumen but because he was an asset to their cricket team as an ex-member of the Manchester Boys.

In his teenage years, he took a course in ballroom dancing at Watling's Dance Academy, where six years later, I, too, learned to dance. We were in step from the moment we met.

Fred told me he was 'grade A' fit at the start of the war when he and his church club friends enlisted in the RAF. He suffered from motion sickness and assigned ground staff duties servicing aircraft, while his friends became pilots. At the end of the war, in 1945, Fred came back from Germany to sad news; all his intelligent, pilot friends were dead.

His father, in Manchester, also died of a heart attack that year, so Fred, fed up of the gloom and doom in the UK, decided to return to Germany, where he believed he had a better chance of finding happiness. Then he met me and had a change of heart.

The notion of motion sickness was comical until I saw him floored on two occasions, first on a ferry crossing the Irish Sea, the other on a plane in a holding pattern over London. There is no doubt an assignment as ground crew during the war, and not a pilot, saved his life.

Fred's proud mother, Lily, told me he made his first public appearance as a four-year-old. He stood on an upturned crate in the local market and sang *Jesus Wants Me for a Sunbeam* in perfect pitch. It earned a round of applause from the fruiterers and doting shoppers, and it sowed the seed for him performing in public.

Fred spent the following years practising on spare pianos and borrowed harmonicas. At high school, he used a tennis racket which belonged to his friend's older sister, Pat. At school, she took singing lessons and then sang in the local establishments. Years later, Fred was surprised and thrilled to see her name,

'Patricia Kirkwood', at the top of a London billboard. He felt proud to know she'd become a star, a stage actress, singer, and dancer. She also performed on radio, television, and films and the first woman to have her own television series on the BBC.

When Fred started work, instead of bringing home his first pay packet to his mother, he spent his wages on a shiny new harmonica from the music shop near his office.

His parents feigned annoyance. They banished him to the bathroom with a stern admonishment, 'Don't come down until you've mastered a tune, or it'll go back.'

Anyone who has tried to learn this instrument will know the squeaks and hooting that ensues. Fred managed a few recognisable ones, enough to mollify his long-suffering mother. They applauded his single-mindedness and let him keep it.

He saved for a guitar, taught himself to play, and joined a beat group who sang and played in clubs and pubs, a youthful backlash against the formal bands of trained musicians in the dance halls. When the groups broke up and enlisted, Fred went, coincidentally, for initial battle training in Squiresgate, Blackpool, where he visited his elderly auntie on his father's side and got acquainted for a few weeks.

During the war, he trained as an aircraft mechanic, not on the frontline. With musical entertainment expertise, they assigned him to play in a band to entertain the troops, mainly in Germany.

99

That's not to say he didn't experience the horrors of war and what it did to the servicemen and women, and even he had a few near-misses.

The first happened in Manchester, while he waited to enlist for the RAF. As one gig finished, a warning siren whined. Everybody trooped to the shelter, where the band played an impromptu concert until the all-clear siren drowned out the music.

After the show, partygoers dashed out to grab the last tram to Ardwick Green. Fred hurried as best he could with his cumbersome guitar case. It was huge, sturdy brown leather, previously used for a cello, which he stuffed with towels to protect his guitar whenever he travelled. In the scrum to board the full carriage, revellers pushed him and his bulky case out, back onto the platform, and the tram left without him.

He lumbered over to the nearby tram station, found a clean place to sit and propped himself against the wall. He made himself comfortable against the case knowing the first tram in the morning would be about around 6.00 a.m. and he tried to grab a few hours sleep.

The next morning, as he sat in the near-empty carriage, he overheard a shocked conductor talking to a colleague, 'The last tram yesterday got a direct hit with a bomb. There were no survivors.'

Fred never forgot that night. He had goosebumps when he recognised his lucky escape. He was under attack, and he hadn't even left his hometown and gone to war.

When stationed as a ground crew operative in an overseas airfield, the officer's mess, sergeant's mess, or canteen doubled as venues for the band. Entertainment officers sought performance-standard musical talent. Barry, in Fred's group, was a professional keyboard player from London. He formed an RAF Swingtet, which depended on available musicians, so it varied in size and quality.

He and Fred enjoyed a visit to London buying instruments, where Fred returned with a clarinet and a saxophone. They played for functions which bridged the gap between dance halls and clubs. They also performed as a backing group for visiting professional entertainers. It was a rare occasion when they had to stop playing to service incoming planes.

Fred's second near-miss occurred while stationed in Germany when he heard the low drone of aircraft engines circling above. He saw an enemy plane make an arc and sprinted for shelter across a field. In his haste, he tripped over a cabbage stalk and fell full length. Bullets thudded along one side of him, and he lay still until the fighter flew away. His knees knocked together for the only time in his life.

One time overseas, after playing guitar and saxophone in the RAF sergeant's mess, he staggered back to his billet. He crossed the airport runway, in the pitch dark, riddled with bomb craters, and tumbled into one 15-feet deep. With no way of climbing the steep walls, the sensible thing was to fall into a drunken sleep in the rubble. Dawn broke, and he shouted for help. His colleagues cheered and made a rowdy performance while they hauled him from the hole, astounded he hadn't broken a single bone.

When the focus of war activity moved away from France, the troops, already trained in trades, trickled back to England and found full employment right away. Fred stayed in Germany and helped to establish a business school for the females, the WRAF. He trained them for future secretarial positions requiring typing, shorthand, and accounts for their eventual return to Civvy Street.

Barry had already established several London connections, ready for the Swingtet to fit into the swinging London, post-war music scene when they demobbed. They were disappointed when Fred refused their offer and returned home to Manchester. They thought it a waste of his talent to go back to an insurance office. After six years, racketing around Europe, Fred longed to sleep in his own bed and have a cooked evening meal at the same time every night.

Jobs had been left open for returning service members. On his return, he decided against the lift insurance office option, and accepted an officer's position in Germany, but then met me and changed his mind.

Fred reluctantly re-joined the insurance company, and I worked in various central city post offices. After Fred had finished work, he walked to My office and waited, ogling me from the back of the room until I finished serving the customers. We travelled home to Gorton together on the bus to our separate homes for dinner and met up again each evening.

Grace and I had scheduled to attend an evening class, but not enthused with paper-flower making, we walked to Fred's house instead to invite him out for a coffee, and on the off chance, meet his mother, Lily.

A middle-aged lady with iron-grey wavy hair and a perfect gleaming complexion opened the door, with a glacial stare. She looked smart in her dazzling white blouse tucked into a navy skirt. The unexpected hostility of her welcome shocked us as we stood on the doorstep.

'Fred,' she shouted out, 'Two women here for you.' The bitchy tone of her voice and her icy expression implied we were hussies as she pointed to the living room.

As he changed his shoes, she stayed out of our way in the kitchen. We beat a hasty retreat, while Fred explained her unfriendliness. 'She's very suspicious. Now you know why I never brought you to see her before.'

The following Sunday, he arrived early to call on me. His mother attended evening church service from six to nine, so we sneaked back to his house. Dark doorways and back alleys were for trollops, so a real bed was tempting.

We had just settled into his bed when we heard a loud clattering of his mother's heels as she trotted upstairs. Fred flung himself against the bedroom door, stark naked when she tried to barge in.

'Go away,' he shouted through the door. 'She's going.' We threw on our clothes and slunk out. Had we sinned? Hardly, we'd only been found out.

The previous Monday, when she changed his sheets, she had found my hair slide with blonde hairs. She must have suspected Fred's game. She pretended to go to church, waited around the corner, sneaked back, and when the bedroom light came on, she charged upstairs to confront us.

What a farce. When we got outside, away from the house, we hung onto each other, and laughed, because it appeared to be so wicked and wasn't. In 1946, talk of sex was still taboo, and impossible for us to share this hilarious story with anyone, not even my sisters. Contraception was Russian Roulette in those days. I remember Mum's mantra: 'Get the engagement ring on the finger before you have sex. He'd be obliged to marry you if he put you in the club.'

We chose a large, inexpensive, spinel, solitaire, which looked the part and sparkled under artificial lights. Fred insisted on getting my wedding ring at the same time, a large, heavy solid 22-carat ring, bought before his demob money ran out. The jeweller suggested Fred put most of his money into the gold in the wedding ring. They told him to economise on the engagement one as the amount of gold in the wedding ring could be pawned for a decent amount, at any time, if required.

A few years later, I was glad of this advice, as my purse got stolen while on the bus home. I never wore the engagement ring at work and always left it in my handbag. I felt a fraud as we could never have afforded a real diamond so large and I was never keen on the ring. It was ostentatious, but Fred loved it, so I pretended to everyone that I was heartbroken at losing it. We never replaced it, even though Fred offered, we always had something more important to buy.

With the rings safely bought, it was now acceptable to go away for a weekend. One day, Mum looked for the ring in my room to show it to her sister. It wasn't there; I had nipped off for the weekend with Fred, wearing it. When we got back, Mum had a quiet word. 'I think you two should set a wedding date sooner than later.' She had been 'landed' with five surviving children and didn't want me to get pregnant and have to get married, as she had done.

Fred hated hanging around, waiting for me to finish work and also didn't want me to go in on Saturdays. I intended to stay at the Post Office for another six months to qualify for a dowry, a six-year service bonus, a substantial lump sum given to girls when they left to get married.

'It's only money,' Fred said, 'I can't wait for six months to marry you.' I forfeited the dowry with reluctance and resigned.

With his usual single-mindedness, he came back from the local vicar holding a special licence to enable us to marry in two weeks, in our parish church. The vicar was curious, 'Why the great haste?'

'We couldn't wait any longer,' Fred replied honestly. The vicar must have assumed I was pregnant and rushed through the licence.

With only two weeks to arrange our wedding, the family, as always, clubbed together. They possessed no suitable clothes, so used their saved coupons, and borrowed hats from somewhere. They arranged the flowers, a car, and a cake - a magnificent effort all round.

With no time to make a dress, Mum accompanied me to buy one. We chose a flattering, pale turquoise crepe day dress. It was plain and V-necked, gathered over the bosom, and knee-length which I could use again for special occasions.

Our memorable marriage took place on 26 April 1947 at The Church of Our Lady in Gorton. A handful of my nearest and dearest came to wish us well. While I waited with Marjorie, my bridesmaid, for the wedding car, we compared hats; hers was navy blue, mine brown. Her borrowed, veiled hat suited my dress and vice versa. It surprised those who helped me get ready for the ceremony when I walked down the aisle wearing a different hat. I never knew who provided my magnificent bouquet of golden spring daffodils.

It was an overcast afternoon, but as I glided down the aisle with Dad, a shaft of sunlight shimmered over me, and the congregation gasped at this enchanting cameo. Overjoyed, this was a beautiful sign, and I knew fate destined this union.

I smiled into the face of my darling husband-to-be, and thought, 'My God, what on earth are you wearing?'

Belted over silver-grey slacks was a soft, wool, camel-coloured safari jacket, suitable for an African wildlife expedition or a motoring holiday in the South of France, but not quite the attire for his wedding day.

When we came out of the church, I hissed to Mum, 'Have you seen what's he's wearing?'

Mum was always on his side and whispered, 'Don't you *dare* say a word to him about his coat.'

After the service, we returned to Mum and Dad's house on the Avenue. We didn't have champagne to celebrate, but my 'sensitive' auntie Annie read the tea leaves in my cup.

She looked at me, smiled and forecast, 'An untroubled and happy marriage. Two keys dominate; you will have an offer of two houses, and as the leaves are under the rim, it could be very soon.'

We assumed she was acting kindly towards us on our wedding day. The likelihood of this coming true was remote as there were no houses available.

For the first few months of married life, we lived in Gorton with Lily, Fred's widowed mother. She valued her privacy to the point of paranoia. Heavy handmade lace curtains covered her windows. Whenever I answered the door, she stormed over and pushed me aside. 'Don't let them in. They only want to see what we've got.'

She kept a clean house, but there was nothing of value to hide in her mismatched well-polished, wooden furniture.

I was not a saint, just lucky that I didn't get pregnant before I got married at 20 years old. We had only been married a month when I overheard raised voices in her kitchen. Lily hissed, 'She'll have a load of brats, just like her mother. She'll bring you down.'

Fred saw my tail end running upstairs and bounded after me. He hugged, dried my eyes, and to soothe me said, 'Of course you can have a baby.' But under his breath, he no doubt muttered to himself, 'but not just yet.'

Ardwick was part of a slum clearance which stretched for miles. The network of cobbled streets leftover from the demolition cut the area into precise segments. A Gothic church stood proud within this wasteland, a perfect setting for an apocalyptic film. From these houses, the occupants moved to the edge of Manchester into newly created satellite villages.

As my auntie's tea leaves predicted, we were offered a vacancy in a dilapidated house in Ardwick. It was in a terrace of four houses in a cul-de-sac opposite the school playground with a rent of six shillings per week. The two-up-two-down terrace had flagged floors, no electricity or hot water, and an outside lavatory in the tiny yard - a real hovel, with a fancy name, Lyon's Court. We almost accepted this rental, but within days, a more suitable property became vacant in Lyon Street.

Granny Rowlands collected the rent on behalf of the rent collector. The neighbours left their cash and rent books with her on their way to work. He collected weekly, and while he drank a cuppa, he counted the money and wrote it up in the books. He was grateful for her assistance, so as fate would have it when the house next door to her became empty, he offered it to her, for me, a newlywed.

The end of terrace house had steps rising to a lobby, but it had always been a seedy area, and she told us a prostitute was murdered years ago on that doorstep. We snapped it up because there was no chance of inheriting Lily's rented council house, we would have needed three children to qualify for one that size.

As this house made a corner, it gave us an extra window in the kitchen/living room. We accepted this rental at ten shillings per week. There was one small problem, the plaster on the dividing wall between the houses had crumbled, exposing the brickwork.

Dad, being a builder, was thrilled to help in our first home, and hastened to plaster and paint the walls before we moved in. Talk about a whirling dervish.

Once Lily knew we had found a place of our own to rent and would soon move out, she avoided us and instead left copious messages. Nothing else changed, she continued to do our washing, and as we never ate together, dinner was still left out for us every evening, but with instructions of how long to heat it through in the oven.

It was surreal; her paranoia rubbed off on me. I became anxious and had dreams that she was trying to poison us. When we left her home, communication stopped. Fred attempted to visit her several times, but whenever he saw her in the street, she always hurried over to the other side.

It was 1947, and Lily had reached 52 years old. We realised that after Fred moved out, and without his weekly contribution, she would have to work to supplement her widow's pension. She had worked in Terry's of York, making ornate chocolate boxes with fancy ribbons, and she might have returned to the chocolate box industry, down the hill, beyond Pin Mill Brow, within walking distance of her bus.

Fred told me he had applied to many large newspapers to be a roving reporter, but they told him he was already too old, even though he had shorthand and typing skills. They told him they took school-leavers at 15 and trained them up themselves. So, that's when he became a lift insurance clerk and wore a pinstripe suit, waistcoat, stiff white collar, and tie until he joined the RAF.

Every week we sent the detachable collars to be laundered. To carry home a specialist box full of starched collars was deemed impressive. I washed his shirts and ironed them by heating a heavy iron on the gas cooker and was careful to ensure no smut ingrained itself in the white cloth.

Fred soon became bored in the insurance position, and one morning, while he sat in the company's toilet cubicle, he glanced at a newspaper left on the floor. An ad for junior school teacher-training positions caught his attention. The Education Committee office was a five-minute walk away. His lunch break couldn't come quick enough. He marched over, completed the application, and they accepted him straight away. The government was desperate for junior school teachers, and they readily awarded Fred the grant to study on an intensive, truncated course, thirteen months, instead of three years.

That evening, he barged in the door, grabbed me and danced around the kitchen, ecstatic to relay his news. As he wasn't usually demonstrative, this showed how deeply happy he was to study and get paid. He had never told me of any aspirations to become a teacher, but I knew he had experience from his time in Germany with the WRAFs. I was caught up in his infectious exuberance and looked forward to further developments.

I thought you'd like to know the song title of this chapter, "What Are You Doing The Rest Of Your Life" Fred and I had chosen as "our song". It has such poignant lyrics which held true for us.

"What are you doing the rest of your life?
North and south and east and west of your life
I have only one request of your life
That you spend it all with me."

(Lyrics written by Alan Bergman and Marilyn Bergman and original music written by Michel Legrand.)

Chapter 9 – Spooky

(Peter Grant)

The women in my family always dabbled in fortune-telling cards, tea leaves, and talked about the supernatural. Auntie Annie used the teacup as a focus while others used the crystal ball. She was a remarkable psychic but only did readings on special occasions; because of being badgered at work during her tea break.

For someone with a keen interest in the occult, it's incredible I haven't seen a ghost. However, I know of three paranormal sightings in the family which appeared to sceptics, disinterested in the afterlife.

One evening, Nan sat in the firelight, holding hands with her new boyfriend, Roy, when a rustling sound made them turn around. They saw Mum dressed in a long white nightgown standing by the door.

Embarrassed, Nan said, 'Oh, Mum, it's you! I won't be long.'

The following morning, Nan asked, 'Mum, why were you standing in the doorway last night in your white nightie with no dressing gown?'

Mum said, 'I didn't come downstairs. I don't even own a white nightie.'

Nan brushed it off, 'It must've been the light from the fire flickering and reflecting.'

When Nan met Roy, it made my life easier. He was popular, friendly, well-dressed and generous to our family. Nan confided to me sometime later, 'I'm glad I've got Roy. I was jealous of you and Fred and your happiness.'

'I like him; you're a perfect match,' I said. They were both expert dancers; both petite, he with short, dark-hair, good-looking with even features, while Nan, measured just under five feet.

I watched Roy's multiple personas evolve and names always have clues. Roy was Roly Robb at junior school, Roy in grammar school, and with the family, Charles as he progressed in business and Charles Roland Robb when he became the managing director of a thriving printing business. Ambitious and successful, which took hard work, sacrifice, and flair, he settled Nan and their family in Marple, a middle-class country suburb.

For Nan's wedding to Roy in September 1949, I made myself a dress with an integral peplum, moss green, figured furnishing velvet, which caused a nasty person to say I might be sat on, mistaken for an armchair. It photographed magnificently, so that's all that mattered. With no time left to insert the zip, someone in the family tacked together the dress opening together, with me in it.

After the reception, I was tipsy, and Fred's wide outstretched hand secured me onto the back of the motorbike as he carefully steered us home. In the bedroom, I giggled and became limp and useless. When Fred asked, 'Where's the zip?'

I flopped about the bed and slurred, 'There's no zip. Rip it off.' He said, 'To hear these words is every man's dream.' But his fantasy was short-lived. Once undressed, I collapsed, rolled into a heap and Fred bundled me under the covers.

Not all my creations were masterpieces. I once made a dress for work out of a fine, wool army blanket. The longer I sat there in the office, the more overheated I became, so colleagues cooled me down by taking turns to fan me. It was the last time I wore it. Such a pity, but this elegant, khaki garment ended on the compost heap.

While Fred waited to attend teacher's training college, he obtained his schoolboy dream of becoming a reporter when offered a job at the *Two Worlds* psychic newspaper. One of our neighbours recommended we visit a medium who lived near us in Ardwick Green, ten minutes' walk away. It was acceptable in those days to arrive on the doorstep unannounced.

The medium was an unremarkable white-haired old lady. Six people crammed into the parlour of her tiny terraced house, in stark contrast to the large hall venues we attended for the newspaper. As we sat in a ring of assorted chairs, we hoped for curious or amusing individual readings or messages for the intimate group.

On Fred's turn, the medium became animated. 'A young man who's just passed over sends his best wishes. He tells me he was not killed in a plane but on a motorbike.' She told us in such a straightforward manner that we believed her. In a peaceful atmosphere, we prayed together and left her modest terraced house inspired and intrigued. Throughout that time, in all our travels, we only encountered welcoming, warm, unpretentious spiritualists.

Later that week, Fred bumped into an old pre-war friend. He cut across the formalities, 'Fred, you'll never believe this. Dicky Bird was killed, not as a pilot but in a motorbike crash. How ironic, he survived the war but died in a local road accident.'

We exchanged glances and expressed great surprise, but of course, we already knew of this through the medium. This message took top place in our search for proof of life after death. I was Anglican and did not doubt that people from another dimension had contacted us. Fred said, 'If someone has proved life after death, it surely must be true.'

One evening, I sheltered in the *Two Worlds* doorway waiting for Fred to finish work. In a side room, a religious meeting underway caught my attention. The theme was reincarnation. I couldn't help eavesdropping, captivated by the intriguing novel concept of no dead relatives or friends' souls waiting for me to join them. They were busy preparing for their next life on earth.

I now imagine a repertory company of souls, at a similar level of spiritual attainment, playing out different roles in our lives, of either a relative or a companion. To me, this concept explained instant rapport or the flash of recognition when first meeting someone.

It's reassuring when nearing my death; I can say, 'Well, that was a thrilling and interesting life, I'll come down and have another.'

How many have experienced strange episodes in their life, dismissed them as happy accidents, and not discussed them with anyone for fear of being ridiculed? Coincidences are not psychic phenomena, only actions so unusual the odds against them happening are impossible to calculate and I find them riveting.

We travelled all over Manchester when Fred reported on spiritualist meetings, and Birmingham was the furthest place we travelled for work on our motorbike. It was unusual for me to have a message at these events, so I held my breath as the medium pointed to me and said, 'A little girl, initial E, wants to contact you. She says there was a china doll that disappeared.' Before I could say anything, she swung away to relay the next message.

I whispered to Fred, 'I think it must be for somebody else. It doesn't mean anything to me.'

After the meeting, Fred interviewed a few attendees who were stunned at the strange, inexplicable accuracy of their messages. For us, it was worth the long trip to witness the uplifting atmosphere of friendship and love which filled that great hall.

The next day, we relayed the medium's message to Mum. We expected her to dismiss it, but she looked puzzled. 'Yes,' she said, her eyes misting, 'We never found out what happened to Elsie's beautiful doll.'

I had forgotten about my elder sister, and Mum reminded me of the heart-breaking story. In 1928, after Elsie fell down the stairs, she became weak and confined to bed. While they nursed her, she kept asking for Joe, another lodger who'd rented a room in the same house with us, and who she adored.

Joe had been ill and housebound and often played with her. It shocked our relatives to the core when Elsie's condition worsened, and she murmured, 'I can see Joe.'

Joe had been dead for two months, and not long after Elsie sighted him, she died. They suspected the three-year-old caught pneumonia, but it was more likely to have been the same infectious tuberculosis that took Joe.

Some suggested his spirit might have come down to collect her, as the unlikely couple had been inseparable here on earth. With no cure for tuberculosis or pneumonia, infant mortality was widespread.

Elsie departed, and so did her china doll. Perhaps someone stole it? It was never found and remained a mystery. With no credit cards invented, I suspect my Auntie Grace bought the expensive toy by instalments. In that area, the doll was considered rare and valuable, and well worth stealing.

Mum was inconsolable after Elsie's death and became deeply depressed, so my aunts tended to me as a toddler. One morning, Mum came downstairs, smiling for the first time in ages, 'I had a vivid dream. Elsie approached my bed and said, "Look, Mum, I'm dancing" and twirled away through the door.' The cloud of Mum's depression lifted and blew away, and I took centre stage, as number one child, for a little while.

Chapter 10 - Electric Avenue

(Eddie Grant)

Our terraced house in Ardwick was basic, but Fred couldn't exist without electricity and needed to have at least one power outlet. We hired an electrician for twelve pounds and ten shillings, and he connected four ceiling lights and one socket. Over a few days, the interested neighbours viewed the installation and, when finished, came inside for the switch-on. With panache, the electrician flicked on the electric light to rapturous applause. A chain reaction from our neighbours kept our grateful electrician in work for months. Heaters and electric lights illuminated the tumbledown terraces, with families taking turns to use their revered plug for the few available gadgets.

This plug assured our top standing in the neighbourhood, and we bought a television in time for the 1947-1948 football cup final between Manchester United and Blackpool. Not the bog-standard nine-inch diameter set, Fred splashed out on the ten-inch. The tiny black-and-white screen was out of all proportion to its bulky housing.

On Cup Final day, Dad and Fred arranged their chairs like thrones, 18 inches away from the screen. We had invited the neighbourhood men, and our tiny living room was jammed packed, with standing room only. Just when the match reached a crucial point, the television clicked off, and the screen went black. Dad jumped up and hit the tv to help it work. It stayed blank, and the men swore and threw their fists in the air. Fred waited a few minutes for the set to cool down and the men to relax. He sighed with relief when the grainy picture loomed into life when he switched it back on.

On my way to the corner shop, I heard applause and shouting echoing in the air. I knew they had won when the winning score of 4-2 brought rousing cheers all over Manchester.

Not content with one plug, Fred fashioned an unsafe extension lead. The cherished plug also meant Fred didn't have to shave using chilly water and a cut-throat razor. We still didn't have running hot water, only a gas water heater in the kitchen. When Fred had lunch with Mum and my siblings four times a week, he had access to their bath and copious boiling water. I had to wash in our enormous pottery kitchen sink. It had a large cupboard above it, so I crawled in, and kept my head down to squeeze in the narrow gap. Fred, oblivious to my contortions, just sat completing another crossword. He only put it aside to hand me a towel and lift me onto the floor.

Whenever I visited my relatives, their greeting consisted, 'Plenty of hot water upstairs,' and I wandered off to wallow in a luxurious bath.

The local municipal baths made provision for us unfortunates without a bathroom, still waiting for the slum clearance and better housing. In winter, they heated the swimming baths, which emitted a steamy chlorine vapour. They built it to cater to a more significant population, and as they rehoused families, the numbers dwindled.

The rear of the building housed a laundry, as hot as Dante's Inferno. The Labour Council built the facility, and I can imagine the councillor saying, 'My voters may be poor, but by gum, they'll be clean.'

When I got there late in the evening, my stiletto heels echoed as I walked around the deserted hall lined with banks of about 50 deep, unused, galvanised sinks. Most people had done their washing during the daytime, and it was pure indulgence to have the place to myself, with access to unlimited, free hot water and soap powder. For months, I frequented this eerie wash house, until one night I trudged home through the streets like Little Orphan Annie, with my sack of clean damp clothes, and that's when, overwhelmed, I felt impoverished, miserable and prayed for change.

The swimming baths in other city areas had even more blandishments for the poor. The trained masseur laid us on huge slabs, and I experienced my first massage. I didn't know what to expect. After he pummelled and kneaded the knots in my back and neck, I stood in my swimsuit as he doused me with icy water from a hosepipe. I came out stimulated, full of life, a unique experience, but one I didn't repeat.

In our first winter, water froze in the outside toilet cistern. Fred took a warmed kettle of water and stood on the toilet seat to pour it into the container to defrost the ice. He wedged the spout between the open box and the ceiling, misjudged the opening and poured streams of lukewarm water over the solid block of ice, which slid off and drenched his clothes. He hated water on him in all forms so you can imagine the expletives.

Fred came across the strangest things and marched into the kitchen one day, with a rolled-up, bright-yellow tarpaulin. 'It's a dinghy to take on our holidays,' he said. 'We can sail from bay to bay.' The concept was odd, coming from a water-hater and non-swimmer.

Our neighbour, Mrs Fisher, had two dainty pre-school daughters, who enjoyed visiting our two stray cats, Horace and Kitty. The girls were quiet, well-turned-out and sweetly fussed over the cats. From the living room sofa, they watched while Fred moved the kitchen table back, unrolled and inflated the plastic dinghy with a bicycle pump. He half-filled it with water using a bucket and invited the girls to take their shoes off and have a paddle.

'Sound as a bell. We'll try it out properly tomorrow,' he said and placed the dinghy in the yard to dry before rolling it up.

When I next ran into Mrs Fisher, she asked, with a raised eyebrow, 'Have you really got a paddling pool installed in your kitchen?'

I laughed, 'Not now. It's in the backyard.' She looked puzzled but relieved and changed the subject.

The venue for the dinghy launch was the park, with what Fred believed was a small lake, at the bottom of a sloping grassy bank.

It was a children's wading and boating pool, and on a sunny Saturday, dozens of children were already splashing about in the water, as their parents sat on the hill and supervised.

Glad of a diversion, they watched Fred take off his shoes, roll up his trouser legs, blow up the inflatable, and push it out two yards. He gingerly climbed in and squatted while I squashed in beside him and rolled my eyes in resignation at the audience. With a gentle shove from the children, we floated away.

I thought, *If this helps him over his fear of water, it has been worth it*. A few yards out, a film of water was already seeping in over our backsides.

'We're sinking,' I said.

The look of terror on his face was pitiful, as he shouted to the children, 'How deep is it?'

In two feet of water, they gathered around and gently pushed us back to the side. We stepped out of the submerged dinghy and now, dripping wet to the waist, dragged our makeshift boat behind us, to wild shrieks of laughter and derision.

I perched on the back of the motorbike with the sodden, rolled-up tarpaulin wedged between us. We hadn't thought to bring towels, so left a trail of puddles as we drove out of the park for the long drive home.

In rented rooms in tenements and slum two-up two-down terraces, doors and windows were left open to the street, to facilitate airflow during the humid, city summer. One hot night, as we slept with our bedroom window ajar, a clatter woke us. Thieves had broken into the factory opposite and to gain access had pulled down the iron factory fire escape that rattled and woke the whole neighbourhood.

With quick thinking, Fred darted downstairs into our back yard and blew his school whistle three times. The shrill screech pierced the night air, imitating a police signal.

From our bedroom window, I watched the burglars slither down the ladder and run away. Fred came in, pushed the sash window closed. 'Sleep,' he mumbled.

The following morning, from our grandstand bedroom window, we saw police officers pushing back the fire escape ladder and busying themselves. On our way to work, we stopped to exchange pleasantries with our next-door neighbours.

'Did you hear that racket last night?' they asked. 'They caught the stupid villains who were trying to nick stuff from a cigarette shop up the road. We didn't bother to come out into the street because we heard the policeman's whistle.'

Fred confessed with a wicked grin, 'Actually, it was me, not the police, but it did the trick.'

The employment exchange deemed me a natural for the Civil Service. My unedifying title was Temporary Grade-Three Clerk at the Ministry of Food.

I dealt with wages and admin, and they partnered me with a middle-aged lady Mrs Storey, who instructed us to call her by her surname and had arranged her desk to allow a bird's-eye view of any office antics. My colleagues thought her severe, and her nickname was "The Dragon".

I got on well with her, sat opposite, and maintained pleasant contact with the insipid girls behind me. Mrs Storey and I raced through our work to leave time for chatting. I felt protected and appreciated her clever, cruel wit, so long as directed at someone else.

She wore plain clothes, flat shoes, and no make-up at work, but outside, she led something of a double life. Nobody knew her boyfriend was a French Freedom Fighter, who had access to scarce commodities such as nylons and make-up, stashed in his officer's mess.

I thought she must have been well-off since she lived in a leafy, affluent area, and her daughter attended a private school.

One day, "the Dragon" was off work, sick, and my colleagues "volunteered" me to visit her with flowers. When she opened the door, my jaw dropped. She was all dolled up with mascara, dark pencilled in eyebrows, and red showgirl lips. With her shiny platinum-blonde hair perfectly styled in a glamorous wave, she was a dead ringer for Marlene Dietrich.

She invited me in, poured us a glass of sherry and cooked lunch. She confided that she didn't own the house but rented the bedsitter with a kitchen and bathroom. A widow, with just one wage coming in, she desperately wanted her daughter to continue her private schooling. So, once a month, they paid a dutiful visit to her late husband's mother, who lived in the countryside. With scrubbed faces, thick stockings, and drab, nondescript clothes, they caught the train. The mother-in-law, a strict Methodist, had Victorian values, and this visit afforded them a regular stipend to cover extra living expenses, with her daughter's fees paid directly to the private school.

When they had done their penance with the old lady, they returned to the station in their drabness. In the waiting room, they transformed themselves with make-up, gossamer stockings, and high-heeled shoes. They emerged, unrecognisable from the downtrodden women who had set out with their begging bowl. Their final wickedness in this charade was to kick back with a large gin and tonic to celebrate.

From Mrs Storey, I learned that for the greater good, sacrificing one's principles was acceptable. I wondered if those performances made a lasting impression on her daughter, this well-educated, well-groomed young girl.

The position with Mrs Storey ended when Agriculture and Fish swallowed the Ministry of Food, and I moved to work in the inner city.

My new title was Civil Service, Grade Two Temporary Clerk and a new friend, Theodore Galgut, (Theo) in personnel, brought me a form. 'Fill that in, pass the exam, and it grants you an extra week's leave,' she explained. Fred tutored me at night, using example exam papers.

I had only a borderline pass and primed for the dreaded, pre-requisite, half-hour interview. I had dealt with many kinds of people and had a knack for adopting appropriate body language. The panel comprised four middle-aged men who sat on one side of a long table. Their faces softened as I sat across from them. I crossed my dainty feet, pushed my glasses up my nose, smiled along the line, and clasped my hands in my lap.

Startled at my composure, they beamed back. I tried hard to give answers they hoped for until they exchanged glances and gathered their papers. One man, while collecting files together, asked me which newspapers I read.

I said, 'I have access to *the Guardian* and occasionally, *the Telegraph.*'

'Access?' he looked puzzled.

'My bosses give them to me each day when they leave the office. They don't do crosswords.'

He seemed surprised and impressed. I answered one last question before I got up.

'What does your husband do for a living, Mrs Rowland?'

'Teaching. He tutored me for this exam.'

As I closed the door, I heard their laughter. We had all put in a decent performance. I didn't know if the hilarity was for my presentation or whether Fred's tuition had been lacking, and I had only scraped through the exam.

Theo, in Personnel, was responsible for my meteoric rise through the Civil Service. She advised me I had an internal transfer to Ag, Food and Fish. She was in her early twenties, trendy and flamboyant, with covetable emerald-green faux-snakeskin court shoes.

In the large office next to her cubbyhole, she announced to me, 'You're wages and admin, and this is your team of four men.' Someone dusted a chair and cleared a space for me on a square table.

Introducing me, she said, 'This is Win from Food, same system.' We sneaked back to her cubicle for a coffee and a crafty fag.

She puffed, 'You like classical music, don't you? I've got the new Brahms violin tape.'

I smiled, 'Menuhin?'

Animated, she said, 'You're in for a real treat.'

We founded a friendship on the spot, two rare floating water-lilies in a lake of men.

A snooty, self-important member of staff bustled around the offices making notes. When absent through illness, we discovered he had no real job; he worked hard at walking around the offices carrying a clipboard and pencil.

My new colleagues referred to themselves, the merged workforce, as a load of demics. Half unfit to go in the Forces and the others damaged, unable to stay in the Forces. They were vulnerable, and I became fond of them. Two served in tropical campaigns, contracted malaria, and suffered from frequent debilitating bouts of fever and sickness. Theo's job was to find permanent placements for them in the Service or Civvy street. Not long after, our department disbanded.

Our charges settled, we two waterlilies were now high and dry. The only job available for my rank was in Shropshire, and somewhere remote and extreme, such as the Orkney's, for Theo. We paid our salaries up-to-date and sacked ourselves. If bosses existed, they were invisible.

In retrospect, there was nothing to stop us from remaining in our surreal sinecure. We could have enjoyed gainful employment, clutched our clipboards and sought for placements for ourselves, while we talked of books and music. Those couple of years working together cemented a long and entertaining friendship outside work.

We contributed to numerous leaving presents in our time there. Theo declared, to be fair, I had earned one. She unhooked the government-issue framed print of *Umbrellas* by Renoir, from the office wall, which I had previously admired, wrapped it, and warbled, 'Happy Leaving Present to you.' There was nothing left of interest she wanted for her leaving gift. The building returned to the owner, and the furniture deposited into storage.

Umbrellas was our first art piece, and we hung the print in pride of place in the hall of our house in Burnage. I'm sure the Ministry of Agriculture and Fish never missed it.

Theo and I shared a joint driving force; education was our right. Her Jewish father, a tall blonde South African, was patrician and doted on his two good-looking sons and smoothed their paths to university and their professions. One son, in a taxi going home, jumped out when it screeched to a halt in front of a man under attack. As the boy rushed to the victim's aid, he caught the sharp edge of a knife and was viciously slashed from cheek to chin by the assailant. He crawled back into the cab, covered in blood, holding his face together, and the cabbie sped around the corner to the hospital. A long, livid scar remained as a caution to anyone who wanted to act as a hero.

Theo and I were overweight. Her enemy was her mother's delicious food, mine was the British Restaurant, opposite our hovel in Lyon Street. Fred carried home delicious, subsidised, two-course, takeout lunches, and dinners, for a few pence. Kind ladies served the food and with no concept of portion control, fed the clean, poor city dwellers of Ardwick.

Fred was their darling. Tall, dark and witty, in collar and tie, he stood out in the sea of mothers, babies, and pensioners. The dinner ladies asked to meet me. In my smart office dress and clickety heels, I smiled at them and acknowledged their past largesse. I, too, became a darling.

I was luckier than Theo, the British Restaurant closed and reverted to the pre-war carpentry section of the school opposite. Women's magazines proliferated, and I chose one diet, fruit, and vegetables for two days, protein for the other two.

131

Her doctor gave her a diet sheet and told her to reduce her food portions. He convinced her concerned mother; there was no danger if Theo's food intake decreased. With no immediate threat of famine or pestilence to the Jewish race, her mother helped her lose weight.

We both lost a stone in a month, and often marched for 15 minutes to the university for a coffee and to see her boyfriend, John Rowlands. He was blonde, gentle and artistic, and spoke a strange computer language with his colleagues.

He had almost completed his PhD and had helped build one of the first automatic adding machines which filled the room. Nowadays, 70 years on, calculators are downsized to a microchip.

It was a thrilling time, soaking up all this culture. We hung out with smart people, enjoyed music, art, literature, and the cinema, and became caught up in a constant social whirl of outings. One of our bosses dropped his unwanted tickets onto Theo's desk, which gave us a once in a lifetime opportunity; front-row seats for a Pablo Casals concert. We sat, only yards away from him, mesmerised, as he played his remarkable pure-toned cello.

Subsequent tickets allowed us to jump the queue for the first Picasso/Matisse art exhibition in the city art gallery. I was in my element; education seemed easy, enjoyable, and mostly free in Manchester. Theo and I revelled in this sociable and exciting lifestyle.

Students were encouraged and subsidised, and Fred's college scarf became the free pass to plays, concerts, and orchestral rehearsals. As a non-paying audience, we queued in the hall, and when the lights lowered, and no more patrons claimed paid seats, we quietly dispersed and filled the empty ones.

Theo and I had both met clever men; we had covered every possibility to further our cultural knowledge. She married John, who became a worldwide lecturer on nuclear physics, and she became a polyglot. Their two sons became musical prodigies; thus, Theo entered her "heaven".

I became a permanent clerical officer, head of my department, in charge of the four men. Nothing changed, we all worked together at speed, which left time for them to talk sports betting and fill in the football pools, and for me to talk books with Theo and our gay friend, Henry, who belonged to an upmarket book club.

A year later, on completion of my probation, I received a letter of confirmation of the extra week's holiday allowance. My payslip also showed a year's back pay. I was incredulous; the staggering amount was enough for Fred and me to buy a new motorbike.

With the luxury of reliable transport, we ventured further along the West coast on our holidays. Most boarding house windows displayed signs offering accommodation, which comprised bed-and-breakfast in the parlour, and then any guests locked out by the "dragons" for the day. This banishment led to the proliferation of shelters along the promenades, and the popularity of Blackpool Tower.

On our longer holidays, we reached mid-Wales, where a broad estuary fought the tide for supremacy. When it rained, the shelters filled with singing from English visitors, often accompanied by Welsh harmonies.

We spent many glorious days riding around the mountains, and after dinner, we took our usual stroll along the beach to see the sun go down. One evening, we were horrified to see farm-carts piled with black tarpaulins. Some bystander said they were bringing up bodies, retrieved from the seashore; it was a sobering moment. The prevailing mood in the town was sombre, and we hurried back to our accommodation, fighting back the tears.

Our landlady said, 'There was a freak cross-current which caused a huge wave to race across the beach. It swept some holiday-makers, including children, into the sea. Some were drowned.'

In our room, shocked at what we had witnessed on the bay, I wept into Fred's chest. The holiday atmosphere had changed. We abandoned our trip, packed our bags, and rode home.

Was this happening from years ago, the driving force to prioritise teaching our children to swim when we moved from the city to the seaside? Thus, is our behaviour seasoned and modified by a single searing incident?

To fill the gap for maths teachers left by the war, Fred and other students crammed two or three-year courses into thirteen months of intensive teacher training. He wrote the lectures verbatim in shorthand, typed up his notes at night and made copies for classmates. Most survived this gruelling course and exams; others had nervous breakdowns. Fred thrived on the challenge, failing this, meant a dreary office life of insurance proposals. He was never going back there.

After Fred passed his training, the Education Committee allotted him a junior school position. Out of the hundreds of schools in Manchester, they gave him my old school in Gorton. My younger siblings, Alan and Linda, attended this school and Fred pointed out the relationship as a courtesy, but it posed no problem, as he wouldn't be assigned to teach them.

Whenever Fred and I took out Alan and Linda, with them being 20-years younger, everyone presumed the two blonde children were ours. For years, at lunchtime, Fred walked home from school to Mum's, hand in hand with them. He played the piano to the budgie, found time to teach Linda ballroom dancing, and completed the football pools with my Mum. The pool's first prize was a staggering £75,000. We dreamed of what we would do if we won. I told Fred I would buy a bungalow by the sea, have two children and a dog.

To quote Marilyn Monroe: '*I'm dreaming the hardest.*'

For the first time, Fred enjoyed being part of real family life and saw them more often than me. I worked in the city, but he kept me apprised of any gossip. In a rare sentimental moment,

Fred confided, 'I wish your Mum had raised me. It's such a warm and loving household.'

Fred was brought up by his mother, as his elderly father, William Bone, worked mostly away from home, through a lack of jobs since the steel industry closure. Knowing Lily, and how cold and difficult she could be, I understood why he travelled abroad to secure employment to bring in the money. He was a generation older than Lily, married and widowed twice already. Everyone expected her to marry William's son, Rowland, more her age; but she married his father.

While William was on assignment at a steelworks in Australia, a piece of metal became embedded and blinded him in one eye. He returned to Lily in Manchester, took a lump sum payment, and retired. He died of heart failure, not long after, in 1945, aged 71, and Fred took special leave from Germany for his father's funeral.

Lily's house was only a five-minute walk from Fred's new teaching position at Gorton Mount School. Still estranged, I insisted he visit her once more and try to resuscitate the relationship. He agreed, and after school went to visit her.

A different tenant opened the door. Fred asked the neighbours, but no-one had been on speaking terms or knew where she had gone. That made sense, she was always a private, paranoid, suspicious lady. We guessed she must have moved to her brother's in York, but we never knew this for sure and didn't have his address.

After work, I often sat cushioned in the rocking chair by the fire, drank tea laced with whisky and chatted to Granny Rowlands about my day. What a waste of an opportunity, as she never shared her own riveting life stories. If I had known, I would write someday about my ancestors; I might have encouraged her to tell me the full details of her sudden flight from her husband and the struggle to raise her family alone.

Her story made a promising saga and became the basis of my fiction novel, The Golden Dog Tag.

When Granny Rowlands died, I chose a turquoise vase which had been the empty centrepiece on her battered, brown sideboard. It had an imposing, amphora shaped beauty, incongruous in her tiny grey hovel with its dusty rag rug. This ornament was too tall and tricky to fill with flowers, but I always admired it.

One afternoon in July 1952, a tremendous crash came from our parlour. The door had been firmly closed, and we burst in to find the treasured vase in smithereens on the floor. It was a mystery; we had ensured it was secure on the mantlepiece.

I became distressed and filled with foreboding because it was precious to me, the one I tried to fill with flowers for Granny, and the only keepsake I wanted when she died. It wasn't just a broken vase; to me, it meant impending doom.

And I was right. We heard during that week, Jack Stafford, my sister Grace's husband, had been killed while on pilot training in Rhodesia, Africa.

Jack and Fred were close friends as well as brothers-in-law and often dismantled and tinkered with motorbikes on our kitchen table. It was Jack who persuaded Fred to buy our first motorbike, and they sourced the cheapest one, a Douglas motorcycle for £15. It always broke down, especially when travelling uphill, and Fred had to hit it with a hammer when it overheated and a piece always fell off. When the engine overheated and struggled to take two people going uphill, I often ended up walking behind the bike.

Relatives assumed Grace's life was over at 22 and believed no-one would marry a widow with a new baby and toddler.

Chapter 11 - What's New Pussycat?

(Tom Jones)

In our house in Lyon Street, Fred was the attendant to all waifs, strays, and nomads of the cat world who lodged within our 'four-star cat hotel.' Horace, our first rescued stray, moved two houses away from us. Fred named him this because his enormous tomcat head suggested a philosopher. I insisted he could keep the strays only if he bathed and flea treated them. They were irresistible little charmers until they became mothers. With several kittens to find homes for, Fred solved this by giving his junior school pupils a talk on cats. Any pupil who wished to home a kitten required a signed note from a parent.

Fred kept one stray, a Persian-type beauty, Kitty. She inherited enough ancestry for a luxurious coat of pale grey and white, without the chore of daily grooming. No longer young, Kitty only had two litters, one in Ardwick and, one later, in Burnage. She staked her claim on us, and without mercy, despatched all contenders.

One night, while she curled on Fred's knee, he put down his crossword and called me over. 'Kitty's stomach's moving.'

She purred when I stroked her silky protruding belly. 'Kittens,' I assured him. 'By the amount of movement, she's in labour.'

His eyes widened in fear. 'What can I do?'

'Settle her in a darkish, quiet place, lots of newspaper, towels and drinking water. Don't interfere, unless she's in difficulty, and she'll show distress by mewing. Later check each kitten is suckling. That's all.'

I spoke as an expert but had no doubt read it somewhere.

Kitty made her birthing room in the unhygienic coal-hole, a tiny room off the kitchen-diner. Crammed in with brushes and cleaning material, she settled in there, and an old drawer served as a safe bed for the five kittens that emerged.

One night, in bed, we heard strange bumping noises. Kitty had dragged her litter upstairs to our bedroom, one by one. After this, we established a nightly routine to transfer the litter into a large base drawer in our bedroom.

One morning, a kerfuffle woke us. Kitty was trying to stop her kittens from climbing out and throwing themselves off the top of the drawer. Fred got to work and devised a ramp system for them. From the bed, we enjoyed a grandstand view of our tiny, fluffy circus performers as they slid and rolled in safety onto the bedroom floor. Five weeks later, we found homes for each of her kittens, and Kitty slept in peace again on Fred's knee.

When Gran died, we realised we didn't want to stay in Ardwick. We never moved into a corporation house on the slum clearance; we strived for a more independent life. While we rented in Ardwick, we saved every spare penny into an endowment scheme for a house deposit. When we had enough for a deposit, we viewed many houses to buy.

One was in a perfect location and a lovely home, but when the neighbour came out, she had bright-red hair, a raucous voice and a gaggle of half a dozen shrieking children. Fred avoided this nightmare and didn't even reach the door. Halfway down the drive, he turned on his heels, grabbed me, and we scrambled back onto the motorbike.

Fred had done his homework, Burnage had the best performing junior school in Manchester, the Acacias Community Primary. The next house we viewed was in a leafy suburb with rows of mature trees lining the roads. It housed middle-class, genteel professionals, teachers, midwives or managers.

Fred scathingly said, 'These professions, perceived as prestigious, long-term and safe, were, in reality, only low-paid jobs.' This was his beef throughout his career; professionals had to endure years of training, gruelling exams and develop the expertise required to qualify in these occupations, but the salaries never matched up. Teaching was to some, a vocation with a steady pension; and didn't seek higher wages. The salary may have been suitable for the single, women teachers, but not at the time for men who supported growing families.

The Burnage house we chose was a large three-bedroomed, older-type semi-detached, at the affordable price of £1,350. We cashed in our endowment to cover the deposit. Unknown to us, the agreement incurred an early withdrawal penalty, which left a shortfall in our payment. Our dreams dashed, we dreaded telling the seller, now in advanced pregnancy.

She said, 'In my state, I couldn't stand putting the house back on the market and chasing another buyer.' With fate on our side, they could afford to reduce the house price to our offer, and we swiftly signed the contract.

Names are important; in how we address ourselves and each other, show hierarchy, or how we hold someone in affection. I married Fred Bone and became Winifred Bone for a few months. Fred was almost a qualified teacher and known to his pupils as Mr Bone. He never liked his name and thought it sounded harsh. We discussed the possibility of changing our surname by deed poll.

Our surname was easy to alter; we had become known as related to my granny, Mrs Rowlands, so we removed the "s" from Rowlands, and Fred loved it. He started teaching as Mr Fred Rowland, but the clerk at the education office thought it was odd to christen a child Fred and changed it to Frederick on all his documents. By default, Mr Fred Bone was now Mr Frederick Rowland, proud and ready to face the world. His change of name invited all manner of good fortune.

We changed our surname to Rowland by usage when we bought the house in Burnage and left behind Fred and Winnie Bone in the hovel.

Location in place, I was ready to lay my newspaper in the cupboard, emulating the cat, to prepare for my planned litter of two daughters. Despite our rigorous planning, fate had other plans, and our children never attended Fred's preferred school in Burnage.

The back garden had tall hedges on both sides, and I cut the teeny lawn by kneeling and cutting with shears as it wasn't worth buying a lawnmower. Facing us at the back, was a sprawling lilac tree from the neighbouring property that spilt over the wooden fence. When it was in flower, which lasted only six weeks, it formed a beautiful view from our south-facing French windows.

We were cat-less for a brief spell when Fred took me to a cat show in Manchester. He became enamoured with a distinctive Siamese cat and was on the lookout for one for sale in our local paper. He telephoned in response to an advertisement and requested, 'It must have blue eyes.'

The owner replied, deadpan, 'Sir, they all have blue eyes. Come and take a look.'

An irresistible silky seal-point kitten, Samarkand Sabu, known as Sammy, came home with us. His madness became legendary. He often edged across the pelmet and slid down the curtains, hanging on with his claws. He eventually got bored entertaining himself and left the curtains alone when he'd completely shredded them. The next phase of Sammy's antics continued, and he would sprawl along the top of a door and drop onto anyone who stood near. Even though we warned any visitors, when it happened, it still made them jump.

In summers, we had a break from his antics when he was an outside predator. He spread out along the sycamore's bough, full length, stock-still until a bird perched. He lashed out with his paw and knocked it for six. There was no malice, in his little cat head, he was just playing a game.

Fred attended school in his blazer with shredded lapels, it broke the ice and amused his students when he explained why they were fringed. Sammy used to drape himself around his neck and held on as he walked around the house. Maybe this was the only time Fred clarified his bizarre actions or why he wore distressed clothes?

Whenever Fred answered the door, any visitor stared at this cat wrapped around his shoulders, which pulled and purred on the blazer.

At Gorton Mount school Fred was in his element. Two of his colleagues, Cliff Carver and Cecil Stowasser, were inspirational and made a start on a book on modern teaching of maths in junior schools. Many students couldn't relate arithmetic to everyday living, and this book would remedy it. After school, the three teachers met in a coffee shop and shared strategies. Fred was always keen to get home but occasionally joined them as their reader and sounding board. I found later; his colleagues published a successful series of educational books.

Chapter 12 - Saving Grace

My sister, widowed Grace, worked at the nursery school at Belle Vue. She often stayed overnight at weekends at Mum and Dad's house. At their insistence, she went to the dances with a friend and they looked after her daughters, Kaye aged 4, and one-year-old baby Jill.

After a few dates with George Wood, Mum assumed, from Grace's stories, they were getting serious and advised her to confess to him she had two daughters.

George always ensured Grace returned home safely and accompanied her on the bus, but she insisted he leave her at the bus stop. He didn't mind the additional journey, even though it took him two more buses back home to Moston. When Grace became more comfortable in George's company, she asked him to meet her for coffee one afternoon and allowed him to walk her back from the bus stop to Mum and Dad's house.

Grace stepped on to the pathway and stopped when she saw Kaye's excited face at the window. She turned to George, 'I'm sorry, I didn't mean to lead you on and not mention right away about my two children, but I had been advised not to.'

'Oh, I see,' he said and slipped his hands into his pockets, wanting to hear her out.

'My husband, Jack, was a trainee pilot, killed in a plane crash in Africa months ago. We're outside my parent's house, and

145

Kaye's the one looking out the window at us. Jill is much younger.'

Glancing at the window, he saw a beautiful child with red hair and rosy cheeks staring back at him.

'Thank you for seeing me home,' said Grace, watching him smile but say nothing. She walked towards the front door and turned, 'It's been very nice meeting you. I understand if you don't want to see me again.'

'No, I'm so sorry, I've been too quiet,' he replied. 'What an ordeal you've been through, and you're so young. Of course, I'd like to meet your girls.'

Grace showed George into the living room, and Kaye rushed over just as Mum popped her head around the kitchen door.

'You must be George. Would you like a cup of tea?'

Grace and her two girls lived in a council house in Wythenshawe, and George became a constant visitor. Jill, walking by now, but not sure of the stranger, hid behind Grace whenever she saw him. Kaye had a bit more confidence and asked him lots of questions.

Months later, in January 1954, we attended Grace and George's wedding at Manchester Central's registry office. Their reception was an informal affair held nearby at Ping Hong's Chinese Restaurant.

My friend Theo and I visited this eatery occasionally as a special treat where we lunched on his divine chicken soup with a crusty roll. Dad had worked at the Ping Hong and renovated the floor tiles around the time Grace and George decided to marry. I presume that was why they chose such an unusual wedding lunch venue.

Just close family attended the reception, held in a large gold and red orientally decorated room with long windows which overlooked the busy street. After warm greetings, we sat ceremoniously on the plush chairs and waited for Fred. The waiter hovered, menu in hand.

'Perhaps he got lost in the library,' Grace said and pointed toward the magnificent rotunda library building, yards away. We laughed, which banished the pomp of the occasion.

At last, Fred strode in triumphantly, brandishing a loosely wrapped vacuum cleaner. He beamed at Mum, 'I got it for you before they sold out. It was half price,' he explained, as he slumped down beside me.

Mum acknowledged her trophy shyly with a smile. An obsequious waiter sprang into action, and pulled out a chair with one hand, grasped the vacuum cleaner with the other and carried it off for safekeeping with the coats.

I pushed the menu into Fred's hand, which he scanned dismissively. The waiter returned to take Fred's order. 'I don't know any of these. Do you have fish and chips by any chance?' Fred asked.

The inscrutable Chinese gentleman replied, 'Of course, Sir,' and retreated. I tried to catch Fred's eye to give him the full power of my baleful glare, but he kept his gaze firmly on Mum, always his partner-in-crime. With no apologies for his tardiness, he leaned over to shake hands and congratulate the happy couple.

When the meals arrived, none of us seemed confident in our choices from the foreign menu, and the plates of food were unrecognisable to us.

The oriental waiter allowed himself a faint smile, and with a flourish, he presented Fred with his meal. It was the most tastefully arranged and cooked fish and chips we had ever seen. Fred generously waved a chip around, but when he reached me, he retracted it with speed, gave a devilish smile, and started eating. Our dishes were exceptional, but we gazed across enviously at Fred's plate. Wedding breakfasts are always memorable in one way or another.

Fred and Mum agreed babies were an inconvenience and an unnecessary expense. Over the last ten years, we accumulated reasons for delaying the inevitable baby I desired. The list of excuses comprised: I was still young; no hot water in the house; we're saving for a deposit; paying for fitted carpets; enjoying a comfortable job; fun holidays and music with entertaining and cultured friends; and other pressing family events. Why disturb the status quo?

As I skirted around my 30th birthday, anxious about swapping the youth of my twenties, time began rumbling like an earthquake. My astrological Saturn return was an indicator to make changes.

'It's time for a baby,' I announced one evening. Fred was raised an only child and had no close relatives and babies were an alien concept. He had fought hard to keep me for himself. At that moment, his stark options were divorce or sharing me with a child. It was crucial to have a happy wife, so with no discussion, no arguments, he agreed.

He checked his watch and said, 'We've just time before we go to the flicks,' and sealed his pledge unceremoniously on the plush, red Wilton carpet.

Throughout the film, I sat there feeling heavily pregnant, clutching my stomach. We're off. We're having a baby.

The following day, he was fidgety while he lunched with Mum. She couldn't stand the angst any longer.

'Whatever's wrong, Fred?' she asked.

'We're trying for a baby.'

Mum reached for the calendar. 'How long have you been trying?'

She kept a straight face when he replied, 'Since last night.'

There were no secrets within our family. Mum told Grace, who then told Nan. They discussed it and gave Fred their findings, 'For God's sake, get her pregnant, or else it will be hell for all of us.'

I missed the boat the first month, but it was plain sailing from the second. Conferences over, we started to knit. I had waited years for this moment. I was really pregnant. Did I feel euphoric? Triumphant? No, I just felt sick, with an increased dislike of tea and coffee.

I worked for Thomas Guest and Company in Ancoats, Ardwick, who manufactured patent medicines, which included Sure Shield iodised throat lozenges and fruit laxatives. Other pills and chocolate laxatives were processed and exported for the constipated people of Africa.

It soon became clear the lower ground-floor office windows were within easy reach of children's hands. During the summer, they left windows open for fresh air, but the wire grid remained. A group of enterprising schoolchildren hooked bits of the brown blocks through these large metal squares and ate them. One day, workmen added a two-foot-high fine mesh on the ground-floor windows, to close the holes for pillaging fingers - those poor children, who presumed they'd eaten chocolate!

A few months into my pregnancy, none of my smart office dresses fitted. It was time to shop for smocks. I helped the boss, Mr Baker, to open the post. The old-fashioned gentleman acknowledged my new pale-blue cotton maternity top. 'I understand these things, sickness and such. Don't worry about resting or coming in late.'

One day, he asked me to get a signature from an employee in the 'Works.' In complete silence, 60 pairs of eyes focused on the pale-blue cotton smock. I shared my joy with these smiling women. I had joined 'the Club', nauseous but elated.

150

This birth thing was 'all very textbook,' according to Fred, who read several books in a short space of time and became an expert in ante-natal care. Dr Spock became his Bible (the writings from the American paediatrician and 20th-century icon of parenting expertise, not the modish, pixie-eared Vulcan from *Star Trek*).

My sisters were flattered with Fred's undivided attention as they relayed their birth traumas. He regarded birth as a mechanical, human activity. In the first trimester, each morning, propped up in bed, he ensured I drank lukewarm water or light drinks, ate plain biscuits, and ignored household chores.

I continued to work to fund larger items for the nursery, and, as being last in the family to have babies, out of storage came the hand-me-downs of fluffy toys, baby clothes and blankets. Expert knitters drooled over more and more intricate babywear patterns. By the fourth month, my nausea faded altogether. One evening, a butterfly wing fluttered in my stomach. I thought it was my imagination, but the flickering returned stronger the following evenings at the same time.

On my routine visit to the Withington ante-natal hospital, I was proud to assist them and acted as the 'Well Woman' for examination by aspiring gynaecologists. They got their diagnoses right for me. Deemed the perfect candidate, wellness overflowed from my glowing skin to my burgeoning bump.

Towards the later stages of my pregnancy, my nightly ritual was to sit at the dressing table and smooth my concoction of baby oil and Coty's Chypre into my bulge to avoid stretch marks. I smiled contently at Fred through the mirror as he watched and waited for me to come to bed.

While I inhaled the heady waft of perfume, the residue of oil sank into my hands. I glanced in the mirror and superimposed on my image was a little girl's face. The static snapshot lasted five seconds.

'I've just seen our baby in the mirror,' I said, elated, 'And she has fair hair like me.'

Fred yawned, 'That's settled then, I'll tell your Mum tomorrow,' and promptly fell asleep.

No-one we knew owned cars, and we took taxis for emergencies only. I don't remember how I got to the hospital. I can't imagine I took a two-bus journey in labour. My probable mode of transport was to ride pillion on our motorbike at bicycle speed, with the lump held side-saddle.

In 1958, the law of the land insisted only hospitals delivered first babies. After ten hours of solitary wandering around the birthing room, I stopped to puff and pant, and the nurse ordered me to sit in bed. After a further number of hours, an auxiliary helped me inhale gas and air and observed the progress of my dilation.

A doctor came in wearing white, half wellington boots. I wondered about the necessity for these, a blood bath? He glanced

152

at his watch and said, 'Five to five. Baby will be here before 5 o'clock when I can leave and have my tea.'

Relieved, confused, I remembered, *so that's what this is all about, I'm having a baby.*

In a light-hearted voice, he said, 'A little prick of anaesthetic and you can push like merry hell.'

'It's a girl,' they chorused.

'That's right,' I agreed. The doctor and the nurse exchanged quizzical looks. I knew she resembled me; I'd already seen her face in the mirror. We had decided to call her Wendy, a name chosen from my knitting patterns and Jane as the middle name, from Jane Austen, my favourite author, in case our daughter turned out to be studious and didn't want to use the frivolous first name.

The Manchester City Council insisted new mothers stayed in the hospital for two weeks after the birth, and to go home invalidated further treatment.

The ward was custom-built onto the existing hospital, with dimensions of an airport hangar, a baby-boomer production line, with meals placed on trestle tables along the centre of the ward. They installed a cot on a stand at the same level as the bed to enable comfortable feeding, baby bathing and changing.

Two permanent nurses and a few auxiliaries during the day serviced this collection of mothers and babies. The hospital served tasteless food. Fred came in for his regimented 'half-hour' visit each evening, and on one occasion, brought in a jam assortment in a special presentation pack. The next day, a few of us sent back the evening meal, asked for bread and butter, and polished off Fred's jam. That caught the authority's attention and brought an improvement in the cuisine.

I overheard an auxiliary, 'Teacher's wives are a soft lot.' My friends in the ward were a teacher's wife and a sweet Indian lady in a pink satin sari.

The matron from the main hospital next door came on her weekly visit. I lay on the bed weak, sobbing with the baby and myself in a dirty mess. Matron charged over to me; a tank ready for action on the battlefield.

'Check her blood,' she ordered. They tended to my baby and found I was weak; my energy had been depleted and desperately needed to recover from the long labour.

I awoke in a side room with no crying infants. When I washed my hands, I caught my reflection in the mirror. This poor ashen-faced woman stared back at me, and I wept for her. After the respite, I had more energy and keen to get back to my thriving baby.

In my absence, they had measured the babies' heads for medical statistics. The mothers were eager to tell me that Wendy's was the largest. They predicted, 'She's going to be very brainy.'

The doctors explained to me my baby had been overdue, longer in the womb, and therefore, older and larger than the others. Her weight was 9lb 3oz, much heavier, and the soft powdered bloom on her skin also confirmed it.

I brought my huge, beautiful, bald, baby home in a taxi, to a bedroom with pin-drop silence and pristine sheets. Flooded with love and compassion from Fred and Mum, I started to enjoy my beautiful daughter, with her large head, full of brains.

At Wendy's christening, the relatives dreamt of drinks and a cold collation to follow. I was proud of them; they kept poker-faced when the minister droned, 'I name this child, Wendy Jane Fowler.' Where did the minister get Fowler from, instead of Rowland? The minister wafted out to the porch.

At the surname mistake, Fred glanced down at me, 'Does he know something I don't?' The group laughed as they pushed the pram home.

Fred was indeed lucky. He left Gorton Mount School when the Education Committee needed specialist maths teachers. They chose him to take the year's intensive course organised by Manchester University held at Didsbury College. He was delighted when paid to study again and knew if he passed, it would alter his life and offered a fortuitous way of progressing from junior school.

Wendy was eight months old and crawling, and Fred had only been in college for a few months when I became lethargic. If it was anaemia, I had to act fast and start the course of iron. I

155

visited the doctor, and, on my return, Mum and Fred stopped chatting.

Mum looked up, 'Anaemia?'

I smiled at Fred, 'No, pregnancy.'

We laughed like mad as we realised it was such a world-changing diagnosis from anaemia.

My sisters reminded me I had boasted of my plan for two daughters. Grace and the midwife assured me another protracted labour was unlikely so soon after such a big first baby. Both offered to assist me if I chose a home birth. Now I had two devoted minders, after none at the hospital.

It suited Fred to attend short tutorials in the mornings, study in the evenings and spend the afternoons with Wendy and pregnant me.

The middle of June was the baby's due date. On the morning of the 11th, familiar twinges woke me at six. At eight, Fred picked up Grace on his motorbike, and the midwife turned up at nine. Fred tucked a single bed against the dining/living room wall, as the morning sun streamed through the open French doors. With everything prepared for the birth; ready for any action in this unique situation, he happily left me and sped off to college. I sat and experienced regular contractions, and strolled around the room, bright and confident, waiting for our second baby to be born. Everyone chatted with shared excitement and exhilaration.

At ten, the doorbell rang, and Grace opened the door to a workman waving a worksheet. From his list, he recited, 'The over-sink heater in the kitchen smells of gas. Check for leaks.'

'Please, come back another time. My sister's giving birth in there,' Grace pointed to the closed door in the hall.

He shook his head, 'Can't take chances. Even more critical under the circumstances.'

Grace escorted him around the outside of the house and into the kitchen to avoid the living room. She made him a cup of tea and signed the form while he located a loose connection and bustled off to his next emergency.

She entered the birthing chamber with tea. 'I've locked the front door. No one else is coming in,' she vowed.

This baby didn't wait around; she was 'coming ready or not.' With a few huffs and puffs, I delivered our second daughter at noon, in time for the triumphant midwife to pop home for her lunch.

My strong premonition was that I carried another girl, as we had only chosen two names, Melanie, from *Gone with the Wind* or Stephanie, having several ancient royal connections.

'Melanie sounds too fruity for me - melony or lemony,' Fred had said. So, we had previously agreed on Stephanie.

Fred returned from college with his course work, and as my last labour was so lengthy, he thought the baby could not be due for a few more hours.

157

He gasped when he entered the sitting room and saw me eating lunch in bed, glowing and serene. I pointed to the cot in the corner, raised my finger to my lips, and waited for his reaction.

He crept over, peeped at the sleeping baby, smiled and collapsed into the nearest chair. The midwife had wrapped the baby in a blanket, so he gave me an inquiring glance, wondering what gender.

'Stephanie,' I whispered. He ate his lunch through a wide grin; here was the other daughter I'd predicted.

I had an easy six-hour birth as Steph was long and thin. She was a healthy eight-and-a-half-pound baby, with a beautiful dome head covered by a shock of spiky brown hair, inherited from Fred's paternal side of the family.

My two sisters and I were mothers now, and none of us worked. We carried on having sociable home lives, and Mum often joined us. Nan and Grace lived two buses away, so when Fred was available, he chauffeured them between our houses on his motorbike.

We had put the Burnage house up for sale before I got pregnant with Stephanie. If a 'For Sale' sign was outside, prospective buyers thought it reasonable to pop in unannounced, often inappropriately. One couple called in on their way home from the cinema, at 10:30 at night, so we took it off the market. After Steph's birth, we put the house up for sale again, in preparation to move somewhere with our two baby girls. We had

158

no idea where we were heading, but we needn't have worried, fate had already mapped that out for us.

Chapter 13 - Daughters Of The Sea

(Doobie Brothers)

After the war, gaps in the medical or educational areas needed filling. Fred and his fellow students on the specialist maths course sought jobs suited to their enhanced qualifications. It was a pivotal time that defined their future. It became our one chance to move and live away from a city.

They poured over the situations vacant paper and divided the various positions between them. Some wanted city posts with the fast-track career prospects of becoming headmasters; others wanted to move to where they regularly holidayed.

Fred had Wales as his first choice and then any places other than cities. He sent off various applications and waited for responses. We soon ruled out our first choice of Wales since the schools required a Welsh speaker and neither of us spoke the language. He also turned down a school placement in Cornwall, suggested by his old colleague, Cecil Stowasser, who was now living there. A lovely area, but from holidays we'd taken, we knew it would be too remote.

A teaching post in the south of England, at a brand-new school at Dibden Purlieu, Hampshire, offered housing earmarked for teachers which clinched our choice. With excitement, we planned our move to the outskirts of the New Forest and showed Wendy pictures of wild ponies on misty moors. We completed the official education paperwork for a move to the South of England, or so we thought.

One ad-hoc application that Fred sent off was for a post at Les Beaucamps, on the island of Guernsey. They were late with their recruitment for teaching staff, and so it was unexpected but exciting, to receive a telegram dated Tuesday 14 April 1959 from the Guernsey Education Officer. It asked him to attend an interview the following week in Guernsey and to travel by sea or air the day before.

Fred asked, 'Where the hell is Guernsey?' Neither of us had heard of the Channel Islands.

Without hesitation, he sped off to the local library and found one book with black-and-white photographs of bathing machines on a beach and a selection of maps. In a travel agency, he discovered a brochure which showed a shimmering turquoise sea and sapphire-blue skies (accurate, but not every day). We were hooked.

Maps of England ended at the Isle of Wight, but those of France showed a small collection of dots. This beautiful, bijou Channel Isle - eight-miles long by five-miles wide, with a population of 45,000, appeared to be much closer to France, only 27 miles from the Normandy coast, perched in the Bay of St. Malo. We were surprised to find it was a whopping 70 miles away from the UK mainland.

To give you a little background, Guernsey, is a Viking name, possibly meaning 'green island,' and has a rich, romantic history, an intriguing wartime past and centuries of conflict between the English and French. With a curious mix of Gallic and British, the Channel Islands have links to both nations yet belong to neither. Remnants remain of fortifications built by the German military during the Second World War, the only part of British soil that Hitler secured.

Guernsey is self-governing and since 1921, has had control over its own currency, the Guernsey Pound, a local version of Pound Sterling, legal tender only in the Bailiwick of Guernsey, but not in England.

We were intrigued, and Fred was eager to go to the interview for a teaching position. He arranged to fly across for a couple of days.

He met other applicants at Les Rocquettes Hotel, where he learned 700 people applied for three jobs in differing schools on the island. Some were very well qualified, and he didn't think he stood a chance.

Fred's CV impressed the Guernsey Education Department; he had played both cricket and football with the Manchester Boys teams, was a park tennis champion, and competed in athletics. He was also a musician in the RAF and taught commercial subjects to WRAFs waiting for demob. These attributes were over and above the desired requirement for a qualified mathematics schoolmaster, perfect because they were looking to expand their curriculum.

He passed the interview there and then and readily accepted the Guernsey position as a maths teacher at Les Beaucamps Secondary School.

From war-time experiences, he had learned the value of a peaceful and settled lifestyle, and Guernsey seemed the perfect place. After a day exploring the island, without another thought, he knew he wanted to whisk us off to this enchanted paradise with windswept cliffs and quaint shops. On his return, he couldn't wait to tell me he had taken the job, and it would be everything I had asked for had I won the football pools.

A few months later, we had sold our house in Burnage, but the paperwork still needed completion, so while Fred rode his motorbike to the south coast to catch the Guernsey ferry, I stayed behind in Manchester with the new-born Steph and toddler Wendy. His bike panniers were stuffed full of clothes and other necessities to cover him until the rest of our household goods arrived after the house sale.

The Education Committee had arranged for him to lodge with a couple, Mr and Mrs Penney, who lived in Le Rohais, an area halfway between Les Beaucamps school and St Peter Port. These pleasant, hospitable people gave him an introduction to his future environment, which included a Breton-influenced vocabulary. They pronounced for him the French road and place names which bore no resemblance to the written word.

Les Beaucamps was the first of the new secondary modern schools for 11-16-year-olds to be built in Guernsey and opened by Princess Margaret in June 1959. It took children from various parishes and was a large two-storey, flat-roofed building, built on a hill with banks of glass windows overlooking the west coast. What an enticement, to gaze out of the classroom window at a distant beach with breaking waves.

The Education Council was most interested in Fred's shorthand, typing and book-keeping skills and years later they asked him to install classes in the school. He taught the girls the necessary secretarial skills to take up secretarial positions in the burgeoning finance industry.

Weeks dragged by and I missed Fred. It was hard work looking after our babies under two years old on my own, but my family rallied round and were wonderfully helpful.

To keep Wendy occupied, we created makeshift books by cutting out coloured pictures from old magazines appealing to young children, and she gaily stuck the quirky shapes onto paper. We thought she might destroy them, but each one was kept clean and treasured.

Encouraged by Fred, she soon sat up and spoke in sentences; she was evolving into a bright golden-haired child who did everything early for her age.

Steph, too, soon showed advanced signs of intelligence; a quieter child, but she watched everything that went on. They were not miserable, crying babies, and a succession of family visitors kept our two girls interested and amused.

The dreary setbacks on the house completion continued. The purchasers, a female teacher, had her half of the mortgaged sanctioned, but her husband, who did not share her professional status, found difficulty raising his half. A frantic search produced a working man's benevolent society that filled the mortgage gap.

The building survey report was positive, apart from what they thought was a suspicious, integral wooden porch with fresh paint. The wary surveyor suspected it covered the dreaded dry rot. Once stripped and declared faultless, they still refused to issue a mortgage until I repainted it.

During this frustrating mess, Fred's letters arrived from Guernsey. It's inconceivable, in this day of instant communication, to think our only contact was by letter. We were both busy and scribbled notes to each other, not exactly passionate love poems. Fred's last letter suggested a time for me to stand by the telephone box on the road to receive his call concerning accommodation.

At school, Fred became firm friends with two colleagues who also came from Manchester, Mary, who taught art, and her partner Judy, both on a one-year teacher exchange. They had harried and cajoled their landlord until he looked into finding rental lodging for us. Their coup was securing rooms for us in a seasonal hotel, owned by their landlord's friend, that had closed for the winter.

The day before Fred's call, a distressing incident occurred. Wendy ran after a man in the street, shouting, 'Daddy. Daddy'.

He turned around, and it was not her daddy. She wouldn't stop crying. Fred had been at home all day with her for a year and completed his course assignments whenever she napped or went to bed. No wonder, she missed him. With the mortgage problems and our new baby, we had not considered Wendy's emotional state.

My letters to Fred explained the delays and his next telephone call was pivotal. 'Come over right away,' Fred insisted, 'Let the ruddy house sell itself. I've got ideal digs for us. You're going to love it.'

Relieved, I immediately agreed. 'That's brilliant. Wendy's pining for you.'

The family bade me farewell at Manchester's Ringway airport and assured me arrangements were in place for them to liaise with the removal company. They even got stuck in and cleaned the empty house.

I was in shock, and a few days later, hurriedly left without a tear, for a new life in the sun.

On the near-empty, decommissioned British European Airways, Dakota, the flight attendants took charge of the children. The bumpy laboured, three-hour journey took us over land, then sea. They provided refreshments, amused when I assumed the Isle of Wight was Guernsey. The flight continued above choppy waves, and I was excited when the outline of an island appeared. We suddenly swooped and touched down.

166

Before we disembarked, a stewardess pointed to my head and reminded me to take my curlers out.

After agonising weeks apart, I was eager to see Fred. The stewardess took control, and I peered through the window until the children were at the bottom of the aircraft steps.

I watched Fred scoop up baby Stephanie in the carrycot in one hand, while Wendy, an eighteen-month toddler, hand-outstretched, clutched his free hand. As I descended the steps, waiting at the bottom was my gorgeous husband, smiling up at me. A stark white collar showed off his tanned face. I was overwhelmed with love.

From the moment I set foot on the grass airstrip, the cool breezy sea air in my face, I felt freedom and an immense sense of belonging.

The taxi meandered its way around winding lanes, past grey and red granite walls, evergreen trees shimmied against brilliant blue skies, but there was no sign of the sea yet. The hotel owner escorted us to our apartment in a large annexe. For a pittance, we had rented a wing from her, with four bedrooms, one converted into a sitting room, plus a kitchen and bathroom. I gasped when I saw each bedroom window framed spectacular eastern sea views. Sunlight poured through the windows, and I instantly became a permanent holidaymaker. The red-bricked boutique hotel sat on a steep hill overlooking the outer islands, and to the right, the magnificent Castle Cornet dominated a harbour crammed with bobbing fishing boats.

The area, Le Mont Bleu (the Blue Mountains), was near to an official viewing area over the other islands of Herm, Sark, and, on a clear day, you could easily make out the French Normandy coast. Three flights of garden steps led you a safe and circuitous route into the centre of town.

I left Manchester in a grey October with its dismal, dark evenings. But here, through the clear air, the blue, white and green shades of the island were dazzling. I marvelled at the glaring light that reflected from the sea onto the red granite rocks. Like Dorothy, I left black and white Kansas in a whirlwind for a bright Technicolour Land of Oz, which was Guernsey.

Wendy settled into her new bedroom with her toys and zonked out. Steph slept peacefully in her carrycot. We sat close, holding hands and watched the twinkling town lights below, unwilling to draw the curtains or end the magic moment.

During the gloomy, bone-chilling Manchester winters, I often fantasised about greenery, light, space, and sunshine, and here I was, on the edge of my dream.

The weekend after we settled into the hotel, Fred's colleagues, Mary and Judy came to gloat on their handiwork. 'We got you the best view in town,' they boasted and pointed at the panorama. 'Leave the babes with Fred and come and see our pad.'

Mary was about 30 years old, the more masculine of the two, with muscular arms and an unusual, thick black haircut, styled short back and sides. The trouser wearer who often juggled with her jingling keys. Judy, slightly younger, was slender, delicate, and pretty, in complete contrast.

Everything was fun for them. It took only three minutes to walk along the narrow lane, just wide enough to accommodate three females who, with linked arms, marched along and sang.

I stopped to admire the towering granite walls on either side, and Mary said, 'They belong to Castle Carey next door to us.'

In their tiny apartment, there was a disclaimer from the landlord to insure himself if they fell off the flat roof: "Nude sunbathing is forbidden". This sign amused me; to be naked on that rooftop, in full view of everyone, would have stopped the traffic just below in St Julian's Avenue. They pushed up the sash window, and we crawled out.

They laughed and said, 'It isn't his, so he can't fence it in.'

I was mesmerised with the jigsaw of roofs and chimneys backed by harbour cranes. We scrambled back in, and they showed me their newly painted, vivid-pink bathroom.

'Very bright,' I said.

'The landlord hasn't seen it yet. We call the colour "hot vagina".

Very apt, I thought and was relieved that Mary, an accomplished artist, and bawdy Mancunian, had refrained from adding an artistic mural.

They delighted in their openness and didn't bother to disguise their relationship. While homosexuality was illegal until 1967, the same restrictions didn't apply to same-sex relationships

169

between two women, though unspoken, it was still regarded as indecent and scandalous in repressive Britain then. Not for them the dark, closeted life of the tormented lesbian, everyone who knew them found it a natural union and accepted their relationship.

Mary often came to visit and one day, *The Two Worlds,* a paranormal newspaper, arose in conversation. It prompted her to tell us she had been a professional medium. She abandoned the practice as it took over her time and life. More important to her now, was Judy, her partner. What mad fun they were relating racy, ribald stories with healthy, earthy attitudes which appealed to Fred.

Mary possessed a unique talent, and I considered it a waste that she wasn't a practising medium, but I saw her point of view. As a medium, a picture of the person trying to make contact appeared in her subconscious, and she sketched outlines of her sightings. We saw other mediums who drew the person's spirit guide, which was often fanciful and not wholly believable. Fred would mutter out of the corner of his mouth, 'Not another ruddy red Indian.'

One weekend, Mary brought in the post and plonked the letter on the sideboard and ordered, 'If you sit down, I'll do some psychometry for you.' Intrigued, I gave her my full attention. She held the envelope and closed her eyes. 'This letter contains a snippet of dress material for a special event and the date's

170

arranged. It'll be a successful and joyful occasion. There's also a warning about dangerous dogs.'

Mary's psychometry came true. My sister, Nan, had enclosed a fragment of silk and someone's wedding invitation. There was also news that two neighbourhood dogs Mum befriended while feeding leftovers, had savaged her calf. There was no impairment of her movement but resulted in ugly, disfiguring scars.

As with all fun things, they come to an end. Mary and Judy were employed in Guernsey on a temporary teaching exchange and moved to London. Sadly, we heard their relationship ended soon after their return.

It seemed as if people played out their pivotal part in our lives and then moved on. As in folk dancing, we took their hands, danced a few steps, changed partners, and moved along.

One day, I took the children on the bus to visit Cobo Bay on the opposite side of the island. Near the cobbled slipway, on the sand, was a dry, sheltered area, I spread the blanket on it and, one by one, we fell asleep. A strange rumbling and agitated men's voices woke me.

Glancing around half asleep, I saw the tide surging towards us over the flat sand.

The fishermen behind the wall had spotted the dilemma, dropped their nets, and sprang into action. As they whisked the tots and me up the slipway and deposited us on a wooden bench, one of them said, 'We wouldn't have let you drown, young lady.'

I bet we looked so sweet; three of us zonked out below the seawall.

Fred drove to the beach after school as arranged, in time to see a group of men waving me goodbye, each wearing their traditional navy hand-knitted Guernsey. Many islanders wore these seaworthy sweaters being warm, hard-wearing, impervious to showers and easy to keep clean.

He peered over the wall at the waves which already lapped the bottom of the slipway, while I excitedly told him about our rescue. We had learned the local tides displayed exceptional height ranges, and since then, have found great respect for the sea.

Fred told the landlady I had been cavorting with the fishermen on Cobo Beach, with two babies in tow.

She just laughed. 'Shocking, what the bloney seamen get up to when the husband's at work.'

In 1959, only two local houses for sale fitted Fred's housing licence; both were identical bungalows on the island's west coast. One was in an unsuitable location; on a coast road corner, unsafe for wandering children and also suffered from the occasional high tide which deposited lumps of seaweed that would stink as it rotted.

The other house was perfect for us, down a lane, a few hundred yards from the scenic Port Soif bay. We decided on the detached, square bungalow, with pebbledash walls, a pointy red-tiled roof with a curved porch, within easy reach of a safe, accessible coastline.

I knew how lucky we were to have a flat, west coast choice, as the south cliff-lined bays were accessible only by steep gravel paths interspersed with long, concrete steps. With a toddler and six-month-old baby, it was as hazardous as living in the city, but there they had wide pavements, buses, and parks. These south-facing bays, although spectacular, were not suitable for my envisioned daily mother-and-baby forays to the seaside pushing a pram.

Fred asked the bank manager, 'When are you available to see the property?'

'Mr Rowland, I drove past the house yesterday, and they have already sanctioned your mortgage.'

Fred was speechless at the uncomplicated lending requirements. He was a teacher, under a permanent licence, and on a decent salary, so it was a formality for the manager and only required a flying drive-by and glance at the house.

The local market two-bedroomed bungalow cost £2,000, and we arranged the repayment to be £16 per month. We had an annual celebration, where Fred actually danced when we received the Cadastre request, the real-estate tax. Compared with the Manchester rates, we only paid a fraction in Guernsey.

The delivery of our furniture from Manchester meant we could move into our house during the crisp first week of January. They had stacked the boxes around the walls, and we stood in the cardboard citadel with our toddler and baby, overwhelmed at the mammoth task ahead. We didn't know where to begin as we hadn't packed the boxes, but, the family had clearly labelled them, so we placed them in the relevant room.

Fred heard a knock at the door. No-one was there, but on the doorstep, he found two wicker tomato punnets which held a steaming pot of tea and a packet of biscuits.

He read out the notelet tucked in one basket, 'Welcome to Port Soif. My house is Bon Accord, opposite. I will pop across tomorrow afternoon to pick up the baskets. It's signed by a Mrs Laxton.'

This thoughtful gesture raised our spirits. We found two chairs and a side table and tucked into this welcome gift.

On the first morning, I walked to the metal front gate, and a motorbike zoomed past, followed by a car. It was no country lane but a long straight road, ripe for any speedsters. Fred's first job was to install a chicken wire fence to the existing metal poles to keep the children from wandering into the road.

I arranged the kiddies and their accoutrements in the spacious Victorian pram and pushed them up the lane a hundred yards, across the deserted main coast road and through the undulating dunes to the beach.

I sat on a towel, mesmerised at the white sand framed by the waving fronds of yellowy-green seagrass, and watched the tide creep in to form a perfect blue circle within the horseshoe bay. We wore our winter coats, but there was still warmth in the

January air. I left Steph in the pram while Wendy and I toddled to the cold water's edge. I couldn't wait to get home to tell Fred we had won the lottery in terms of location.

When Fred returned from school, we prepared to meet our kind benefactor who had left us the pot of tea the previous evening. As she stood on the doorstep, we shook hands and formed opinions of each other. I got a surprise, Mrs Laxton appeared kind and approachable, with her wiry steel-grey hair, slight, sparrow-like body and scrubbed ruddy face. The first of my Guernsey fairy godmothers had arrived.

She made her way to our kitchen with a strange sideways rocking motion, like a crab, and Fred rushed over to pull up a chair for her. Noticing our concern, she confided in her strong Glaswegian accent, 'During a gale, the car door blew against my leg and trapped it.'

She had been a history don and had taught at Edinburgh University, where she met her late husband who became an Anglican minister. Now a widow, she knew several wealthy ex-parishioners of her husband's congregation who deemed her worthy of their largesse. In her case, they gave her recent releases of expensive hard-backed books. These were a good investment, creating symbiotic relationships and an accidental reading circle.

Often, to grab my attention, Mrs Laxton stood in her window and held up the latest new volume, emulating a chauffeur waiting with a name board in airport arrivals. No libraries existed yet on the island, only reference archives, so I borrowed romance novels from the stationers. To get my hands on the bestsellers from Mrs Laxton was manna from heaven. I felt blessed and grateful.

With Jill, my newfound friend, whom I will introduce later, we received brilliant quality reading matter. At our unconventional seaside book club, we discussed them at length on the beach, sat on towels, and drank flask coffee as we supervised our offspring paddling in the surf.

I returned the prized books to Mrs Laxton in the late afternoons and delivered a précis over a small sherry. She transmitted my critique to her wealthy friends, who sported a veneer of culture. She thought it hilarious that they discussed these books with conviction at dinner parties, never having turned a single page.

Amid busy growers and country folk, we were transplanted city dwellers. I appreciated that fate had given me accomplished companions. By osmosis, I received the further education I sought.

Mrs Laxton, now 83, caught the flu. I popped backwards and forwards and liaised with the doctor. One morning she called me by her daughter's name, 'You're just in time for sherry, Monica. Draw the curtains.'

I telephoned our local doctor, who she called, "Young Johnny Bolt". He diagnosed she had suffered a stroke and a fall in the night. I persuaded her busy daughter in England to come over immediately. She stayed with her mother for only two days before she died.

I presumed Monica, who, also being a minister's wife, would be austere and religious; but as we sorted out her mother's things, we found a box of ancient corsets with strings. We bound ourselves up and pranced and paraded about, shrieking like schoolgirls. We stopped larking about when we realised this wasn't seemly, as her funeral had yet to take place.

'I feel that Mum is with us, revelling in this,' she said, with a cheeky smile. So, we carried on enjoying ourselves, sorting out the ancient array of underwear.

I didn't go to the funeral, not being a member of Mrs Laxton's church set or part of her late husband's congregation. Preoccupied across the road, my neglected kitchen floor needed a clean, and while I was on my knees scrubbing the tiles, the intense scent of hundreds of freesias and jasmine bombarded me. Overwhelmed, I thought, *What a bright idea of hers. She's brought her funeral flowers to me.* I savour these vivid memories.

Chapter 14 - Boys Of Summer

(Don Henley)

Raising children on a sunny, subtropical island was peaceful and had its magical moments. Surrounded by water, ditches, sandpits, and puddles, it had its hazards too. My priority was to teach the kids from the earliest age how to swim or at least float. I gave baby Darius flotation lessons in the warm, hollowed-out rock pools. At five years old, Wendy thought she could swim well enough to remove her rubber ring and was sensible, keeping close to the shore while she developed strength and proper strokes.

None of the schools had swimming pools, and as our children passed through infant, junior then secondary schools, parents raised funds for each pool to be built. We had three children and contributed so much money over the years that Fred calculated we probably now owned outright one of the pools!

With the girls now comfortable in the sea, and respectful of its changeable tides and currents, Fred drove us to swim in several of the safe sandy swimming bays during the summer months. There were many balmy summer nights, where I dived off the harbour walls and piers with them, during glowing, multi-colour, west coast sunsets, with Fred photographing our movements.

At 36, I wanted to press the pause button and stay there forever. I finally had everything I ever wanted, blessed with two healthy daughters, a bouncing son, and an intelligent, indulgent husband, whose working hours coincided with our children's. My substitute sisters, Jill and Betty, provided lifts and babysitting. We gained a dog and a cat; our family was complete.

In the winter, my homely Methodist ladies group gave me culinary lessons; how to dress crab, which involved removing the cooked crab meat from the shell and claws. My next challenge was ormer bashing; how to tenderise them with a rolling pin by repeatedly beating the fishy steaks between a moist tea towel.

They gave me the recipe for another of Guernsey's definitive delicacies, a local delicious buttery tea bread called Guernsey *Gâche* (pronounced Gosh). In Guernésiais, *gâche* means cake, and made with raisins, sultanas and mixed peel; yummy when layered with Guernsey's golden butter. Visitors often take home the *gâche* and butter as tasty souvenirs.

Port Soif bay is a crescent of powdery white sand, flanked by huge rocks, sentinels on both sides of the narrow mouth that leads to the Atlantic Ocean (next stop America!). I believed it was the best beach on the island, and I walked or sat on it day after day, with our dog and children. Most of the time, it was empty, so I claimed it as mine.

During the summer, Jill and I alternated the beaches according to whether it was high or low tide. During high ones we paddled, swam or messed about on the seashore at Port Soif. On alternative weeks, we strode five minutes over the headland to

179

Portinfer, where Jill lived. It was a rocky beach, but as the tide receded it left vast swathes of sand with enormous, warm, rock pools. The girls loved the low tide weeks and picked their way through the little rocks and sand patches to the sea and marched in, without fear, belly boarding for hours in the crashing, rolling waves on their polystyrene surfboards.

When we were exhausted and thirsty from the sea activities, we sat on our towels to dry off and had snacks. I always took a large bottle of diluted orange squash, which I doled out into coloured plastic beakers, and we shared a packet or two of iced gems (a tiny biscuit with an iced swirl on top). Fred often joined us straight from school and sunbathed still wearing his blazer, long trousers, and lace-up shoes.

Shore larks, seabirds, and ravens loved the acres of common land behind our bungalow, and we often lay in our sun loungers watching them swoop catching bugs on the wing. The rough grass and brambles beyond our garden hedge supported limited grazing for the cute brown and white Guernsey cows. One afternoon, we rushed inside to shelter from a freak storm. It was so near, lightning tripped our electric switchboard in the house, and when we re-entered the garden, we could see four legs sticking out of the hedge, tragically, one of these gorgeous cows had been hit and killed.

I had always lived in a predominately female household, so having a young son was a novelty and an unknown quantity. We gave him a carefree idyllic childhood, where he played in sandpits with toy diggers, free to be dirty, tear his clothes, and have pockets filled with fish bait, disgusting snails, and worms. He had infinite patience and an excellent eye for drawing. His perspectives were accurate, and he moulded perfect models out of coloured plasticine. *I wondered if, in later years, he would take up sculpture and be the next Henry Moore or Rodin.*

In high summer, on June 11th, we often celebrated Steph's birthday with a party in the garden for her friends. In photographs, her birthdays seemed to be always on bright sunny days. When the food ran out, the children trooped off to the beach, leaving Betty and me to clear up.

After one party, a panting boy came running in. Darius, now three years old, had fallen in a deep hole, filled with water, in the nearby scrubland. Betty and I ran up the lane on India rubber legs. To our relief, Darius came towards us, surrounded by a posse of our party children. This apparition, plastered in white sand, resembled a moving statue. Rivulets of tears made tracks down his cheeks.

The vast hole he fell into became treacherous when filled with rainwater and natural drainage from the sandy terrain. The holes were wide enough to take door-sized rafts which the children paddled around on and craftily slid planks across them to get onto the floats and to create an exit if they fell in. We parents were unaware that behind our houses, our children were playing in such a dangerous place.

I simmered with anger and frustration all night, which spurred me to devise a short but forceful letter to the *Guernsey Press*, the leading local newspaper on the island. No-one else had bothered, but I wrote a protest. 'How much longer were we expected to endure this scene of devastation, a danger to our children?'

The following day, the banner headlines quoted my phrase: 'Spoliation of Port Soif.' All hell let loose. By lunchtime, a reporter interviewed me and took photographs of the desecration. Television cameras filmed me with the horrific holes in the background. Steph, who was home with chickenpox, held my hand, and out of nowhere, an assortment of young urchins joined us in the filming.

Fred and I had previously arranged a nibbles and drinks party that evening for six friends. In the afternoon I received a call to advise me the televised piece was going to appear on the local evening news. My guests came early to view it with us. We sipped our wine and gave the screen our full attention knowing TV segments lasted only seconds.

Fred quipped, 'The sight of this concerned mother, shielding her innocent charges, must've brought tears to all but the hardest heart.'

The television clip showed pompous States members who waffled and asked for an inquiry. During the excitement, we had prepared no food, so we gathered in the kitchen, ate bread, chunks of cheese, and drank wine.

It was a momentous day for me, but I had opened Pandora's box. Within days, the sand-hills were bull-dozed, pits filled in, seeded, and levelled. Until it was old news, cars stopped, and drivers shouted, 'Well done, Win.'

Neighbours confessed they didn't want to get involved in politics, as their husbands either worked for the States or the builders, and they needed to keep their noses clean to protect their jobs. Reputation is everything on such a small island, and no-one wanted to rock the boat over this.

With sudden change, there's often someone who loses out, and this time it was the children. They were upset at the ban of rafting amongst the bulrushes and the loss of their autumn blackberry picking. Ingeniously, they turned to even more dangerous pursuits of secret, perilous, rock-climbing and throwing crab and lobster pots off high pointed rocks into the sea.

Jill's husband, Richard, a carpenter, took on smaller projects in his spare time and created us a much-needed loft conversion. The pitch on the roof allowed for one sizeable room, a staircase and landing, achieved without significant building work. The girls slept in the double-aspect dormer bedroom.

A spacious area with under eaves access in the sloping roof remained undeveloped until Darius lost his bedroom downstairs when we knocked a wall down to extend the lounge. We added another dormer window on the landing which gave walk-in floor space and a single bed just fitted under the eaves.

Darius positioned his headboard adjacent to their bedroom door, and as the girls stumbled upstairs from their nights out, they often patted his head on the way into their bedroom, 'Goodnight, Darius,' they chorused.

Infuriated with this indignity and to give him privacy, he bought a door, built a partition wall, and squared off the landing to make himself a proper bedroom. His bed was on one side with open access to the eaves and his wardrobe rail, with room available to stack his diving, fishing, drums and painting gear without limit.

Darius was a practical teenager and loved working with his hands. Self-taught, he developed carpentry skills when the local DIY shop sold off a flat-pack kitchen. The carcasses and doors were ash-coloured, sturdy wood and piece by piece bought during the sales, he created a top-of-the-range fitted kitchen for us.

As a competent artist, he commandeered the garage for his spray-painting hobby, where he customised motorbike helmets. It was lucrative; the girls chose flowers and butterflies in pastel shades, and the boys requested go-faster stripes, flame-spewing dragons, and macho images. For extra funds, he later painted local seascapes using oils and regularly supplied a gallery in town. Wendy dated a boy who played drums and Darius soon bought a set and found his musical niche.

I attended his school play of *Joseph and His Coat of Many Colours* where Darius was the young drummer for the evening's performance. I came home so proud, and Fred was thrilled to have another musician in the family.

As he was so proficient, it was never a hardship to hear him practice night after night, bashing out rock numbers from Deep Purple, Black Sabbath and Bad Company, never missing a beat. He has gigged in the evenings with several groups and continues to use his multitude of talents.

Two things cast an icy chill on our passionate marriage: paint charts and wallpaper books. Catching sight of these, Fred became deaf and colour-blind. I ignored the risk to our marital happiness and carried on the preparations.

With Betty's cooperation, I strategically placed paint tins around the house, warning signs of impending changes.

Fred avoided chores and hated decorating. He raced through the task, balancing like an acrobatic circus act, as he painted ceilings with the roller in either hand. Tall enough to reach, standing on an old chair, he leapt on and off like a gazelle.

We built a safe contraption of ladders and planks on the stairs, so I squeezed in and reached the back two square yards of the ceiling. A catastrophe struck; I'd caught the cuff of my old shirt in the loaded paint tray's handle, which flipped and tipped half a can of white emulsion paint over Fred's head.

Shocked, then demented, he tore off his top clothes and flung them on the protective newspaper on the floor. Through gritted teeth, he shouted, 'Hose,' and sprinted into the back garden in his underpants.

The full force of the spray dispersed the paint. He was a non-swimmer, feared all water, especially icy cold, and when his steely brown eyes narrowed, I shrivelled with remorse.

I gingerly handed him a towel, transfixed at the difference between his chalk-white torso, which never saw the sun, and his mahogany, tanned head, which now dripped with diluted, white emulsion. The decorating was completed surreptitiously during the deep freeze that followed.

There were no witnesses to this embarrassing accident, but I roll about laughing each time I picture it. If captured on film in today's world, it would have gone viral on YouTube.

Betty was a frustrated interior designer. When changes were afoot, her husband, Ray, hid in his workshop behind the television sets that waited for repair. To avoid her, their four boys made an excuse about camping with their various scout associations. When they returned, she sat with polished nails, perfect hair, and basked in the glow of her expertly applied latest fashion in wall colour.

She came to grief when one of her dizzy turns, toppled her off the ladder onto her head and knocked her unconscious. The ambulancemen thought she only escaped death because she wore one of her boy's large, leather, aviator helmets to protect her

186

precious hairdo. There were no more ladders for her unless a tall son supervised.

When the children were young, Betty came into our kitchen and found the children sobbing. She hugged Steph, 'What's wrong?'

With tear-stained faces, they blubbed, 'Our cherry wallpaper's gone.' The kitchen feature wall had squares containing colourful fruit and vegetables, and I had replaced it with a smaller, modern, patterned paper. Betty commiserated with the children, 'Never mind. It was time for a change.' To her relief, I had chosen a muted design; as large geometrics, like the one in our hallway, sent her reeling.

When the '60s shift dresses were high fashion, my friends and neighbours, who were not dressmakers, begged me to make them one each. They provided the materials, and I charged one pound, an adequate payment, for a sack. I got bored when it turned into a business that crushed the fun out of it. I'm so glad I didn't pursue my childhood ambition and become a full-time dress designer.

My friend Betty was the exception. We came up with a plan. She was an expert dancer and organised dances for charities. When she visited her parents in Manchester, she bought back lots of remnants at silly prices on the markets, which she shared between her, my girls, and me. She had an upright carriage from ballroom dancing, was a stock, *Simplicity* pattern size, and had a slim figure. To make evening dresses for her was a delight. Her thick curly auburn hair and white skin completed her elegance.

For many years, each daughter's dress I made had a matching outfit for a doll, cut from the remnants. We unearthed a stash of slides and photos, and I was thrilled to be reminded of those homemade clothes and dollies dresses that photographed so well.

One day at primary school, Wendy had knotted the two rope swings together behind her, and when she had finished swinging, she jumped away. She hadn't realised she had tied the skirt of the dress into the knot, and the propulsion when she leapt off, ripped it from hem to waistline.

She shrugged and said to the horrified teacher on duty, who pinned the dress together, 'Don't worry. Mum won't be cross. She'll mend it or make me another one.' She was right; I salvaged it with one secure line of sewing.

My most ambitious project was making a cover with fitted sides for Fred's baby grand piano. The vast expanse on the piano top tempted us to use it for a dumping ground. He hated to see framed photos and books cluttering them because they rattled when the piano was played and often caused scratches.

Fred supported the heavy canvas as I fed it through the sewing machine, and then he carried outside. Our neighbours stared in amusement when he crawled around the lawn wielding a large paintbrush and red paint which coincidentally matched our carpet.

'He's painting his piano cover with the leftover car paint,' I explained. They were beyond surprised at anything eccentric Fred attempted. I was proud when we sold the piano in pristine condition; he was right, of course; the cover had saved it from any scratches.

My driving test was a humbling and terrifying failure. I took driving lessons. At first, Fred took me to a car park on the headland. He erected a series of expendable cardboard boxes to stand for gate posts.

His wry sense of humour prevailed. 'Whoops! There goes Mrs Le Page's gate post again.' After another disastrous manoeuvre, I stopped for that lesson.

He deftly collected and piled the damaged boxes on the back seat and sighed, 'Don't worry. We'll try again tomorrow.' After our nerve-wracking drive home, he had to prise my fingers off the steering wheel.

A patient, professional driving instructor gave me lessons and told me I had two nasty habits to overcome, I slowed at any gateways and moved into the middle of the road, so I explained it was in case a dog, cat, or child ran out.

My other fault was to line up the offside front wheel to the curvature of the lane, leaving the same distance from the wall, or pavement, as if creating a perfect line on a sewing machine. I promised I would take a more direct approach in future and not weave in and out.

Guernsey drivers are very understanding and leave plenty of room when they see the white and red learner 'L' plate on the back and front of the car, or the yellow 'H' sticker which symbolises it's a hire car and maybe a visitor behind the wheel.

We also have a quaint system of "filter in turn", which works well on the narrow, but busy, crossroads. Fred's advice was, "if ever you get lost on the island, just carry on until you reach the sea, then turn left or right. You'll get to your destination around ten minutes later".

I didn't expect to pass my first driving test, and I didn't. I crunched along the high pavement edging, scraping the hub caps. The driving test examiner cringed at the screech, 'Ouch, your husband wouldn't like that. I'm sorry, Mrs Rowland, you haven't passed this time because you're unfamiliar with the island. Practice in St Martins for the next time.'

He assumed I was new to the island, but, by that point, I'd lived here for several years. With only one examiner and more people buying cars and learning to drive, if you failed the test, you had to wait six months to retake it.

I started the torture of lessons again but stopped because I took a well-paid job on the bus route, so I never took another driving test, nor did I ever familiarise myself with St Martins.

My life had revolved around the garden and house, I could walk to the beautiful beaches, and I never hankered to be anywhere else on the island. So being a non-driver had no impact as there was always someone around to ferry me wherever I wished to go. If it wasn't Fred, there was Betty or Jill, then later, Wendy, Steph or Darius. Even nowadays, if I go out to play cards or have a social lunch, my bridge partners will make a point of collecting me.

The Guernsey Tourist Board heard Jill had nursing experience and persuaded her to become a landlady and take in diabetic visitors. She and the Tourist Bureau recognised the potential of this niche market for guests who had specific food requirements. She was an inspired, competent cook and studied and offered special diets; strict, simple, and cheap. Grateful visitors booked her rooms and catering year upon year.

One time, she explained to me the Bureau was desperate to accommodate a pair of holidaymakers with diabetes. Their usual guesthouses could not take them with their condition, and Jill didn't want to refuse.

For extra cash, Jill had already taken in two Scottish carpenters on a bed-and-breakfast basis. She only glimpsed them at 5.00 pm, when they came out of their room, transformed after work and left in a cloud of aftershave for their evening on the town.

She pleaded for me to take them in as a favour to her, 'Are you sure you can't fit them in anywhere? They're fun-loving lads. It's just for a fortnight, and I don't want to lose them as long-term guests.'

We agreed to accommodate Jill's temporary, cast-off guests, Frankie and Johnny, (as in the ballad), for two weeks only. We set about rearranging the sleeping arrangements.

These boys came home one afternoon and asked for Fred. Jill, who was visiting us, told them, 'He's not home from school yet.'

'Not home from school?' they repeated, surprised.

'Yes. Fred teaches maths at Beaucamp School.'

'We thought he was a professional musician,' one of them scowled, 'We wouldn't have come otherwise.' They held teachers in high esteem and presumed he would judge them on their behaviour or how they spoke.

This misunderstanding arose when they saw Fred, who was always home before them each day, tuning his bass guitar, sorting out reeds for the clarinet, polishing his magnificent tenor sax. He was sometimes rehearsing new pop numbers ready for his night out in the band, bow tie at the ready. The nightlife in Guernsey during the summer in the '70s was in full swing, and Fred regularly performed in a dance band at various hotels entertaining visitors.

Frankie and Johnny came for a fortnight and stayed the summer. They had a car and took Wendy to the outdoor bathing pools at weekends, where she would watch them, triple high dive off the boards to catch the eyes of the ladies. The extra income they brought, we spent on linen and household replacements. The bonus from these two youthful men was fun and laughter.

192

Fred's secondary school held their annual sports day, and as he did not need to be there to organise any event, he just showed his face and crept away. With no dogs or children to attend to, he made it home in record time to spend a naughty afternoon with me. In one minute, he had drawn the lounge curtains. It was pre-planned, and at home I was ready for action. Fred stood in his underpants, and I emerged from the bedroom, dressed in what I thought was a sexy, frilly, pink baby-doll nightie.

After a few minutes, two heads appeared around the lounge door, 'It's us, Mrs R. We just popped in to pick something up.' The carpenters, stood there, mouths open, at this unexpected afternoon peep-show. Stifling laughter, they mumbled, 'Won't be long,' and fled.

The moment had passed, and we both felt stupid, childlike and exposed. Fred sighed, glanced at his watch, 'Time to pick up the kids,' got dressed and opened the curtains.

I never wore the ridiculous pink frillies again but caught winks and knowing glances from the two lads.

We had been interrupted for the second time, *in flagrante delicto*; (in fragrant delicious as Fred called it).

Chapter 15 - You're My Best Friend

(Queen)

In winter, Fred often dropped me at Betty's house on his way to school, where we saw Joy, the female, white, standard poodle who lived opposite. She was a regular sight in her owner's jewellery shop, in St Peter Port; a diversion for the shoppers, groomed and polished to match their wares. Standards were rare on the island, so it was unusual when we met a second large one on the beach, a very friendly male.

Months after this sighting, we were excited to hear from Betty, that Joy had a bumper litter of puppies. Betty told the breeder how we loved Joy, and she invited us to view the pups. With the puppies having first-class pedigrees, we knew buyers would snap them up, at prices beyond our means.

Joy paraded her gorgeous, fluffy pups. They had already earmarked puppies for overseas to spread the gene pool around the world, and two stayed on the island for continuity. Joy inherited an impressive, long pedigree, descended from the Dame of Sark's white champions. A photograph exists of them with the Dame and Nazi officers in Sark, during the German occupation.

The breeder saw our enjoyment and interaction with the puppies, 'I hear you don't have a dog at present. Would you like one of these?'

I looked over at Fred who played at fending off the marauding bundles. Besotted with these fluffy runaways, he smiled at me, nodded at the suggestion, and that was that.

I was thrilled, but then reality set in, 'Yes, we'd love one, but it'll be out of our price range.'

'How much can you afford?' I mentioned a derisory amount, but still expensive for us.

'Good, it's settled. You can be first to pick a name from the list.'

At the first name, Polly, I stopped her, 'I have fond memories of a sweet lady with that name.'

We became the proud owners of a white poodle puppy, 'Polly of Minikena', named after the breeder's house. The bush telegraph had delivered again, as she held out the wriggling puppy, 'I believe you met her father on the beach. He's been the perfect match for Joy, hasn't he?' He certainly was.

Polly had intelligence, was so loving, and glamorous, but it was so expensive to have her professionally groomed, in compensation, I made do with home perms for my hair. She loved travelling with Fred or Steph, sitting tall in the back seat of the car. At one point, a funny rumour circulated that Fred, a teacher, was brazenly having an affair with a blonde, glimpsed in his vehicle. Of course, he was, she also had a fluffy tail.

One day a colleague approached Fred. 'You've got a standard poodle. Can you manage another? Her owner died, and the dog's dreadfully overweight. Colour blue, I believe.' Fred knew this meant a bluey-grey, a splendid contrast to our white one.

We met Golly at the vet's surgery. They told us she had been terrified of being groomed and clipped, so they anaesthetised her to perform a complete overhaul before we took her home. It didn't bode well, and I must confess I was disappointed; this poor mutt was the most sub-standard, standard poodle I'd ever seen. Her temporary minders had slimmed her, but it left her coat the texture of grey, wrinkled underfelt. She waddled over to us, and even under semi-sedation, she seemed to be short-sighted, which turned out to be tunnel vision.

She instantly captured my heart with her vulnerability. I thought, *You poor thing. I will make up for the trauma you have suffered.* She blinked; her black eyes full of trust. Overwhelmed with protective, maternal feelings, I whispered, 'Hello, Golly, you're coming home with us.'

Rather than feeling sorry for her, the children loved her quirky nature. The satisfied vet handed over the lead. We nicknamed her "Goggles", to reflect her failing eyesight.

On her first night in a different home, I slept on the sofa and put a bed on the floor nearby. When she felt my hand touch her back, she settled. After an exhausting day, we both slept until late morning, when on waking, without hesitation, she left me and scrambled into the garden to join the noise and laughter of the children and Polly. A proper dog's life had begun for her.

She wasn't the most attractive dog, but what she lost in beauty, she gained in brains and humour, and we absolutely loved her. I tried to clip her using some quiet electric clippers, but the buzzing still terrified her, so I worked around it, and gently moved my hand over her fur, and cut the protruding hair with scissors. Her coiffure was always a work in progress, she allowed bursts of time for me to snip her coat, and I managed one leg a week. I trimmed her body fur whenever the television got boring. This practice stood me in good stead for dealing with other pets when they got too frail for visits to the doggy beautician.

Goggles eventually became blind, and I demanded, 'We can only keep her if the floor is clear of clutter, and the furniture never moved.' For the children, this was inadvertent training in tidiness, which became second nature for them.

Goggles was familiar with the wooden steps leading onto the beach. We instructed either 'up' or 'down' to raise her front legs and feel the way. She was so intuitive and brave. For fun, the children gave her these same commands on a flat surface, and she performed them like a sweet little show pony.

She had one unpleasant habit. Whenever she got downwind of rotting, stinking fish at the far end of the beach, she made a beeline for the smell and rolled in it. It was a game, and we couldn't catch her. To lessen her fishy odour, we had to hose her down after the walk.

When Fred and I were on holiday in Australia, we had a call from the children. They had taken Goggles to the vet to investigate a suspect cyst. The vet told them, only on rare occasions did they operate on blind dogs.

'But this is Goggles, and we promised Mum we'd take care of her,' they pleaded. 'We'll take full responsibility.' The vet operated, and she made a full recovery.

She was the most lovable dog and gained a few more quality happy years with us. We revelled in stories of her antics, often repeated in our household. So, when she died, it was consoling to know we gave her the best life we could, she had been safe and knew we really loved her.

Chapter 16 - The Heat Is On
(Glen Frey)

I didn't practice extravagant hobbies but needed a small outlay to finance the ones I had. My requirements were material and cotton for sewing, plant pots for gardening and special oils for mixing paints. The children always knew to buy me presents of large tubes of oil paints in titanium white or cadmium blue. The seascapes, cubists and modernists I copied, used lashings of paint.

We were fortunate to have a celebrated artist, Brenda Munson, living and working in Guernsey. Her work displayed a true artistic reflection of the granite byways and alleys of St Peter Port. She ran oil painting lessons from her art material shop and ladled the oil paint on with a palette knife; this was within my talent but beyond my budget.

Jill juggled well with her limited cash flow, and Richard provided us with free hardboard offcuts to paint on. I suggested she try watercolour paints as they were less expensive, but the technique was different, so she eked out her oil paints and created small delicate landscapes.

Our children had reached the expensive stage, and I needed to find a job. I had reached the end of my allotted ten years of their childhood that Fred and I had agreed. So, I hot-footed it to the employment office, where a loud, diminutive elf-like Glaswegian with khaki hair greeted me at the office reception. While I sat in front of her wondering if it was an amateur dye job or her real hair colour, she broke my thoughts when, out of the blue, she said, 'You believe in the occult.'

Startled, I nodded.

'I predict I'll be of enormous help to you in the future.'

I laughed, 'Forget the future, I need help now.'

She picked the job sheets from the under desk filing cabinet and looked down the list and presented me with the perfect job: ordinary clerical, with average pay, and only ten minutes cycle ride from home.

A fortnight later, her employment bureau had closed, and she joined me at the small horticultural supply factory. Within a week, we were both redundant as they shut down the factory for reorganisation; grand terms for our piddling outfit, which was little more than a packing shed.

Before we left our jobs, my Scottish elf remembered Lloyds clearing bank had advertised for a temporary position and gave me the manager's name, so as soon as I got home, I telephoned him.

He said, 'Since you're available now, you can start tomorrow. We'll sort out the formalities then.'

The following day, he interviewed me in his authoritarian style and glanced at my homemade C.V., which outlined typing experience and time as a civil servant. He looked me up and down before he leant his six-foot-four frame over the desk.

Narrowing his eyes, a few inches from my face, he enunciated every syllable, 'Do. You. Chat?'

I didn't answer. What do you say to that? He was a little odd; the whole experience was slightly weird. But when I left, I knew I had the job.

They scheduled decimal Day in the United Kingdom and Ireland for 15 February 1971, when they subdivided the pound, shilling and pence into an easy to calculate 100 pence to equal one pound. My workload for the year was to transfer the customer details onto the bank's card system in time for this transition.

After I had completed this project, they offered me a full-time position, which I declined, as the children were still at school, and I needed part-time hours. I had enjoyed the job and working with conscientious colleagues.

To keep up the income stream, for minimum wage, I took a summer morning job at Cobo Bay Hotel. It was an enjoyable, leisurely ten-minute scenic cycle ride from home along the coast. I stacked breakfast dishes into a huge dishwasher, then hung the piles of clean sheets on the outdoor washing lines. I could hear the shrieks of laughter and envied the holidaymakers below me as they frolicked on the beach.

After two months, Jill commented that I was acting downtrodden, like a scullery maid, 'Even though you have a menial job, there's no reason to enter fully into the role.'

That week, I had an impassioned plea from one of the Lloyds Bank colleagues, 'Please come back to work for us. Otherwise, I can't have a honeymoon. There's no staff to cover for me. They have arranged for you to go on the switchboard on a nine-to-five basis.'

I eagerly accepted this arrangement, especially when I found out the salary was a staggering increase compared to my earnings at the hotel.

The other draw was that many bank employees had been recruited from England and awarded two free flights per year back to London. The travel benefit applied to all the staff at local clearing banks.

When I asked if I could change the route from London to Manchester, twice the distance, they readily altered my allowance and reduced it to one flight instead of two, which gave me a free annual visit to my parents.

Years had gone by since they cleared the land behind our house at Port Soif. We heard several rumours that someone had earmarked the vacant plot for new homes, and we waited for the inevitable.

While at the bank, a pompous sub-manager, who took the early lunch hour, approached me, 'It will be advantageous to go straight to the States offices at lunchtime. You mustn't miss the notice pinned there.'

He piqued my interest, and I rushed to find out. The announcement decreed the builders had accepted the reclaimed land at St Sampson on the North-East coast, with permission to erect ship landing stages. In exchange, the States received the builders' Port Soif holdings, and they now designated it a recreation area, with proposed plans for a community clubhouse, cricket, and football fields. It was a real 'Thank-you, God' moment, and I skipped back to the bank.

In retrospect, I thought I had done the States a disservice, thinking nothing was in the pipeline for the Port Soif hinterland, but they had expedited the exchange behind closed doors. It was a triumph for me and the neighbourhood and scotched the rumours of mass housing construction. The Rovers football team eventually built a modern, low-rise clubhouse. A circuitous gravel footpath for dog walkers took them past a new wildlife pond with a nesting place for local birds. Boy scouts also used this nature trail as a shortcut to the beaches.

I relished the sporting activities on the Rovers' playing fields and their accompanying seasonal noises. In summer, the thwack of cricket bats with genteel clapping; in winter, the raucous shouting during football training and subsequent matches.

My lively young colleagues in the bank kept me stimulated and treated me as an equal. They valued my time as part of a well-oiled establishment which soon stretched to ten years. The extra income financed our loft conversion, a fitted kitchen, and several Italian holidays. But I never saw my wee Scottish benefactress again.

One evening, my heart beat faster, my body seared with heat, and hot flushes swept over me. It wasn't a heart attack, as I first thought, the menopause had arrived, when I least expected it.

I was unprepared for the emotional changes and chaos it would bring. During the motions of everyday routines, I became drenched in sweat dealing with family crises at home, but at the Bank, in charge of my emotions, the menopausal hot flushes did not manifest.

Compared to the surrounding teenagers, I acted stylish and mature and became the bridge between the lofty bosses and the banking hall, but my recurring sin was my daily return from lunch five minutes late. One summer lunchtime, I sat watching the boats which rocked in the careening hard and fell asleep in the sunshine. Workers returned to their offices and picked their way over my snoring body on the walkway behind the seawall. The apologies and excuses I gave to the sub-manager became more and more bizarre, which he shared with the counter clerks.

One day, fed up at my tardiness, he shouted, 'Win. You're late again. What is it today? Did your house catch fire?'

I replied, 'Well, I was rushing back, and the elastic in my tights snapped, and they started to fall down. I had to keep my knees together and slow my pace up the High Street.'

He tried not to laugh when I lifted my skirt to show him and then shuffled towards the bank lift.

Prompt at 5.25 pm each evening, after I left work, a blight descended as I reached my other life, at home. Fred dutifully placed my dinner on the table as I came in, ravenous. I avoided most tantrums and took up tearful tree-hugging.

Enough sense remained to remind me of my erratic, flaring temper, and I often defused the tension by deliberately thumping and cursing at the walls. Witnessing my craziness, Jill said, 'You're lucky. If I did that, they'd cart me back to the loony bin.'

At work, my two worlds collided. Something got to me in my bank cubby hole, I threw a bundle of cheques into the air, stamped on them as they landed, and stormed off to the restroom, shouting, 'Enough! That's it, I've had it.'

Once calmed, they sent me home with orders to consult my doctor, who saw the sweat which streamed from my temples to my chin, and my hair stuck to my head.

'Bum,' he ordered and injected my backside with Hormone Replacement Therapy (HRT) which had recently reached the UK from Australia. I was only 40 and had responded to the family genes for early menopause.

The bank manager, informed of the cheque throwing incident, rang me, 'Poor Win, you've been overdoing it. Don't worry; I'll deal with everything here. Please take some leave and get better.'

The following morning, I stunned the staff by arriving on time, smiling, wearing a smart and sassy A-line shift, trailing a cloud of Chanel perfume which lingered long after I'd left the building.

HRT was a new drug, and calculating the correct dosage was trial and error. Individuals responded in different ways. The first time I overdosed, it resulted in turning me into a wanton hussy leaping on Fred when the children left the room.

I consulted with the doctor, who sympathised, 'Your husband won't be able to maintain such an intense level of activity without injury.' He reduced the dose, and I stopped tearing Fred's clothes off.

The Methodist Church Ladies Guild Choir performed hymn concerts to a captive audience at our old people's homes. I read the lessons and Psalms in what the locals called "my pleasant English voice".

At my first community church dinner, I was the only one holding a full pint glass, with what the committee referred to as 'the demon alcohol.'

My table of ladies whispered, 'Congratulations.' They thought I was brave, but I was just ignorant and embarrassed. They had been dying to have an illicit, satisfying glug all evening. The barman in the kitchen must have had a sense of humour and gasped at the order: 39 glasses of water and one cider. The beer mug had been his creative, theatrical flourish.

On HRT, I left the ladies' choir when my voice dropped from soprano to growling bass. Still musical, it created hysterics within the ranks, a boom, boom, rolling jazz bass, wholly unacceptable for hymns. It never came back, and I grieved the loss of my singing voice, the only musical ability I had.

They reduced my hours and duties at work, being otherwise a healthy employee who never took sick days from the office, apart from my annual holidays. Impervious to infection, not absent for melodramas, nor bad-hair days, I soldiered on, even when my home hair-tint turned my head psychedelic colours.

The office gossip soon spread, and on a pretext, the manager came to my desk to view my new hairdo. He cocked his head to one side, like an expert assessing a rare work of art, and, with a hint of a smile, asked, 'Good morning, Win. New hairstyle?' He reached the door, turned and with a straight face said, 'Bright purple suits you.'

'Thank God she's back to normal,' said Bert, the sub-manager. I was his buddy and an appreciative audience for his acerbic wit and an invaluable help writing apology letters on his behalf. He thought my choice of words were inspired; not only were our errors forgiven, but we left the customers with the impression they were slightly to blame.

As a widower, he fancied his chances with the nurse at our mutual dentist, and I boosted his confidence enough for him to approach her. After each dental visit, I returned, singing her praises. Enthusing about one to the other pushed them to make a match that ended in a short, but joyful marriage.

Bert retired at 65 and travelled with his new wife in their campervan. Unfortunately, he died not long after, without experiencing much retirement time. His untimely death, so soon after retirement, was a wake-up call, and I insisted Fred retired at the earliest opportunity, even if we had to manage on a smaller pension.

Chapter 17 – Tragedy

(Bee Gees)

Tragedy seems to strike when you least expect it. We witness the fall-out, standing by, frustrated, and impotent. One such time for me started with a hectic car treasure hunt. These were popular fundraisers where parties in cars set out with a list of clues, places of interest, and a few quirky items to bring back. Teenagers often popped in to see us with requests for odd things.

Steph was never keen on racing around in cars and dropped out of one hunt to study for O-level exams the next day.

The following morning, Steph's best friend's father telephoned. The night before, a car crash had claimed Sharon's life. Fitting of car seatbelts was not standard regulation, so the teenagers' chances of survival in a speeding car were slim. The car driver, when flung against the granite sea wall, was killed outright, while Steph's friend, Sharon, sustained her fatal injuries when thrown into the road.

After I hung up, I wondered how to tell my teenage daughter that her best friend was dead. Talking to a child about death, whether it's a goldfish or grandma, is always a terrible task.

I mustered the nerve to tell Steph and stumbled upstairs with a cup of tea. I had never taken drinks upstairs, and this and the stark look on my face alerted her to bad news.

She sat up in bed, 'Who?' she whispered.

'Sharon was killed last night in a car accident.' I told her the sparse details I knew, and she found out more, when, grief-stricken, she joined the others at the grammar school.

Steph returned to her classroom and for weeks, sat next to an empty desk. Distraught, she sat but passed no more exams that year. The school staff did nothing; they had no procedure in place for student counselling. Unlike today's mass outpourings of grief, schools are more informed of the psychological effects of a student death, and therapy offered to the pupils. There was no such provision in those times for poor Steph and her classmates.

I couldn't help or do more because I never knew the girl or her family. I worked full time and only met her a few times. During the school holidays, Fred, and Sharon's mother, took turns shuttling the girls between homes on opposite sides of the island.

Wendy returned from a weekend in London to this shocking news and her distressed sister. This tragic event, coupled with other situations, had repercussions. When off-island, Wendy insists we are in contact daily and informed when anything unusual has happened. She never wants to come home to bad news.

A crowd of mourners attended the funeral, and the pathways and church adorned with hundreds of flowers. Treasure hunts with time limits fell out of favour and stopped.

Steph passed her driving test at 17 but wasn't keen to drive. Through a lack of travel confidence, she stopped taking holidays which involved flights or boats. Fred was a rock, always there if she needed a lift. She felt safe with him driving her around, and we had a frequent and convenient island bus service.

With help from two married therapists who befriended her, with their coaxing, she lost her fear and started driving again.

Chapter 18 - On The Beach

(Chris Rea)

Evacuated during the German Occupation, many islanders returned after 1945, but some children had grown up without their parents and relatives and hardly knew them. It was difficult for everyone to rebuild their lives and livelihoods. Many properties sustained damage through wood stripped from them for fuel, and rationing had only just finished when we arrived on the island. During the early '60s, there was an air of relief and optimism as the island slowly recovered, and tourism started up again.

At that time, I understood why the teachers preferred the south coast, as the north and west were not that appealing, being undeveloped, flat, windy stretches of marshland near the sea, waterlogged in winter. Banks of greenhouses dominated the landscape, which housed tomato plants and freesia bulbs. It was a stark landscape as growers left the land uncultivated around the greenhouses to let in maximum sunshine. In summer, they whitewashed the glass panes to stop the plants from shrivelling. It was a thriving industry, and in winter, when the greenhouses were empty, small engines chugged, steamed, and sterilised the soil, which left free time for the housewives to socialise.

They exported tomatoes to England, graded by hand, and packed in wicker baskets lined with coloured tissue according to their size. In the late-1960s, they shipped almost half a billion

212

tomatoes, but the price of oil increased, making it too expensive to run the greenhouse heating boilers. The UK also started to import tomatoes from Holland, as cheaper North Sea fuel allowed the Netherlands to provide low-cost heating to their growers. As the island's bulk tomato shipments dwindled, it was not unusual to see piles of tomatoes going to waste or given away on hedges at the side of the road. As a result, growers cultivated other fruit, vegetables, and flowers.

Spring in Guernsey always came earlier than the UK and galvanised the women into action. They systematically picked the fields of daffodils buds, packed and exported them. In the greenhouses, women bunched freesias, five stems wrapped in damp cotton wool, secured with a tiny rubber band, packed into boxes and sent off to decorate and perfume English houses. I often received misshapen stems, which made crazy, looser flower arrangements. Year on year, thousands of daffodils split and grow in gardens, fields, and hedgerows which brighten our landscapes and our lives. I lived within an enclave of greenhouses, marshes, bowls of flowers, and kind, sweet ladies in pinafores.

In the collection of small bungalows with long gardens in Port Soif Lane, the large families had mostly boys. Everyone was charming and friendly, but they were all busy as many helped in their family businesses. A punnet of tomatoes, carrots and lettuce appeared on my doorstep every few days, sometimes green beans or anything left over from a glut and there were always flowers, of course.

213

I tried to thank my neighbours, but with no real success. I was a housewife and Fred, a teacher, so we had nothing tangible with which to reciprocate. They didn't expect anything from us, and I found out later, they felt it an honour to have a teacher in their midst. Unlike the growers, he wore a collar and tie and worked a short day. They expected nothing in return from this cerebrally superior being who had spare time and sat in the garden reading books.

At Port Soif, I planted a cottage garden to save money. My first lettuces tasted bitter, coarse, and inedible. The grower next door said to his wife in his local idiom, 'She'll not grow nothing yer. Its bloney white sand. We're part of the beach, eh?'

Salt-laden winds from the beach often lashed the house and garden. My neighbour's mother was replanting her backyard, and she removed and donated a row of blackcurrant bushes to start my shelterbelt. Not only was it a substantial windbreak, but for years, the fruit made several jars of delicious jam. I had tried everywhere to find information on seaside gardening but to no avail. I soon created a shrub border, but it was trial and error to grow in sandy soil on a windy site.

The light soil needed humus to enrich it, so I smothered the beds with old newspapers, wool, and cotton clothes. Cuttings wrapped in a bed of newspaper retained moisture, which stopped the natural drainage through the sand. I gleaned snippets from any plant and tried everything to grow in the garden.

My moniker was 'the compost queen.' When Fred noticed the elm leaves had fallen in the school premises, he drove us to a safe country lane in the Talbot Valley where we could shovel the blown heaps of leaves, into huge black plastic sacks. The children relished this fun activity and looked forward to our autumn weekend leaf-gatherings. By spring, the leaves had rotted, and the gang of children delighted in throwing the free leaf mould over our flower beds.

Fred soon traded our motorbike, and our first car on the island was an old, wine-coloured, four-door, Peugeot, with the number plate 4. Number 1 belongs to The Governor of Guernsey. In 1960 there were few cars on the island, so there was nothing unusual in owning a low registration number. Decades later, our children wished Fred had kept number plate 4, as there are now over 86,000 vehicles on our Guernsey's roads, for a population of 63,000, and is now worth a small fortune!

They didn't paint cars or treat them as they are today, they faded with the intense summer sun, and seawater sprayed up from the coast roads rusted the chassis undersides. Whenever the Peugeot's bodywork faded to pink, Fred repainted it with dark-red, gloss house-paint. If we could see road tarmac through the floorboards, we exchanged the car. The car dealership, usually low on sales in January, often sold Fred a summer hire car with low mileage and took the old banger in part exchange. He seemed to pay a regular small amount, for a nearly new car. He learned from the red Peugeot and requested the next vehicle colour to be as pale as possible, so it didn't show the sand and salt that settled from the beach.

Liberation Day is one of the most important holidays on the Island. The UK's Prime Minister, Winston Churchill, announced the end of Second World War on 8th May 1945, and the much fought-over Channel Islands were freed from German occupation the day after. This freedom from hostilities is celebrated gratefully every year on 9th May by the islanders in Guernsey and Jersey. There is always an excellent turnout as revellers spill out on to the seafront in St Peter Port, closed to everyday traffic, to watch the military vehicle parades. Local people mingle and enjoy dressing up in military and nursing uniforms and clothes of that era.

Guernsey has three annual shows on consecutive weeks in August. The South Show, for locals to present their cakes, home-grown produce, and crafts, the West Show promotes and encourages agricultural interests and the North Show, held at Sausmarez Park, a favourite event, has Guernsey cattle, goats, and agricultural produce. On the last Thursday in August, crowds of islands and visitors watch the Battle of Flowers, where colourful flower-laden entrants compete for the coveted 'Prix d'honneur.'

When I first arrived here, they created the floats with local flowers, which culminated in an actual 'battle' or skirmish. The crowds stripped the flowers from the displays and bombarded each other with them. Nowadays, islanders decorate fewer floats with real blooms and now use thousands of paper flowers as a colourful substitute. An illuminated parade takes place in the evening, culminating in a firework display. After the event, there is no battle, but prizes awarded for various categories. Different-sized themed floats are installed at strategic viewing points over the island so everyone can enjoy the unique spectacle and hard work, for a while longer.

Lé Viaër Marchi is another annual summer event, where stallholders show their artisanal crafts and vendors supply Guernsey's famous dish, "Bean Jar". Attendees are guaranteed a special atmosphere at this unique event where traditionally dressed dancers sing and mingle with the islanders and holidaymakers.

I often feel like I'm on holiday here, especially when taking the scenic route around the coastline. Guernsey has a 33-foot tidal range, one of the largest in the world, which transforms the shoreline every six hours, from sandy beaches at high tide to the slow revelation of red-granite rock formations when it's low. The sea colour shifts hourly depending on the time of day and the sea state. It can be light turquoise to rival any Caribbean seascape, ranging to deep forbidding grey when storms chase across the horizon.

During the 1960s and 70s, the larger Guernsey hotels organised professional shows for the visitors and invited top-line English performers. Fred earned extra income during the long summer holidays when he played saxophone or clarinet in a four-piece band. He was also a rolling improvisational guitar player, so he never got bored when he wasn't blowing a wind instrument. If the hotel management only wanted to pay for three, he played bass to the drums and keyboard.

Fred was well-informed on most topics, but two terrible flaws emerged, after our marriage, that often caused me to cringe - clothes and occasions. His underprivileged background led to his schooling 'on the Parish' (funded by the Council), which included a provision for school attire and sportswear. He always wore uniforms and knew nothing else about fashion. Even when he played in the band, he wore a white formal jacket.

At home, it was all about comfort, and he sported virulent-green corduroys, which everyone called 'Fred's frogs.' When they became too tatty, I engineered weird accidents, which resulted in a 'frog' interment on the compost heap.

One night, the young drummer in Fred's band was moody and miserable. He had recently lost his father and confided that family members had glimpsed his ghost standing at the garden gate. Their priest had been unhelpful and avoided involvement, so this lad was feeling troubled. Fred knew how to deal with lost souls and advised the boy to arrange a family get-together for a brief prayer, and say out loud, 'Don't worry about us. We're coping very well. Be at peace now.' A quick but decisive farewell. The next time the drummer saw Fred, he gave him a beaming smile and thumbs up; all was well.

The entertainment organiser of a hotel asked the band to turn up in fancy dress for the following Saturday's dance. The theme was St Trinian's, with attendees dressing as schoolgirls or schoolboys. Fred, with our encouragement, borrowed from the girls, a white blouse, a pleated skirt, tie, and black tights. We couldn't disguise his size 10 feet, so he slipped on his usual black, shiny, band shoes. He wore my shoulder-length blonde wig, which we tied in bunches with ribbons, and with coral lipstick, he looked the part.

When he arrived at the hotel, he leapt gracefully onto the podium and unpacked his saxophone. As he bent over, there was complete silence, broken only by a snigger from the side of the stage. He turned around and noticed that no-one else in the ballroom was in fancy dress. No-one had notified Fred that they weren't dressing up that night. With no time to go home to change, he entered into the spirit of things, didn't explain, and just played until midnight as a six-foot St Trinian's schoolgirl.

Even before her first birthday, Steph showed she was strong-minded and fiercely independent. When spoon-fed, she always

219

pushed the spoon away with her tongue and turned her head away. She then grabbed handfuls of food and plastered it into her mouth. To minimise mess, we placed her in the highchair, stripped down to her nappy and bib. A few newspaper pages placed around the chair legs caught any droppings. She supped nutritious soups from the non-spill plastic cup or sucked soft fruit and vegetable crudities. This caper amused Fred, who turned the cleaning up operation into a game. As a teacher of countless young children and pets, it guaranteed success.

For Steph, learning to walk was a steady, serious, personal progression; from a crawl, then support from furniture to furniture as she staggered round. On her first birthday, a doting neighbour, Mabel, visited us. The large spots on her dress transfixed Steph, and she got up and waddled across the room to pick them off the fabric.

Wendy, thrilled to see her sister get up, shouted, 'Look, Mum, she's walking!' It was a delight to capture the first time Steph wobbled unaided, and we caught her first smile.

It had been a brave move to uproot everything familiar and relocate to an island where I didn't know anyone, apart from Fred. A few afternoons, as I rested on the deckchair in the garden, I wistfully watched the planes which flew in the direction of Manchester. I longed for a spare thirty quid to fly back to visit my family, a fortune in those days.

Someone I met and chatted with told me years later that she saw I was lonely and miserable, obviously missing the vibrant family in Manchester. She often wondered if we had left Guernsey and returned to Manchester.

That day, my guard must have been down, my façade had slipped. I didn't recognise the misery of loneliness because it had never happened to me before. By coming to Guernsey, I thought I had burnt my bridges and couldn't allow myself regrets; I was supposed to be grateful.

On the surface, I had what I'd wished for, a beautiful haven to bring up our girls and to live the perfect life with a dutiful and faithful husband. But I lacked the companionship, liveliness and sharing of stories with my sisters and our close family ties.

My melancholy soon lifted when I had spirited encounters with people who turned into lifelong friends. I still vividly remember meeting Jill Vaudin. Our meeting appeared symbolic, straight out of a film. We gently collided on Port Soif, the horseshoe bay, deserted apart from us, two mothers with small children at opposite ends who paddled through the clear water to meet in the middle of the crescent.

We were both English, with sun-bleached blonde hair and regional accents, and after usual banter about the weather, we mistook each other to be visitors to the island.

I continued with the conversation, I'm Win,' I said, and waved my hand over the dunes towards the lane, 'I live over there. These are my girls, Wendy and Stephanie.'

She smiled, showing a row of perfect teeth, 'I'm Jill, this is Gregg, and we live over there.' she said, pointing in the other direction.

We studied each other's faces, matching sleeveless sundresses and flip flops and laughed. I explained I arrived on the island just over a year ago and wondered why we hadn't met before as we lived so near. *What a waste of a year, I wish I had met you earlier,* I thought.

'Tea, then?' I suggested. We gathered our belongings and set off down the lane. I found her open and intelligent, liked her instantly, and we became friends for life. These seaside rendezvous with our children became a week-day thing, with weekends reserved for our husbands and family outings. We got to know each exceptionally well, and she became a substitute sister.

In the summer of 1961, as we strolled across the beach and monitored our children playing in the rock pools, I told her I was pregnant, and she was overjoyed and said, 'It'll be a boy and won't cost you a penny. I kept all of Gregg's things.'

'We only have girls in our family,' I countered. 'We'll probably call her Felicity after my Granny Rowlands.'

Jill, a trained nurse, assisted my midwife, Miss De Jersey, at the birth of our third child. Fred read a book while I was behind closed doors puffing and panting. A little squeamish, he didn't want to be there at the actual birth, so when the midwife shouted

222

through the door, 'Fred, I'm having problems with the baby's shoulder, can you standby?'

He stood outside, petrified he would be required, and propped himself against the door jamb and listened to my whimpers. If he'd been a drinker, he would have downed a swift one for courage.

Our eyes were on the clock as we willed it to move forward. We raised cheers when the hand clicked through midnight, and finally, to my surprise, not another daughter, but our son, arrived in the early morning, on Wendy's fourth birthday, 28th January 1962. He, like Wendy, was a bald bouncing baby and weighed in at a massive 10lb 2oz. The midwife suggested, 'Win, don't have any more babies, they are getting bigger and heavier each time.'

She took care of the baby's umbilical cord but noticed my placenta had not come out and telephoned for an ambulance. While I was still high on gas and air, they sent me off to the hospital to remove it. The ambulance crawled along, and there must have been so many potholes in the roads, I remember it was the most uncomfortable ten-minute journey. I pitied anyone in real discomfort riding in those old ambulances.

In the ward, I welcomed my first cup of tea for months. I sighed with relief, and, as if on cue, the placenta popped out as my doctor entered the ward. He studied the dawn sky, 'Splendid. All fine here then. Spot of golf for me,' and breezed off.

At home, the midwife filled in her forms and asked Jill, 'What's the boy's name?'

Jill pondered, 'She's never mentioned a boy's name, but she mentioned a composer with an unusual name, Darius.' Miss De Jersey thought it sounded classical and wrote it in her notebook.

I returned home mid-morning, exhausted and climbed into bed. In a loving gesture, Fred moistened my mouth with water before I collapsed into a deep sleep. In the late afternoon, I was strong enough to feed this huge, greedy boy.

Fred brought in the carrycot, 'Darius?'

I nodded, 'Oh, yes, I like that name.'

Miss de Jersey popped in to check on her enormous charge and announced she had named her life-size teaching doll, "Felicity".

Jill hosted Wendy's birthday party at her house. The previous day, in the first stages of labour, I had managed to bake a birthday cake, but Jill said it was as heavy as lead, so she fed it to the seagulls.

The birds are still well fed today from the various "failures" when I've tried out recipes without having the right ingredients. In the olden days, it was a serious problem to have a cooking disaster as food was expensive and little surplus to try again.

I have now got to the age where I don't want my cooking to be an adventure; I want it to be a foregone conclusion!

Darius was a few months old when Jill introduced me to her friend, Betty Denoual, another like-minded Mancunian. We had so much in common; we never ran out of conversation. Jill often couldn't get a word in edgeways; her head just moved from side to side like a Wimbledon spectator. The three of us became inseparable. Fate had brought me a gift of another surrogate sister.

I once asked Betty, with four boys who were always in scrapes, 'How do you cope with the worry?'

'If they're still screaming, they're still alive,' she joked.

Betty and Jill had taken an intensive catering course with their other friend, Marguerite. She, and her husband John, bought dilapidated properties and turned them into guesthouses. They spent their summers catering for guests, and winters renovating their next property. One evening we dined at their latest venture, and the toilets were in use, so John led me upstairs.

'Don't look or step back,' he warned.

Of course, I glanced behind me. There was no back wall, so I could clearly see the next building and a church steeple. As I stooped, it was refreshing to feel the chilly air circulate my nether regions. It was a room with a view, both ways!

We had several visits from my relatives who came to share our idyll at the seaside, a fortnight at a time, in our bungalow, a few steps from the sea. Grace and her family stayed with us and often went to the beach armed with flasks and a packed lunch of free tomato sandwiches. While belly-board surfing on the incoming tide, they were unaware their belongings had been floating in the shallows. Their cheap camera got waterlogged but didn't spoil

225

their day. We often rescued tourists' belongings from the fast invading tide. Grace and her girls returned sun-flushed, sandy, and sopping wet, beaming from the day's adventures. They jumped around on the lawn and were hosed down with cold water to rinse off the sand and seawater.

My nieces, Kaye and Jill, are the unbreakable links to some of the happiest times throughout my life. On another visit, they spent many weeks of their summer holidays with us while Grace and George stayed in the UK and worked. Flame-haired Kaye was tall for 15, confident and sensible. Jill was also lofty, fun-loving with straight blonde hair. They claimed and entertained their charges, Wendy and Steph, leaving me with my king-sized son, Darius, six months old.

Weeks passed before Grace telephoned, desperate for news, and wanted to know if her girls were ever coming home. I was selfish, as it hadn't crossed my mind to phone her as we were having such a happy time.

I cut across her tearful voice and lied, 'I've booked the girls' return flight for Thursday if that's all right? Will you promise next time, both you and George will visit us?'

It spurred me to book the girls' return flights after the call. They visited one more time, but, two years later, fate intervened, and they emigrated. They became "ten-pound poms" and cruised to Australia, followed by Linda, our youngest sister. These "poms" provided an immediate workforce for the post-war boom industries. Ninety thousand volunteered to emigrate over three

226

years, and seven-eighths settled. A number took advantage of what they expected to be a free cruise on a chartered liner. They were shocked on arrival when expected to find work. There was a time limit, and if these 'Boomerang Poms' returned home before their statutory two years, they refunded any costs. A small number didn't settle, returned to the UK, homesick, they realised the grass really was greener and returned to Oz – another boomerang.

George found work in Sydney which enabled them to leave their decrepit hellhole of a hostel. It took some getting used to the searing humid summers. Years later, they moved to the new capital city, Canberra when George worked on patents for the government. With enthusiasm, they integrated to become full Aussie citizens and found permanent gainful employment.

It was always a thrill to receive Grace and Linda's thin blue airmail letters telling me their latest news and I dreamed one day of being able to visit.

Chapter 19 - Witchy Woman

(Eagles)

Steph left the Grammar school in the mid-1970s and joined me at Lloyds Bank. Roy, the bank messenger, was the archetypal figure, a puppet-master pulling strings. His encyclopaedic knowledge of the building fabric, and its daily services, heating, and lighting worked with clockwork precision. During the bank's renovation, much of the work took place overnight, and he marshalled the cleaners like an army and announced their theatres of operation, so in the mornings, we found everything pristine and ready for business.

When they decorated the high banking hall ceiling, the staff and customers were bemused to see an enormous tent-like canvas sail over their heads. With any slight knock of the fabric, anyone below became sprinkled with white dust. Roy consulted his union rule book and found staff could be awarded "a dirt allowance" at the end of the disruption, which earned him respect and gratitude from the team.

During the refurbishment, only one incident intruded into our cushioned lives. A girl working at a desk stationed against a wall screamed and jumped up with terror. A Kango hammer probe pierced through next to her with a loud crash and metallic rattle and stopped. They led her away to rest, suffering from shock. The workers came and viewed this lethal wad of steel and pile of plaster, which stuck out half a yard, and inches away from her

228

typewriter. The ramification of what could have happened filled us with dread. Following the near-miss, any dangerous renovation work continued after working hours.

The manager sought Roy's attention. 'After all this dirt and disruption, I think we should celebrate with a Christmas party.'

Roy said, 'Leave it to me, Sir.'

He consulted with the two sub-managers. They agreed to hold the party in the long banking hall upstairs, which housed the investments and foreign exchange. He co-opted some strong young men to help decorate with lights, tinsel and balloons. Roy's wife, the lively Bunty, laid out a delicious finger buffet. The foreign exchange counter served as the bar, with Roy as 'mine host.'

Non-drinkers volunteered to man the music station and organised hilarious games and dances. My drink was more rye than dry, which seemed to be the standard ratio, judging by tottering steps and shrieks of laughter. What a party!

Steph and I, both a little tipsy, helped each other navigate down the pier steps and sat on a retaining wall and waited for Fred, our lift home. I stopped singing when anyone passed us and started up again with increased volume, which made them jump and turn around. Steph just giggled to herself.

Fred came over and helped us into the car and straightened our paper hats. He drove off but soon stopped and wound down the car windows, afraid of being overcome with our alcoholic fumes.

The following day, Roy was waiting for the sub-manager and said, 'A quick word, Sir.' He wished to prepare him for any leg-pulling or reference to his part in last night's party, which he wouldn't remember, but I certainly did.

When they played *The Stripper* the sub-manager, under an alcoholic haze, hurried to the centre of the crowd, tore off his tie, and waved it around his head several times before throwing it in the air. The dancers alerted to this spectacle, formed a circle and clapped to the booming, vibrant music. He removed his shoes and socks in time to the beat and tossed them with elegant abandon to the far corners of the banking hall. When his trousers were ready to fall, the music screeched to stop. A punchy number started the dancers off again, while he was discreetly dressed and taken home.

I don't know what Roy told him, but the sub-manager kept his head down all day and left work early.

It became an annual event, anticipated by everyone, but we never experienced another floor show of that calibre from a senior member of staff.

The next successful event masterminded by Roy was a staff, fancy-dress ball held in a hotel, with relatives, and friends invited. Fred, my guest, was dressed as a waiter. I sewed playing cards onto a long red dress and turned up as Queen of Hearts with an appropriate crown. Months of anticipation and preparation was a large part of office banter and caused much amusement as we begged and borrowed articles to complete our outfits.

Our wee, Scottish friend, Kay, was on maternity leave, very near her due date, but didn't want to miss one of these popular parties. She drove into town but was stopped by the police in a road check.

'No excuses, please leave your car, Madam,' said the earnest policeman. She hauled her lump out, and he was astonished to see her dressed as a tomato. Her shapely pregnancy filled the red satin balloon smock, and she completed the outfit with green shoes and tights, with an emerald green hat formed into a calyx with a stalk.

'Fancy dress?' she apologised self-consciously.

The red-faced policeman helped her gently back into the car, ushered her through to the vehicle line and waved her off. At the dance, when they judged the outfits, she came a popular second.

Steph won the first prize. She entered as a slinky '60s Playboy Bunny, with high heels, black-mesh tights on her gorgeous slim long legs, under tiny black shorts, with the strapless top of a retro black swimming costume. She outlined her eyes with smoky kohl, and, on her head, she sported black and white bunny ears which I sewed onto a headband covered in synthetic fur. A white, round, enticing fluffy tail completed the sexy ensemble. With a male judging panel, how could she possibly go wrong?

Only once was I unable to appease an angry customer in the bank. A slight mistake occurred in his standing order. His anger on the phone was totally out of all proportion to the misdemeanour. The manager told me not to worry; I had just misread a figure. The furore would blow over.

The following day, colleagues behind the counter greeted me with a pantomime; they crossed themselves against the devil and drew magic signs in the air in front of me. The sub-manager called me over, and there was total silence as he told me the furious customer who caused trouble from the day before, had suffered a fatal heart attack in the night.

The counter staff knew of my occult interests and capitalised on it. They drew chalk marks around my chair and teased me all day, and that's how my nickname became, "Winnie the Witch".

While working at the bank, we had a superb rooftop view, from where I could watch the finale of the Battle of Britain air display. On the maintenance walkway, there was just enough room for four of us to follow the Royal Air Force Red Arrows as they performed their synchronised formation flying. The annual September event commemorates the Battle of Britain and is an opportunity to remember those who are currently fighting for our country and raise funds for the RAF.

The air display lasted for two hours and showcased World War Two aircraft and other relevant modern planes (this collection changes from time to time). Spectators overlooked St Peter Port and crammed the surrounding areas to view the town harbour displays.

Before Health and Safety took hold and moved the display further out into the Little Russell (the sea channel outside the harbour), they held the exhibition over the town and piers. It was noisy, which added to the excitement, the pungent diesel fuel permeated the air and red, white and blue vapour trails dissipated among the boats and out to sea.

The bank staff took turns every year during the lunchtime to watch the skilful airmen. Spectators often stood on the walkway next to the harbour's careening hard, with its uninterrupted view. Caught up in the moment, I surprised myself by jumping and screaming with the crowds when the jets flew past each other with what looked like inches to spare over the towering crane arms. The Harrier Jump Jet was a favourite, with its vertical take-off and landing. The pilot's face seemed so close we could see his features clearly as he manoeuvred the aircraft towards the pier steps, hovered in mid-air and bowed its nose to the spectators.

One day I returned home from work to an air of excitement; Darius had brought me a significant catch. The outlandish air of young Darius's new fishing hobby brought its fragrance to the mix. To please him, with future larger catches in mind, I boned or filleted every tiny fish he brought me. I often cooked and ate the four-inch delicacy, two mouthfuls, with gusto as he eagerly supervised.

Before long, he had grown into a tall, teenage fisher-boy, now proficient at diving in a wet suit and using a speargun.

233

Encouraged by me, his catches had increased in size; I was fearless; no fish was too demanding for me to tackle.

'Your fish is in the bath, Mum,' he smirked. The family trooped behind me to enjoy my reaction. A dark grey, four-foot conger eel stretched out in the bath, with its limpid eye staring up at me.

Darius proudly dragged and draped the fish over the kitchen table, where its head and tail almost reached the floor. With the bread knife, I spent the evening sawing it into meal-size, gelatinous portions. It jerked with the first cut, and I jumped back, dropped the knife and screamed. Darius laughed and assured me it was a nervous reaction from the fish; it was positively dead.

I packed large empty ice-cream boxes with the unattractive, grey fleshy fillets. I cooked and tasted one piece, but the rough and gamey flavour was not palatable to me, so I offered the local delicacy to the neighbours. They pounced upon it and salivated as they carried their booty away.

Chapter 20 - Highly Strung

(Spandau Ballet)

Jill, one of my closest friends, was going through difficulties and sorrows. A manic depressive, any traumatic incidents triggered off her bipolar bouts. Her son's birth was the first as far as I know.

Tragedy struck when Jill's mother died in a car accident in England. Not wearing a seat belt, she suffered fatal internal injuries, while her father escaped with just a broken ankle. The one pleasing event out of this tragedy was that his secretary nursed him after his wife's death. Unmarried and now retired, she never found anyone who measured up to him and seamlessly slipped into the role of carer. Jill's brothers told me she deserved this happy ending when she became his wife.

Losing her mother in such a sudden fatal collision, caused a significant mental reversal for Jill, and her deterioration was devastating to watch. My dear friend was lost to me, sometimes for years, during treatment. We accepted her strange behaviour because Jill wasn't always highly strung, only when her stress and anxiety levels rose.

They sectioned her for nine months while she grappled with her mother's tragic event. Richard, her husband, had relatives nearby who stepped in and cared for Gregg, a tiny tot, still at school.

When they released Jill from the psychiatric hospital, she resembled a zombie, silently staring at the wall or ceiling. The person I loved seemed so distant, replaced by a stranger which was unsettling. During the worst bouts, they gave her electric shock therapy, a brutal and still-used remedy in the armoury against mental disorder.

We were on a constant emotional rollercoaster and learned to relax and appreciate the tranquil phases. After each episode, I naively thought Jill had hit a low point, and it would pass. She needed to go voluntarily into the mental hospital; otherwise, it incurred a legal wrangle for her to be released when she improved.

Convincing Jill to go the asylum willingly was a struggle. During the more challenging times, when it seemed almost impossible, we called Betty, who always dropped everything to help. One time, on arrival, she calmly said, 'Hello, Jill, want to go for a ride?'

Jill looked up animated, 'Are Win and Darius coming?'

'Yes,' we chorused, and she bounced into the hallway to get her coat. We telephoned Richard, who met us at the psych ward.

Jill looked at him and declared, 'I'll only go in if I can take this magazine with me.'

He nodded, and she signed the admission form and gaily waved goodbye with a copy of *Punch*. We breathed a sigh of relief as we loved this woman. She wasn't mad all the time, slipping in and out of her delusions, but she was seriously ill.

Jill was separated from Richard whilst in the mental hospital for longs periods at a time and felt she had grown apart from him. She hated the way he searched for signs of her next bipolar attack.

One day, she glanced over and saw him reading the *Poultry World*. That pushed her to consider her future. The realisation of spending the next 50 years with him was inconceivable; things had to change.

She planned her escape and divorced him amicably. Jill rented a room in a dingy converted Georgian mansion on the outskirts of St Peter Port. It had a communal sitting room with a television, and she often got bitten by fleas as she sat in the stuffy, old sofas, She scrubbed every inch of her bedroom with disinfectant and bug killer sprayed everywhere. The company where she worked soldering computer parts, provided subsidised meals in their canteen, so she was more than adequately fed during the week.

She moved as soon as she could and rented a room in a home with a family in St Peter Port, yards from the seafront, overlooking the harbour and facing the islands. Jill resumed her healthy life, and the couple she lived with and their two schoolchildren, enjoyed the expert catering of their new lodger.

She lived there happily for a few years until the manic episodes became frequent and more bizarre. Her neighbours were intrigued when she erected a line outside her two adjacent bedroom windows with her underwear pegged, blowing like flags in the breeze. The final straw was when the landlady, alerted by her bedside light flickering on and off, found Jill happily dismantling their fuse box.

Her tablets made her feel dumbed down, not the real Jill, and they found she couldn't be trusted to take her medication regularly. After this disturbing wiring incident, her brothers, who lived in Salisbury, in England, arranged for her to leave Guernsey permanently. They found her a lovely new house near them and supervised her medication.

Unfortunately, while in England, once more she threw away her meds, gave herself a holiday from them, and travelled to Guernsey by boat. She caught the bus straight to visit her brother, Tim. He was abroad, on holiday, and decorators worked there during his absence. They presumed she was an approved family visitor, and when they left for the weekend, they gave her the house keys.

When Tim arrived home after the weekend, he was livid when he found unmissable signs Jill had been there. Chaos reigned, as she had rearranged most of the furniture in his house.

Jill, now divorced, was no longer Richard's responsibility, so Tim telephoned us to find out if we had seen her. We didn't even know she was on the island but forewarned; we were not surprised when, just after dinner, she arrived, hyper, full of beans.

I greeted her with a hug and lied, 'What a lovely surprise. We weren't expecting you. Have you eaten?'

She nodded, sat at the dining table, and carried on chatting thirteen to the dozen to Steph.

Fred sloped off to phone Tim to advise him Jill had arrived.

Tim said, 'No-one should get involved because in cases like these, the Police have jurisdiction to repatriate her as a missing person.'

Within ten minutes, Fred returned to us, followed by a uniformed policewoman.

We exchanged greetings with the policewoman as though we were old friends. Jill, oblivious to the plan, chatted with Steph until Fred suggested we go to the Police station.

'Yes,' said Steph, playing along. 'It's a social event, and we'll get cakes.'

Jill and Steph followed the nervous policewoman into the police car, relieved we were old hands at dealing with these episodes and knew how to handle Jill's hyper disposition.

At the station, they served tea and biscuits, and Jill left with her new friend, the policewoman. She returned to Salisbury, got back on her meds, and enjoyed her life. I had slowly lost another dear female friend. She visited us once more in Guernsey before she needed to move into a care home which catered for Alzheimer's patients.

My other closest companion, Betty, had been going through the motions of a happy marriage to Ray. Even though to us, they didn't seem particularly compatible, I never expected her to leave him. One evening, Ray made a surprise visit to tell me Betty had packed her bags and had gone to England, without a word to anyone. I didn't know anything about Betty's leaving and couldn't be of any comfort. Later in the week, he visited again to tell me how wicked she had been, leaving her poor boys. He got no sympathy from anyone; the "poor boys" were in their twenties and already independent.

I was used to her phoning or being around most day and believed we were soul sisters, so it crushed me when she left so unexpectedly without discussing it.

None of her friends had heard anything from her, but a month later, at Christmas, I received a postcard with an English south coast address in Seaford. Her note finished, "I understand if you don't reply".

I wrote back the same day with, "What utter rubbish. When can I come over and see you?"

On my visit, she related why she left so suddenly and without telling a soul. She had met Eric Evans while ballroom dancing and their time together had been exhilarating for both. He came from the UK, a skilful dancer, sophisticated, well-travelled and adventurous. They met regularly in secret on his rented houseboat at the Beaucette Marina in the north of the island.

Betty had taken an enormous step and abandoned her old life, gifted her portion of the house to her sons and left with only a few clothes in a suitcase. During the late '70s, she was barely 50 years old and felt it was time to put herself first and follow her dream.

She and Eric moved in with his daughter until they bought a motor cruiser. They sailed through the French canals to the Mediterranean and stopped for months at a time when they found economic ports to stay at length with low mooring fees. She would buy fresh fruit, vegetables, delicious local bread and cheese to eat with other sailors they got to know. They spent many evenings swapping stories about their varied travel adventures. When invited to be part of the crew to cross the Atlantic to reposition a cruiser to the Caribbean, they accepted and spent weeks sailing around the tropical islands. It was bold and risky to leave everything she had known, but it paid off handsomely, she really was having the time of her life.

Chapter 21 - Who Says You Can't Go Home?

(Bon Jovi/Jennifer Nettles)

On a visit to my parents in Manchester, we had time on our hands, and over a pint at his local, Dad told me this little story. In my experience, ghosts only appeared to sceptics, but Dad, a practical, down-to-earth bloke, saw one in broad daylight.

He had recently retired and offered a dream job, to renovate a cottage. It became his baby, a labour of love. No structural building was required, only plaster and paint on the internal walls. Twice, while beavering away, a bent old lady, in a black shawl and skirt, bustled past him.

To his employer, he asked, 'There's an elderly lady who rushes about the house. Is she a relative?'

His boss casually replied, 'Ah, yes, she's our resident ghost. Does it bother you?'

'No,' Dad laughed, 'No wonder she didn't return my greeting.'

After our pub visit, Dad and I walked around his garden, and I wondered what the pungent smell was wafting over his vegetables. Dad, a keen gardener, was a lover of compost, and all things putrefied. He told me that the week before, a mate of his, who worked at the local Belle Vue Zoo, arranged to drop off a load of elephant dung.

Dad had a sizeable garden, but it had a little gate and a narrow path, not suitable for a lorry to drive along. Hence, they dumped the pile of dung on the pavement, spilling onto the road, leaving space only for foot soldiers and interested bystanders.

Mum was so embarrassed and wanted the muck shifted from the front as soon as possible. She had great faith in her gardening mad husband and to appease her; he rallied neighbours and friends to help him wheelbarrow the load round to the back of the house and distribute the smelly contents over his vegetable patch.

Dad paid the helpers in cash backhanders. The potty ones refused the notes; instead, they left thrilled with their barrowful of golden elephant dung.

While I was visiting, my brother, Alan, with a chemistry degree, who could brew alcohol out of any fruit or vegetable, came round to see me. He had worked for years in Saudi Arabia and became an expert in desalination, making seawater fit for human consumption. He had left ex-pat work and returned to Manchester. He bought an old car, and with Dad, they spent hours touring neighbourhood dumpsters for discarded windows. It was a splendid barter system; people took out, and people put in. Fair, above board and encouraged today, another way to make friends and recycle.

Nan loved to nurture her tender perennials, and Alan and Dad took me to see the perfect gift they had built her, which was a lean-to greenhouse. They used the windows they had found in skips and stacked in her back garden until they had enough to fit it together like a jigsaw.

It was sturdy and chock-a-block with her seedlings. Alan had proudly displayed their handiwork to a friend and waited for praise. His mate walked around it, took a moment to study the arrangement of mismatched wooden panes, and pronounced it 'artistically challenged'.

Alan, hopping mad, retorted, 'What did you expect for nowt, the bloody Taj Mahal?'

Over the decades, we often received reports from the family of incidents involving Nan, her offspring, and their crazy spotted dogs. During one visit to Guernsey, Nan and her family occupied themselves, equipped for exploring, with bus passes, maps, and the occasional lift from Fred.

Disaster seemed to follow Nan wherever she went. What started as a pleasant day quite often took an unexpected turn. After a beach day at Petit Bot, Fred waited for them to get off the bus at the top of the long, winding hill from the bay. Fire engines whizzed past, bells clanged, and our trio approached the car puffing and panting from the climb. Their plump bodies quivered, and their eyes shined with excitement as they told him, 'The bus had driven halfway up the hill when clouds of smoke poured out of the engine. When the bus burst into flames, we were terrified and jumped off.' Fred drove home at a snail's pace, a precaution against further mishaps.

The following day, *The Guernsey Press* reported, 'This was the first time a passenger bus had set on fire in Guernsey.'

They loved camping, so we booked them an all-inclusive holiday in Alderney, the northernmost Channel Island, a sleepy swathe of wilderness with a sandy beach and flower-strewn buffs teeming with rabbits and puffins.

We received the occasional phone call, and their trip was going so well until the day of their return flight to Guernsey. Thick sea fog came in and enshrouded the island, which delayed the flights. The boat had arrived safely through the fog and the campsite, on changeover day, was full to overflowing. The obliging camp owner, accustomed to the vagueness of the weather, retrieved Nan and the family from the misty airport and distributed sleeping bags to them and offered space to sleep on his lounge floor.

Holidaymakers delayed at Alderney airport, who had to get back urgently, had taken any spare places on the return boat.

Nan telephoned in high glee to let us know about the extension to their mini holiday. The fog lifted two days later, and a priority flight from Alderney took them straight to Guernsey Airport for their connection to Manchester. Short of time, Fred and I packed the rest of their belongings and met them at the departure lounge. With a quick hug, we saw them off through passport control.

We rarely waved visitors off, but this time, we waited in the upstairs observation lounge and waited while Nan and her brood trooped on board. A minute later, they trooped off, waited around, and trooped back on again. The plane's engines roared into life, taxied and became airborne. We mopped our brows, and on our way out asked at the departure desk about the mysterious passenger movements.

The clerk tapped the side of his nose with his forefinger and hinted, 'Not now. See *The Press* tomorrow.'

The next day, the headlines stated, 'Manchester plane delayed a short time for a hoax bomb scare. The first one reported in Guernsey.' Of course, it was, Nan was on it.

Years later, Nan visited on her own. After a most enjoyable fortnight, we drove her to the airport, and when she checked in, was horrified to find she had left her passport on our kitchen table. Not as mortified as Fred, who emphatically assured her he had time to return home to retrieve it. He took a shortcut and got stuck behind a tractor. With no space to overtake it, fuming, he burbled on behind. With one daily flight to Manchester, he didn't want to go through this performance again tomorrow. The tractor turned in a farm gateway, and Fred zoomed away. Guernsey airport staff were helpful and held the flight. Once more, we watched Nan board, but this time, no hiccups, the plane got airborne.

The next time she visited, we prepared to leave in plenty of time for the airport. Fred rolled his eyes, 'Delays all round. Teletext says, wait for news.'

Nan and I sat in the garden and drank tea. Fred stayed inside glued to the television to check the progress of Nan's scheduled departure.

'Everything's on again,' he shouted from the living room. 'Quick, they haven't given us much warning.'

He bundled Nan into the car, her bags already in the boot, and we drove the shortest route to the airport. We had already done the check-in by phone; they had her boarding card ready and ushered her through the gate. That time we didn't wave the plane goodbye, just drove home and had a large, stiff drink.

The report in *The Guernsey Press* the following day stated, "Slight delays at the airport yesterday".

Nan's visits filled Fred with dread and foreboding, but from my lifetime of her disasters, I knew she was a survivor; indestructible.

Nan and Roy's marriage didn't survive. They divorced, and Roy married his secretary. It wasn't a long marriage as he died of a heart attack in 1983, aged 57. He worked so hard but never reached retirement age.

Nan thrived on her gardening, but made unwise choices after her divorce; twice, she bought unsuitable houses, each had extensive, rambling, wild and neglected gardens, probably leftover cravings for the countryside she had tasted in the evacuation.

In her later years, she moved to a smaller house at the seaside in Burryport, Wales, and busied herself filling pots with layers of bulbs, ready to make a vibrant splash in the springtime.

She too, in old age, slowly succumbed to late-onset Alzheimer's and in March 2016, she died in a care home, aged 87. With the illness, Nan had been cut off from me conversationally for a while, so I had already come to terms with the loss of my accident-prone and lively sister I had known, and her final act of death had no real impact.

Chapter 22 - Lily Was Here
(Candy Dulfer/Dave Stewart)

Fred's mother, Lily, was still estranged from us when we left Manchester for Guernsey. The children presumed their paternal grandmother was deceased as we never mentioned her.

Twenty years later, in 1976, while the children were still teenagers, we received a surprise call from my Mum in Manchester about Lily. She was living in York and had contacted a solicitor to sort out her estate. She wanted to bequeath her money to a cats' home.

The solicitor suggested, 'You must have a living relative who could benefit?'

'Yes. I do have a son, but I don't know where he's living,' Lily said and relayed details about the estrangement.

He researched and traced our marriage record to St Thomas in Gorton, Manchester, in 1947. He wrote to the vicar who provided Mum and Dad's address in Gorton, which, as fate would have it, hadn't changed since we got married. They shouldn't have been contactable there, but somehow Suttons Trust never downsized and moved them.

Mum gave the solicitor our Guernsey details and phoned to alert us to expect a letter. It surprised us when Lily, eager to communicate, and out of character, didn't write, she telephoned. Fred said he would visit her in York as soon as he could, during the next school summer holidays.

We experienced an awkward situation where we explained to the children their paternal grandmother's resurrection. Everyone accepted the story, a point of amusement for our friends.

Lily had gone to live in York with her brother, Fred, as we suspected. They lived in a rented tall terraced house, and he had saved to build them a home. Unfortunately, the building didn't go ahead as he died in 1969 of a heart attack and she stayed on in the rented house.

For several years Fred spent a fortnight in York with his mother, and Janet, her landlady, and companion, and they took leisurely day trips along the east coast. Lily paid Fred's airfare and expenses in cash from a suitcase under the bed. She didn't trust banks, but he persuaded her to let him take the old notes into their safekeeping, while still legal tender.

From the first Christmas after Fred's visit, she sent us cards and intricate, hand-knitted gloves she'd crafted during the year. These gloves were smart, hard-wearing, and worn every winter by the family until they disintegrated.

Wendy was working in London when she heard the news of her grandmother and wrote to her suggesting she visit York to meet her, even for a day trip. 'Don't come,' Lily wrote back, 'I can't cope with visitors, and I don't want to be changing bed linen at my age.'

No-one apart from Fred was welcome. She saw none of her grandchildren. Fred left photographs of us with Lily, but she stressed she had no interest in us. Despite her feigned

250

indifference, after she died, he discovered a photo of Steph in her handbag.

On 4th January 1984, we finished celebrating Fred's birthday dinner when the nursing home telephoned with the news of Lily's death, who had just turned 90.

It was icy in January when we arrived to organise her funeral and sort out her belongings. She lived next door to a funeral parlour, easy for Fred to pop in, pay his respects, and oversee the coffin sealed. I hadn't been to York and wondered if her home might have a hostile atmosphere. While in the undertakers, I was alone in her house, and I imagined her with me, smiling, and that she came to say goodbye. Throughout the brief visit, I felt calm and welcomed as we sorted through piles of ancient coal bills, balls of string, rubber bands, and neatly ironed brown paper hoarded for years.

We visited the solicitor to thank him for his kindness. We found a Dickensian-type gentleman, rosy round cheeks and twinkling blue eyes. Benevolent and trustworthy, we thanked him for suggesting Lily look into diverting her estate from a prospective cats' home to us (Sorry cats!). Fred and I split his inheritance five ways, giving a nest egg for our children. It had taken us six years to save for our house deposit, and I didn't want them to do the same. A few days later, we attended Lily's funeral with the two carpenters who rented her outhouse. Our four self-conscious voices sounded thin, and we were embarrassed but relieved when the short service ended.

251

Chapter 23 - Riders On The Storm
(The Doors)

The red granite rocks surrounding Port Soif bay protected our lane from the sea, but not the wind. Each spring, we inspected our roof tiles for cracks and losses. Our neighbourhood roofer sold us a stock of red clay, second hand, but unbroken tiles, matching ours. He and Fred stacked them in the garden, out of sight. These tiles enabled us to leave our storm insurance intact, and we slept easy in our beds even as the noisiest of storms tore through the island.

Guernsey has experienced a few violent storms and has lost over 100 ships on the west coast reefs since 1734. A lesser gale wrecked the 974-foot oil tanker, Torrey Canyon, on Cornwall's on the UK's south-west coast in 1967. One hundred and twenty thousand tons of crude oil spewed out. It was a monumental, ecological disaster, spreading a thick layer of black oily poison, suffocating and drowning hundreds of seabirds, and sticking to anything in its path. The oil coated miles of Cornish beach and seeped across to the Guernsey coastline and filled the air with a stinking, chemical smell which permeated everything.

To rescue the vulnerable seabirds, they declared a national emergency on their behalf. The Guernsey vets and volunteers cleaned and housed the seagulls, and Islanders helped by donating spare towels and linen. For months, we stored cloths in the car boot in case we found an oiled bird.

The shiny black surface floated in and smothered rocks and beaches. An enormous boom caught and contained the oil until syphoned into containers. It filled a small disused quarry and remained there for 43 years, until November 2010, when reports indicated the bioremediation process was successfully breaking down the oil into carbon dioxide and water.

For decades, a tidemark of oil lined the rocks on the west coast, and it took time for the mixture of sea and sand to erode the residue.

Guernsey residents had a Christmas morning surprise in 1973, when the Elwood Mead, a super-freighter, ran aground on Grandes Rocques. This luckier ship was pulled free and taken to Holland for repair.

The following month, in a turbulent storm, the M.V. Prosperity, carrying a cargo of timber, was shipwrecked with the tragic loss of eighteen lives. The ship's bow section broke away from the hull, and when the tide receded, hundreds of planks of wood scattered over the beach and dunes. Islanders used every kind of comical conveyance to take the wood away.

'Spoils of war,' they gleefully told each other. They were wrong, and the law clamped down; it stated, 'Please bring back any timber illegally removed.' Few planks got returned, and the authorities took no legal action.

When the Amoco Cadiz, en route from the Gulf of Persia to Europe, ran aground off the coast of Brittany on 16th March 1978, she split in three and spilt almost 220,000 tons of rock oil which left a 40-mile slick. British and French tugs joined forces for a week using 100 tons of dispersant to save the Channel Island beaches and some on the French coast. Rough seas helped to break the oil up, but at the time, this incident resulted in the most extensive loss of marine life ever recorded after an oil spill. Two weeks after the ecological disaster, they recovered millions of dead molluscs, tons of sea urchins washed ashore, and nearly 20,000 dead birds had succumbed to this oil catastrophe.

Despite more stringent safety regulations, in 1978, the Orion drilling jack-up rig was on tow, being moved from Rotterdam to Brazil via the English Channel. It broke free and beached on the massive boulders which create the Grandes Rocques peninsula.

During Steph's taxi home from a jolly night out, the driver told her, 'There's a marooned oil rig on the rocks next to the hotel.'

'Oh, really?' she replied, in a drunken stupor. 'It's that kind of night.'

Steph checked to see if she could see it from the upstairs window. It was unmissable, and its brightly lit spires dominated the landscape, like Blackpool Tower against the inky black sky. She woke Darius, who had no idea of the event, and they held onto each other as they battled towards the headland against the gale-force wind.

A platform supported a steel ladder-like structure which stretched metres into the sky. This grotesque construction wedged between the rocks could be viewed from many vantage points along the West coast.

Late into the night, trails of islanders trooped along our lane to the beach to watch this unique scene, caught in the darting spotlights from the circling helicopters.

When the stormy seas subsided a few days later, the tide lifted the rig, after nail-biting manoeuvres, and floated off the rocks. As they towed the lumbering behemoth, the spectators showed their relief with cheers and festivities. The Grandes Rocques Hotel, in prime position, yards from the exhibit, must have enjoyed a roaring pub trade.

Guernsey also suffered freak incidents in the Great Storm of October 1987, when hurricane-force winds, devastated the area which encompassed Northern France, Southern England, and the Channel Islands. It wrenched millions of trees out of the ground in the UK, and the Scilly Isles lost their arboreal windbreaks which took years to replace.

A house in a prime position on the cliffs with panoramic views lost a garage, plus an expensive car when they were whisked into the sea and disappeared. The newspaper showed the owners with perplexed expressions as they stared at the space where the vehicle and garage had been.

We were always wary of blustery winds as our heavy clay roof tiles had sometimes rained through the air and smashed to smithereens, which made it dangerous to go out. One night, across the road on a neighbour's house, half the roof tiles that

255

faced away from the wind got torn off. The pregnant owner was horrified at the thumping noise and woke facing an open sky.

Another neighbour found her wooden shed had vanished. Her husband shrugged his shoulders. 'The insurance will replace it,' he said as he waited for the wind to drop before taking his Great Dane for a walk.

An hour later, her next-door neighbour knocked on the door. 'We have your shed. Come over.' It had been plucked and deposited intact, in the centre of their field. She paused for a moment and decided, 'It may fall apart on moving. Keep it to store the children's bikes and toys. I was waiting for a good excuse to replace it with a summerhouse.'

Chapter 24 - Mambo Italiano

(Rosemary Clooney)

Wendy returned to the island from London in July 1978. She had left her musician boyfriend, her banking job, and took temporary work while she contemplated her next career move. She longed for a change of scene and to learn another language and chose Spanish, but fate had other ideas.

Two weeks later, on a Sunday morning, Steph and Wendy came downstairs, already dressed. I looked from one to the other.

Steph said, 'Last night at the disco we met three visitors wanting to extend their night out. Nothing stays open later, so they sat and chatted with us. There are two Italian men and one English woman, and they've flown in from Italy on a private plane. They've offered us breakfast at La Fregate and a flight around the island this morning.'

Fred chimed in, 'No flying today, unless this fog lifts. I can't see the bottom of the garden now. We're lucky that the newspaper plane got in.'

The girls drove to the hotel, but as expected, the visitors were grounded, and we hoped to meet them later in the day. Unfazed, Wendy and Steph took them on an island tour, which included the unique Little Chapel, created in 1914, by Brother Déodat who fashioned it as a miniature version of Lourdes grotto and basilica. The Rosary is decorated inside and out with shells and donations of pieces of colourful pottery.

257

As we hoped, the three visitors arrived at our house in the afternoon, talking in a flurry of different languages. Susan, a chatty blonde Englishwoman in sunglasses and a short summer dress, translated our conversation into Italian for her boyfriend. Carlo, their pilot, was a mature, swarthy man with a mass of curly black hair. Christian, their friend, monopolised Steph. This slight, young man with light brown eyes and tufts of sun-streaked brown hair, spoke French, their language in common. He and his parents owned and ran a restaurant in the mountains on the outskirts of Bergamo, a charming, cypress-cloaked Italian city near Milan.

The travellers were en route to Manchester, Susan's hometown, to visit her parents. Warm memories of family holidays prompted her to include Guernsey in their itinerary.

Wendy chatted with Susan as they meandered around the garden until the fog lifted. They had transferred their overnight luggage to the car, so she took them straight to the airport's private plane section.

She rushed back from the airport, animated, and breathless. 'Susan offered me a job and is looking to recruit someone to work with her in Italy, and she thought I fitted the bill. She's promised to ring in a fortnight when she gets back to Bergamo.'

Wendy felt destined to go there and never doubted it. We did; and hoped it wasn't one of those spur-of-the-moment job offers which never materialised. It became a running joke; everyone waited for the call. We didn't have mobile phones, not even an answerphone, so after two week's had passed, Wendy didn't leave the house for fear of missing Susan.

Everyone who knew of her opportunity waited with us. Jill and Betty visited and lingered, with fingers crossed. The joke was on us. On cue, the day after the fortnight, Susan's call came.

Wendy nodded to us and repeated for our benefit, 'Yes, I can meet Mr Luoni for lunch in London tomorrow.'

That's all we needed to hear. We uncrossed our fingers. How were we to know Susan's call would impact each of our lives? Fate was busy at work again.

Wendy met the sweet and benevolent Mr Luoni over a long, luxurious lunch at the Tower Hotel. They visited a garage where he ordered a blue Honda Civic with a retractable stereo. She collected it the following week, primed and ready to begin the two-day journey from London across Europe to the pre-alps of Northern Italy.

She had no fear of travelling alone, and neither did we question it. After the car ferry to France, she drove through the forests of Baden Baden in Germany and stayed overnight. The journey took longer than she expected; she had calculated the mileage as the crow flies, not the time taken to drive along treacherous snaking Swiss mountain roads.

Spellbound with her first sight of dazzling Lake Lugano in Switzerland, she booked into a lake-side hotel and the next morning crossed into Italy, skirted Milan and arrived at the office in Bergamo in Lombardy.

In August 1978, few people in Bergamo spoke any English, so Wendy's priority was to learn Italian. Mr Luoni now had two good-looking blonde English secretaries, the ultimate status symbol in business circles in northern Italy. Unlike the usual perception, he wasn't a hustler, and he and his wife treated the English girls like daughters and spoiled them.

The engineering business exported steel and heavy equipment to construct significant projects, such as hospitals and airport runways for North African countries. From day one, Wendy translated shipping and packing lists from Italian into English with the help of a dictionary.

After a month in Italy, Wendy asked Steph to join her. There was no persuasion needed for Steph to leave the bank in Guernsey and join her. We have a photo of her waiting to board a plane with her matching pale-blue luggage, her leaving present from the bank.

Susan found part-time work for Steph at the Bergamo British School, where she taught English as a foreign language, to both adults and children. The children were too rowdy to teach seriously, so Steph made them sing English songs, to impress the parents who heard their little darlings as they arrived to collect them.

Steph learnt Italian quickly and easily and took on prestigious private clients, such as lawyers and architects; to be tutored one-to-one by a real English teacher was such a coup.

I lived with a curse, a terrible blight. In my garden, I sprayed roses against black spot, but I had no defence against this new affliction. Fate had stolen all the women in my life, shattered my support group.

While Fred and I were living the dream in our idyll, our friends' relationships crumbled around us, and they left the island. Even two of my sisters, Grace and Linda, were not immune and emigrated to Australia, and my precious Mum was now absent to me through cruel dementia.

Fred seemed unaffected; his emotional needs were met by me, our children and my parents, leaving him free to concentrate on his cerebral interests and hobbies. But I became depressed, and the vibrant island colours gradually faded.

My next life lesson had begun; how to cope without my female network. To divert the misery, I learned French at night school, another gap in my education. I substituted the undemanding exigencies of my colleagues in the bank until the future looked brighter. Joyful times, colour and optimism returned when we started to plan a visit to our daughters in Italy the following Easter.

Four months had passed, and even though Wendy often telephoned from Italy, our house was quiet. I cancelled Christmas on a whim and decided against the fuss.

When Darius offered to bring the tree down from the attic, I replied, 'Don't bother. Thank you, but I think I'll have a Christmas off this year and relax.'

'Okay, Mum.' He exchanged knowing glances with Fred.

Cards, letters, and gifts, including the girls' annual horoscopes, had been despatched overseas to catch the European posting deadline. At the bank, I explained breezily, 'The girls are in Italy, so I am off the hook for this year.' My colleagues looked sympathetically at me and nodded, knowing it was only bravado.

After dinner, a few days before Christmas, while knitting and half-watching the television, there was a knock at the door. Voices of carol singers echoed along the hall and Fred scrabbled around in his pocket for small coins to give them.

Darius laughed. 'I'll do it. They're not very good, are they?'

A minute later, he flung the lounge door open, and Steph and Wendy leapt in, screeching, and laughing, which tailed off as Fred, and I remained seated like surprised statues, and me with knitting in mid-stitch.

'What do you have to do to get a cup of tea in this joint?' Steph asked and marched towards the kitchen.

I flung my needles onto the table and followed her. I touched her arm to feel she was real before I had hysterics.

Wendy entered the noisy scene and said, 'That's more like it,' and joined in the proper greeting.

Darius offered to bring out the tree and ornaments from under the eaves. Christmas was suddenly on again.

The next day at work, a colleague said, 'Are you alright, Win? You look quite pale.'

'Carol singers kept me up late,' I mumbled. Typewriters stopped clattering. I laughed as I told them the story. Being friends, they were thrilled for me.

Wendy and Steph almost didn't make it over to Guernsey. They overslept and missed their midday plane from Milan to London. The last flight to Guernsey was late evening, so they had a few chances to connect. At every opportunity to phone, Steph stopped Wendy from calling us, 'This is supposed to be a surprise visit, so it has to be a surprise.'

At Guernsey airport, Steph pushed Wendy into the taxi, so she didn't have time to telephone.

Having cooked up the carol-singing jolly wheeze, they were the ones to get the surprise when greeted in shocked, stony silence, and no festive decorations up in the house.

Overjoyed, I broke all records, baked a cake, bought more food, and made it a lively, memorable family Christmas, but with no gifts, as they were already winging their way to Bergamo.

Mr Luoni had established an office in Lugano, Switzerland, and Wendy often delivered documents to be legalised and waited days in Swiss cities for them, much on expenses. Sometimes Steph accompanied her to Bern or Geneva, and they spent their time sightseeing, lounging, and eating in the posh hotels and restaurants. For them, it was akin to attending a high-class finishing school, where they learned languages, visited museums, and art galleries.

Fred, as a teacher, had plenty of holiday allowance and I juggled and swapped my holiday entitlement until I accrued enough days to take a fortnight in Italy at Easter and again in the late summer. One time, I mentioned in the bank that for my holidays, I was only visiting my daughters. A colleague chimed in, 'Only in the Italian lakes, that's all,' and boasted on my behalf.

On our first visit to Italy, Wendy had to go into the office in Bergamo and left Darius, Fred, and me aboard an open-air boat to take us to Montisola, the fairy-tale wooded island on Lake Iseo, and arranged to collect us at the same spot in the late afternoon. What could go wrong? We spent a fabulous time exploring this enchanting place, where the drinking water from the fishing village fonts was mountain-fresh and cold.

We caught what we presumed was a return boat. But it didn't return. It just kept sailing on, stopping at picturesque villages, with unrecognisable names, cobbled streets, and vine-draped courtyards. We didn't know the name of our departure point and didn't speak a word of Italian. The captain puffed on his cigarette, swigged his coffee, removed his shoes, and steered the boat with his feet to a cacophony of wild, distorted music. We had hysterics, and the other travellers joined in our infectious laughter, with no idea of the joke.

I thought I was "condemned to float through the Byzantine Italian lakes for eternity, never to return", when we came to a sudden stop. The captain pulled down the shutters, the faulty music stopped, and everyone disembarked.

Lovere was a bustling village, and we found a lady with a *gettone* (a telephone token), who phoned Wendy's office in Bergamo on our behalf. The helpful lady repeated what the receptionist had told her, 'No-one of that name here.'

Desperate, I had a brainwave. I poked my finger into my chest and announced to our helper, 'La Mama.'

Within seconds, Wendy's bemused voice came on the line, 'What the hell are you doing in Lovere? It's miles away, on the far side of the lake. Pick somewhere central to eat outside, and I'll find you.'

Her office receptionist had been instructed not to accept any suspicious calls. I knew, in Italy, mothers over-ride everything.

My lesson from this story is, 'Never stray from your minder without a dictionary, address label and a *gettone*.'

Mr Luoni insisted Wendy used the spacious company Alfa Romeo when we visited. These were enthralling times, as we whizzed around the countryside in the snazzy Italian car. One time, when we took the smaller Honda, we dared to go to Monte Carlo on a public holiday. We tried various hotels, but not a room was available anywhere. We had a late dinner at the African Queen in Beaulieu, and when the restaurant closed, the four of us spent the night outside Nice station in the car, our bodies arranged like a jigsaw puzzle.

The fluorescent café sign switched on at 6.00 am and woke us. Stiff and sore, with crumpled clothes, we were their first grateful customers of the day.

Steph caught the train back to school in Bergamo. Wendy, Fred, and I continued in comparative luxury along the Riviera.

When I walked through the city of Milan, I experienced the same vibrant feeling I had when I visited Manchester. We were eager to see the impossibly grand Cathedral, Il Duomo, and hurried across the tiled palazzo in front of the entrance, and stopped once to gaze at the exquisite, ornate carving and masonry. I entered the portico and glanced at the tiled floor. Picked out in mosaic were the astrological fishes of Pisces; they stood out, illuminated, while everything else faded.

At that moment, a massive wave of euphoria swept through my body and transported me into another era. A passion and religious fervour lifted my spirit to sublime heights. I had a vision of myself living as a spiritual person. I recognised the core of my existence, my dedication to the Almighty. The feeling only lasted a minute and back in my own body, within the dim light inside the vast, grandiose interior, tears poured down my face as I caught up with my family. We returned to the car in silence, stunned by our experiences in the beauty of the cathedral.

I wondered, had my soul been here before? A few minutes can widen your spiritual horizons and your global placement - such sweeping statements for such a brief episode. At the risk of being labelled a crackpot or loony, I must include another example here.

On a frosty cloudless day, while I walked across the common at the top of Port Soif, in an instant, I knew I was living in New York State at the turn of the 19th-century. My two companions, sons or brothers, jostled each other playfully as we hurried across open ground in the cold air towards tall buildings. I noticed we wore black formal Jewish coats and hats. In one second, I recognised I was a male Jew and a Piscean.

Shocked, I stopped walking as I realised I had just lived the essence of myself in a man's body, in another age. This experience was a massive revelation to me, and I was puzzled by yet another astrological Pisces significance. Is this a pointer to the theme running through my lives?

Over the three years we visited Italy, Darius changed the most. On the first holiday, Wendy left him at the local outfitters in the expert care of two young stylish Italian girls, who relished the experience of giving this English boy, the dishevelled Darius, a stylish makeover. They checked his measurements, conferred, and waved their hands with joy. Italians love clothes and dressing up, and I'm amazed at how many exclusive outfits they have for every activity, even cleaning the car.

When we returned to Guernsey, Darius was unrecognisable. We left home with a gangly, jean-clad, scruffy lad with lank hair; a six-foot blonde young god in a white suit returned. *Saturday Night Fever* reigned in the late '70s, with his bell-bottomed trousers and his height attracting so much admiration, he developed an appropriate swagger. Steph and Wendy had their work cut out fending the girls off him in the Italian discos.

I feared his unkempt mates would mock him. On the contrary, they were mesmerised. They scared their mothers, bought new clothes, sported smart haircuts, and used more soap in a day than they had done all year.

When Betty left Guernsey, we kept in touch. In Europe, we met in the most unlikely locations. One time, Betty and Eric met us for a few days in Bergamo.

Steph spoke Italian so fluently, when she fought with her boyfriend, Camillo, it was a grand sight to see her shout and gesticulate like Sophia Loren.

Why on earth did Betty and I agree to take a day trip with Camillo, who spoke no English and drove like a maniac? He probably wanted to impress Steph!

He sped along the shores of Lake Garda upwards towards the Bernina Pass, and we as we climbed, we were in awe of the spectacular panorama, with our guide gesticulating wildly at the scenery.

We reached a magnificent vantage point and got out of the car. Betty said to me in her best Lancashire dialect, 'Ee lass. We've come a long way from Boggart Hole Clough.'

I collapsed in fits of giggles. The difference between the two places was incomparable. One, is a wooded urban country park in a Manchester suburb, the other, the breath-taking glistening glaciers of this high mountain pass. We laughed at the absurdity until tears came. Camillo presumed we were too overcome with emotion at the beauty when he saw our tear-stained faces and slowly bundled us into the car.

Without seatbelts installed, we rolled around from side to side. Betty and I clung together in the back; often thrown onto to one another as we rode the dizzying, hairpin bends. Once more, he pointed out places of interest, turning to look back at us, and Betty shuddered, 'I wish he'd keep both hands on the bloody steering wheel.'

I can still picture the majestic mountains reflected in the lake as we skirted it, at Grand Prix velocity, back to Bergamo.

To bring us back to earth, some islanders call Guernsey 'The Rock,' find it claustrophobic, and plan their escapes several times a year to stay sane. They yearn for the anonymity of a large city or exotic locale with a different beach and warm sea.

Not me. The island is surrounded by a vast expanse of ever-changing seascapes, with the next stop, America. Whenever I stand on the headland at my horseshoe bay, I marvel at the infinite stretches of empty sky and sea.

Le Nic au Corbin, (raven's nest), the giant, deep-red, granite rock forms the head of the bay. In winter, as a tall medieval crown, it stands guard to break the unremitting waves and gale-force winds as they force sparkling white spray into the dark thunderous sky.

One afternoon, the magnified colours of the sea, sky, and rocks gave me a moment of great joy, and I screamed with delight at this mesmerising sight. Polly, the dog, was stunned; her long white curly ears stood up in the wind like a startled cartoon character. I staggered home, battered and windswept.

'Nice walk?' Fred asked, without raising his head from his book, unaware of my scarecrow hair, bright eyes, and salt-encrusted face.

One evening, one of Darius's friends, Nigel, came to tell us Darius was involved in a car accident and at the hospital. We rushed to his bedside, where he lay, unmoving, under anaesthetic.

We heard Darius had been speeding along the west coast at Cobo and clipped an edging which sent his car flying, where it landed, balanced upright on a massive granite boulder. With no compulsory seat belts, (this came into force in 1983), he sustained bruises all over his body and bashed his face against the driver's door.

The surgeon took us to one side, 'We're waiting for him to come round. He has a broken nose and a cracked cheekbone.'

He had stitched Darius's nose, and later, if required, cosmetic surgery was an option. Their primary worry was the fractured cheekbone. If it dropped, it would have resulted in one eye positioned lower than the other.

'Tomorrow morning, we'll decide if we need him to be airlifted to England for treatment by a specialist,' the surgeon explained.

Fred and I sat up all night, holding hands in our version of silent prayer, and waited until time to phone the hospital.

The surgeon answered, 'I was about to call you with the good news. The body is a fascinating thing, the cheekbone knitted together overnight. There are no more worries for us. Pop in and visit him when you're ready. The nurse said it was a minor miracle.'

We agreed. For weeks, Darius's body was painful, but it hadn't troubled him as much as his bruised face, the focus of his pain.

He received many visitors in the hospital and held court when home. A nasty scar crossed his nose and nostril but healed. When I reminded him of the cosmetic surgery option, he shrugged, 'It would've been a disaster for a girl.' He didn't bother having surgery, the scar evened out, or perhaps we just got used to it.

We were so busy at the hospital; we didn't think to inspect the car or visit the crash scene. Nigel, who saw the whole scenario, handled the police and all the arrangements, for which we were extremely grateful.

As expected, they banned Darius from driving for a while and gave him a fine. His speed was excessive, well over the 35-mph limit. Fortunately, no one else was involved in the accident. He learned his lesson, not to speed on these narrow roads.

Instead, years later, he shifted focus and took it to the other extreme, and as a commercial pilot, now flies an Airbus A320, a jet with runway take-off speeds of around 170-mph.

On Monday after Darius's accident, Wendy rang from Italy to tell me about her incident, which happened that same Friday evening.

She had received Betty and Eric's pin-pricked postcard from Elba and planned a weekend on their boat. After work, Wendy drove through Bergamo to collect Steph and Lynn, their English friend, for the journey. As she drove through a crossroads, a car hadn't stopped, so sideswiped her, denting the doors. Their speeds were low, so no injuries sustained, just a few hours delay while Wendy waited for a replacement car to continue the planned trip.

It's no coincidence their car accidents happened at the same time. Wendy and Darius share their birthday, four years apart. With the same astrological aspects, they experience the same things, propitious or unlucky. Often, they travel on the same day, having booked without the other knowing.

Both natal charts show Sun Conjunction Venus. Fred interpreted this as the 'Marilyn Monroe effect,' and anyone who knows them is witness to their traits of extrovert personalities and charisma.

The Italian dream came to a natural end when Wendy's instinct alerted her to arrange to leave. She could see the company might fold because of the non-payment of company invoices from work completed in the Middle East.

Sometime that summer, Fred took early retirement. I left work, and Steph came back to fill my shoes at the bank. She didn't stay long. She snagged a much better position when she passed her Italian language exams, which enhanced her credentials, and she was off to a more well-paid job.

Fred, Steph and I took advantage of an offer of direct flights to Faro from Guernsey. Wendy, on her notice period in Italy, negotiated to keep the blue Honda and took a circuitous diversion home, driving from Bergamo back to Guernsey via the Portuguese Algarve to spend the holiday with us. We spent a glorious week exploring the coastline, hospitality and sights.

How's that for timing? Mr Luoni's Italian-Swiss empire crumbled the following year. Funny incidents and iconic sayings from these incredible family holidays have amused us for years. Fred and I were fortunate to have enjoyed the experience and unforgettable times with our adult children. It broadened and enriched each of our lives.

Fred was one of the first of his teachers to opt to take retirement at 60. A pension advisor wisely advised him to stay another year to get a more substantial payment. Fred heeded his advice, so when he retired, it increased his pension, his social insurance payments were up to date, thus entitled to a full Guernsey pension. Little did I know then I would still receive a teacher's widow's pension 20-odd years after his death.

We spent time and holidays investigating alternative countries for cheaper ways to live. The poorer countries were already levelling in the costs of living. With my sisters in Australia, it was the obvious choice, and less expensive, but our three children were in the UK, and we loved living in Guernsey, so we stayed.

Chapter 25 - Come Fly With Me

(Frank Sinatra)

Steph was the first to visit our relatives in Australia on holiday in January 1983. For over a year, she saved until she amassed the princely sum of a thousand pounds (eight hundred for airfare and two hundred to spend). The bank permitted her to save two weeks from last year's holiday allowance to make the six weeks required.

The money and the time constraint had stopped anyone else in the family from going.

When Steph received a booking confirmation, she turned to me, 'You must take it, you should be the one to go.' I appreciated her generosity. After her sacrifices and dedication to get the money together, there was no way I could take it - but what a tremendous heartfelt gesture.

Steph chose Garuda Airlines, a budget airline which ran a bus-stop type of operation from the UK to Sydney. Her routing took her from Heathrow to Zurich, Abu Dhabi, Singapore, Jakarta, Bali, and finally, Sydney. As she saw the palm trees of Bali, she wanted to stay there and not continue the arduous journey.

For Steph, it was a nightmare; she felt wretched as she snatched a few hours of sleep and tried to adjust to time changes. She solved the problem, lifted the arms of three seats, and stretched out. On the frequent stops, she feigned sleep. It worked, no-one disturbed her during the rest of the flights.

There was no such strategy to solve the food problem. There was variety, and it was plentiful, but most were rice-based and either fish or curry, the food she couldn't stomach. A selective eater, she sustained herself for two days by picking at anything she fancied.

In Sydney, my sister, Linda, rescued this weary human being, suffering from jetlag, disorientation, and starvation. Steph slept for 12 hours, woke up desperate for a hot bath, despite the 40-degree heatwave.

Dozens of photographs prove she recovered to enjoy a varied and fun holiday, where she met with visiting Guernsey friends. Her four younger cousins adored her, two in Sydney and two in Canberra, where she divided her time and was spoiled rotten.

No one went hungry on Linda's beat. Before Steph undertook the arduous journey home, Linda enjoyed the challenge of cooking and packing a picnic which delighted and sustained her niece for the two-day plane trip.

It was a once-in-a-lifetime, happy memorable holiday for Steph. After hearing her holiday stories, I couldn't wait to go and experience everything for myself.

The older we got, the more adventurous Fred and I became. We journeyed several times to Australia but travel in economy class was long and tedious for Fred who had long legs and didn't sleep well crunched up on planes. I am an excellent traveller and have an automatic reaction where I can sleep on any moving vehicle. Drinks came sporadically from the plane galley, and we tottered about to keep the blood flowing. For long hours we sat, seat-belted to our stalls and waited to be fed and watered. No wonder they called it "cattle class".

With a budget of a thousand pounds, I persuaded Fred to take an around-the-world flight. Wendy accepted the booking challenge and arranged a circuitous trip to Australia with a series of mini stopovers to break our journey. It was obligatory to stay on the same airline, and if we missed a connection, the next flight was guaranteed, but you had to keep travelling in the same direction, we chose east.

Overnight flights were plentiful and reduced our accommodation costs. Flights arrived at dawn, we took a hotel for one night and left the following evening, which gave us two full days to explore any resort.

To get our bearings somewhere new, we usually took the local sightseeing bus, which left space for a day and a half on the beach or attractions. We never doubled back on our routing, and it gave us a few different mini-holidays or a recce for future ones.

My astrological forecast showed a mix of Saturn for delays and Jupiter for good luck and expansion. Which planet would dominate?

The London-Singapore-Sydney itinerary experienced a few delays. These ranged from a half-hour to three hours and became the norm. We chuckled in the Singapore Botanical Gardens, where an English translation of a placard urged parents: "Do not to throw your children in the pond".

The city is vibrant and busy, day or night, but it's the safest place I have found as a solo traveller. Older women are welcome, not invisible; they seem to have a veneration of the wise and elderly. Fred and I marvelled at the huge shopping complexes with fantastic air-conditioning, so much choice and affordable prices. If I do get to return, my first stop would be to see their new art gallery, and I wouldn't mind any flight delays as I could relax in the presence of nature in the "Jewel", the variety of exceptional spaces created in Changi Airport. Just the names are enticing, the serene havens of greenery called butterfly garden, cactus, and crystal gardens.

We continued onto Canberra for a sociable and action-packed holiday with my sister Grace and her families. We travelled to Sydney to spent time sightseeing with my youngest sister, Linda. Time always raced by when visiting my relatives and we were delighted when the Thursday evening before our first scheduled flight home, the airline agent rang us.

'Your plane hasn't arrived in Sydney yet. There'll be a significant delay. Are you settled in your accommodation?'

'We're staying with my sister, so we are comfortable,' I said. An understatement, we were ecstatic to be indefinitely delayed.

'Do you have any urgent time constraints?' she continued.

'Not at all. We are heading back home with some stopovers, but we're retired. Our time's our own.'

'That's excellent news. We'll call you in a few days but ring us if you need anything. G'day.'

It had been raining during the week, and on cue, with this excellent, unexpected good news, the sun appeared. Linda took the following day off, which gave her an extended weekend. With the pinched extra days together, we toured scenic Sydney harbour on the ferries. Again, the 20 year age difference between us as sisters was noticed, with people referring to Linda as my daughter.

We checked in for our flight at dawn on Sunday morning. The girl on the counter confided that other passengers delayed on our flight had taken the seat vacancies going north-west. We reminded her that with our round-the-world trip ticket, we had to go north-east. With this news, she needed time to allocate another dozen passengers and us with flights. With a few hours to spare, they took us in a bus to a hotel on nearby Coogee Beach, where we sat on the sand and observed a picturesque procession of Italian families strolling along the promenade to church. The dapper men wore black, the wives and offspring in their finery. For a fleeting moment, I imagined I was back in Italy.

Our first stop was former Western Samoa, and we waited on the airstrip for a transfer to American Samoa. The propeller plane flew low, which gave us panoramic island views. A nervous couple flying with us had never travelled in such small aircraft, the norm for us islanders.

The Rainmaker hotel, a colonial building, open and elegant, and set amongst jungle foliage, lived up to its name according to the last two days, the staff told us as they mopped the hall and installed walk-boards over sodden carpets. It disgusted Fred and me to find on every surface were revolting lumps of discarded chewing gum.

We strolled along the road, but there was no beach, just a grimy working port. Disappointed, we hurried back to sample the food. Fred checked the tickets and dollars, 'Don't unpack. We're out of here on the midnight plane.'

Our two-day Sydney delay, with no allowance for the passing the dateline, left us only a few hours here, in someone else's island paradise. A mecca for gum-chewing, big-game fishing Americans.

We were relieved to land in Oahu, Hawaii, and after circuitous detours, dropping passengers at other hotels, we arrived at our hotel in Waikiki. Our budget did not allow for a beachfront, so we had booked a modest hotel, on the second block behind.

We surprised the receptionist, 'You're not due here until tomorrow. It's probably the dateline mix-up again. Aloha - Welcome to Hawaii.'

She threw garlands around our necks and settled us into the real sunny, palm tree paradise, and added an extra day to our booking. We walked to the beach and phoned Wendy from what must be the phone-box with the most picturesque sea view in the world. We enjoyed the few days there, the excursions, the hilarious Kodak Hula Show and then we were off eastward.

The air stewardess told us San Francisco was a windy city. It was not only windy and foggy but unexpectedly cold. Jack Kerouac, the American beat writer, once said the coldest winter he ever spent was a summer in San Francisco. Good job we hadn't returned the jogging suits and sweatshirts we bought cheaply from a Canberra charity shop when it turned cold. We needed them when we marched along the main beach road, south of the city.

An ambulance siren wailed behind us and made us jump. Paramedics raced through a gap in the sea wall to the beach below us.

Fred peered over. Ashen, he hurried me along and described the scene. 'There's a woman below. She's dead with a bolt through her neck. I doubt anything could have saved her.'

Shaken, we took the free trolleybus up the hill zig-zagging along sharp curves past beautiful, pastel-coloured Victorian mansions back to the hotel. I was relieved to have missed that shocking sight.

A month earlier, in October 1989, an earthquake shook the city, leaving its mark everywhere. Quakeproof buildings were intact, but pockets of devastation remained. The massive pillars which supported the overhead rail track had been demolished and smashed whatever lay below. Lines and girders hung in grotesque shapes. The buckled pavements gave us a view into cellars as we struggled along, like extras on a disaster movie set, with steep undulating hills and incessant whirring sirens.

Those eerie scenes reminded us of bomb sites after the war, where the rubble remained long after and became playgrounds for impoverished children. The buildings were misshapen, like illustrations in a child's book, all higgledy-piggledy.

We were unaccustomed to American-style hotels that have no formal dining area, room service and just a bed. Instead of relaxing, drinking coffee in our room, our usual routine on holiday, we got dressed and crossed the road to get our reviver.

The worker's cafe became our regular eatery. An enormous room had scrubbed trestle tables, old wooden chairs and long windows which overlooked the street. We gave our order and leaned on the counter and viewed the performance as the Chinese chef prepared our delicious breakfast.

He needed to be speedy. His usual customers wore overalls and uniforms, stood and glanced at their watches while they waited for their takeaway. We became a novelty to the staff for a few days, as we sat relaxed and lingered over breakfast.

We didn't do the area justice on a limited budget, but we rode on free trams and trolleybuses, enjoyed the scenery, and saw as much as our time and cash allowed. On the Wharf, Fred was in his element when we stumbled across a Sunday morning gathering of musicians and treated to an impromptu concert.

On the penultimate day, my spinal disc gave out from bending over cases once too often. I managed a cautious shuffle to the trolleybus which stopped outside the hotel.

We reserved the last day for the art gallery, three minutes' walk away. They gave me a stool, so I viewed the paintings in comfort. No-one else entered to see the pictures, so we sauntered around and absorbed the atmosphere. Above the artwork, through a hole in the wall, we watched the shoes of people walking by outside. I perched on my stool in the basement with the priceless Jackson Pollocks and other modern art hanging on the crooked walls. It was as surreal as the paintings.

We ordered a taxi from the hotel to the airport. A driver, wearing a peaked cap and white gloves, waited by an open rear door of a cream stretch limousine. As our first trip to America, our request got lost in translation, and what we knew as a regular taxi, was their limo. We climbed in the enormous car, and it was the only time we enjoyed such a luxurious ride.

The porters sprinted to help such an imposing car when we arrived for our flight. They looked surprised when this tall man, dressed in the faded-navy sweats, got out, followed by a bent lady, similarly dressed. They were even more shocked when Fred left without tipping. It never entered his head to tip them, believing they earned a decent wage. He was unaware staff in the service industry often made up their wages with cash from generous customers, a practice for the rich, as a status symbol of their wealth and not expected from the working classes.

On our arrival at Guernsey airport, Steph and Darius watched me stagger along, bent over to support my aching back, and my arms leaning on a luggage trolley.

'Oh, no. Not a broken dolly again,' they said and turned to greet Fred still in his faded-blue, casual, jogging outfit. They creased up, laughing at his baggy, comfortable attire. He loved this suit; this was one item that never found its way to the charity shop. It was washed and worn until pale and fell apart.

As recommended by the airline, I applied for flight delay compensation. The travel agent cut me short, 'Don't explain, Mrs Rowland, our rep was on that flight. It took her a week to get out of Sydney.'

I bet it did; I imagined this smiling girl, waving the passengers on ahead, to ensure the plane filled up, and she would be required to stay behind and be the last to leave the magnificent harbour.

Two years later, on my venture to Australia when Fred had a new computer to play with in my absence. At the latest art exhibition in Canberra, my mind was playing tricks; had I already seen these paintings? When the enormous Jackson Pollock loomed, it clicked when I read the wall plaque beneath it, "We are proud to display these paintings on loan from the San Francisco Art Gallery while their building is under reconstruction".

I wanted to brag; *I've already seen these in San Francisco.* Still, it was exciting for me to have a second chance of viewing them. Not a lover of Pollock's work, but under these conditions, he became an old friend.

Chapter 26 - Another Day In Paradise
(Phil Collins)

Good things come to those who wait. Fred and I were constantly dreaming of our next adventure. Australia was such a whirlwind, and we made plans for another visit.

Wendy lived in the Thames Valley, in England, as computer software and hardware companies were the new and thriving businesses. She said, 'My travel agent is from the Seychelles and suggested you take that route for something new. The islands are unspoilt, and you would love it.'

The Seychelles, a string of 115 coral islands scattered on the Indian Ocean like gems, is thousands of miles from anywhere on the African coast. It once drew pirates looking for somewhere to bury their stolen loot. In the '60s and '70s, the islands were the playground of the rich and famous and when we visited in the '80s, it was still pretty, untouched and untamed. These days the island nation, apart from its wild beauty, has become known for its proximity to Somalia, its pirates, a magnet for tax dodgers and a money-laundering hotspot. Still, I expect it has retained its magnificent beaches.

Wendy's boyfriend, Dave, had mainframe computer work scheduled in Malaysia, so before meeting up with him there, she travelled with us to enjoy a few days in the Seychelles. The timing was perfect.

We had booked onward flights to Sydney via Singapore, with Wendy's next destination as Kuala Lumpur.

Our budget hotel in Mahé was on a winding road back from the seashore. The larger beachside hotels at Beau Vallon had pools and lounging areas open to the sand. We spent days on this powdery sugar-white beach and walked amongst the leafy coconut palms, admired the lush mountainous scenery, and only returned up the hill to our hotel to eat and sleep.

We hired a beach buggy to explore the island and enjoyed wandering the bustling, brightly coloured streets of Mahé's capital Victoria. As I bought impossibly scenic postcards at a beach shop, Fred admired a nut on display, twice the size of a coconut, smooth, mahogany coloured, with a cleft on one side, making two mounds; it resembled a human backside. The coco de mer palm is a plant which produces this erotic-looking nut and thought to be the tree of knowledge.

The shop assistant told Fred if he stroked the coco de mer, it activated its powers and brought you back to the islands. So, Fred stroked it for longer than usual with an ecstatic expression and placed it back on the shelf.

Down on a deserted, crescent-shaped beach, where the bent palm trees touched the sand, we sat and took in the serene, wondrous seascape. We watched the elegant lizards and birds and, at sunset, the gentle fruit bats gliding across the skies in search of a ripening mango or papaya.

My birthday fell on one of those idyllic days, and Wendy had brought along a miniature birthday cake with a candle, so we cut the cake, and ate our two-inch square slabs. Fred and Wendy sang *"Happy Birthday"* to me as we enjoyed the dramatic tropical scenery.

Those few glorious days flashed past. In the evening taxi to the airport, Wendy, exclaimed, 'Oh no! I've misread the flight time. I thought it was 7:50 pm, but it was 17:50 pm. We're two hours late'.

An official at the airport greeted the taxi, 'We were expecting you, but you've missed the flight. They waited as long as they could.'

We took our cases from the taxi and wandered across the open-air terminal to the check-in desk. Another confident wide smile greeted us at the counter. The girl said, 'There's a weekly flight to Singapore, or if you need to go tomorrow, you can fly one-way to Abu Dhabi and onto Singapore. It will cost a thousand pounds each.'

Fred dismissed this price as ridiculous. While we mulled over our options, the official sauntered across. His sparkling-white uniform matched his teeth in mesmerising contrast to his black face.

'I suggest you stay,' he said with a gleaming smile. 'You can catch the flight next week.'

Our mood improved instantly. We agreed it was a great idea. Why not? We had the time, and now fortuitously, we also had the money.

I said, 'If we have to stay, I want that lovely hotel, right on the beach.'

Wendy checked the time for the UK, found a phone box and rang her London-based travel agent who was still in the office. He booked us into the Beau Vallon Hotel, giving us a budget price for this superior hotel.

Our taxi-driver realised our dilemma, hadn't left the airport and waited on the off-chance for another fare. The local driver was thrilled to give us an island history lesson as we meandered to our beachside hideaway.

The hotel porter showed us to a spacious triple room on the ground floor. It was perfect!

And the sudden extra funds? The day before, Steph had telephoned us, 'There's a letter from the York solicitor. The residue from Grandma's estate is in the bank.'

We expected it to be about £600, but Steph told us it was £6,000 - immense wealth for us.

Good fortune showered us. We reckoned Fred had caressed the coco de mer in the shop with such fervour, not only so we would return, but that we would never leave.

Wendy called Dave in Kuala Lumpur and told him we had missed our flight and were staying another week. He dismissed it as a practical joke and expected her to walk in at any moment, but she didn't.

The Aussies were more laid-back, prepared for anything, 'Yeah, no worries. See you same time next week.'

Steph capped it all with, 'Everyone else gets stuck at Luton Airport. Trust you lot to get stranded in paradise.'

In this sneaky extra week, Wendy learned to scuba dive, and we took part in an exchange hotel scheme on a nearby island. On the boat trip across to Praslin, we watched the flying fish skip across the crystalline surface of the aquamarine sea. In the open boat, the locals sat on their enormous colourful, plastic bales, packed with food and goods bought from Sir Selwyn, Selwyn-Clarke's market in Victoria.

We stayed in a wooden chalet, one of many dotted around a dense jungle. It was well furnished, but we hardly slept a wink. Dogs barked, and unseen animals snuffled and grunted most of the night around our cabin. We stayed for just one night and took the first islander plane out, back to our haven on the beach.

Torrential rains blew in one day, but it didn't dampen our spirits. Wendy and I tried fun things, we canoed, used a paddle boat and swam several times in the warm, tropical rain.

When the sun returned, under a canopy of palms, Fred just lay in the shade, with a book in one hand and ice-cream in the other, savouring every stolen moment.

There was a sudden thud and, a few seconds later, Fred glanced around and saw an angry-looking man standing beside him, waving a coconut in his hand.

'Are you mad?' he said, 'You nearly killed me, throwing these around.'

Another two coconuts whizzed passed both of them and clunked into the sand. They looked at each other sheepishly and then up into the palm tree which confirmed it was just natural ripening.

Fred said, 'See; it wasn't me, but it looks like we've both had a lucky escape this time.'

I still believe in fairy godmothers, magic, and voluptuous coconuts.

Chapter 27 - Golden Years

(David Bowie)

Mum was physically fit as a flea, but she spent the last ten years debilitated by dementia. Dad coped with it admirably, they were happy, and during their retirement, they ignored her loss of memory and carried on with their routine. I visited as much as possible. My brother, Alan, lived nearby and most days accompanied Dad for a drink at their local pub. Mum and Dad celebrated their Golden Wedding Anniversary with their worldwide relatives in England, Wales, Guernsey and Sydney.

On one of my visits to Manchester, Mum, confused, didn't recognise me and startled, she pulled away when I hugged her. I explained I was Win, her daughter and belonged to her, which she accepted. The following day she was taken aback to see me in bed in the spare room. I smiled at her, and she realised I should be there. Relieved, she said, 'I know. You belong to me.'

The warmth between us re-established. We clasped hands and linked arms as we strolled around the garden, and followed Dad, who pointed out his healthy vegetables. Even with dementia, she always smiled, wore her posh pinny, and held a clean tea towel when she helped Dad, 'our Billy,' with the washing up.

When my sister, Nan, visited, Dad produced an old, unopened bottle of Drambuie, received years ago as a present from Roy. Beer was his tipple, and he left Nan and me to sample the liqueur and chat, while he washed the dishes. Not drinkers, we knocked it back, without knowing its potency. When Alan came to take us for a drive, Dad greeted him with, 'These silly beggars have got drunk on Drambuie. You won't be taking them anywhere today.'

Nan and I rolled about in laughter, and Mum joined in, unaware why she was laughing. It was such fun to relax, let my hair down, whenever I got together with my siblings.

A couple of weeks later, Mum broke her ankle, and Dad had to admit he couldn't cope with her at home. A few days after they had bandaged her ankle, they transferred her to a brand-new Alzheimer's care home. It was 11th November 1988, she was 84 and had been in seemingly good health when they had last seen her, and Alan and Dad were keen to find out how she was settling in the new home.

A junior nurse greeted them, 'You must be related to the lady who came in today who just died.' She burbled on, 'I got her nicely settled in the wheelchair, she just had a stroke. It was instant.'

Alan and Dad held onto each other in shock. They had been out all day and hadn't returned home for any messages.

Death is rarely convenient, and I travelled from Guernsey for Mum's funeral even though I had been there two weeks earlier. I juggled with the concept that fate had kindly engineered that I saw her shortly before she passed. Her death through dementia for me was just closure. I had done what I could and visited often, but the loss of my mother happened gradually over many years. It was sad when she no longer recognised me and so Alzheimer's, and her life concerning me had just become a giant question mark.

Dad and I visited the funeral parlour to pay our last respects before they secured Mum's coffin lid. As in life, there is sometimes humour in death, when the young undertaker took me to one side, 'Will you give me the thumbs up when you see your mother. There are two old ladies in there; we don't know who's who, as the labels fell off their toes.'

After retirement, Fred never stopped learning and jumped at the chance when Wendy offered him a unique work opportunity. She worked in a computer company near Reading, in the UK's version of America's Silicon Valley. The requirement was, she explained, was to Anglicise an American dictionary for a new word processing software package. Fred flew over to collect the stack of floppy disks and bring back a brand-new Compaq portable computer.

Now when I say portable, this thing was heavy, cumbersome and the size of a small suitcase which fitted precisely in the overhead luggage compartment. It had expensive, state-of-the-art technology, and Guernsey flights had seen so few of them, and therefore treated as precious cargo.

He also hauled back the latest, substantial Oxford Dictionary which we used as our benchmark. We didn't include the word if it was not in this tome.

294

For weeks, we trawled through the pages, comparing and adding words to the software and amending any Americanisms to the Queen's English.

On completion of the assignment, Fred was thrilled to travel with Wendy to a software development office in Paris for the handover. Afterwards, they spent a memorable couple of extra days together, sightseeing. Fred was never into fancy cuisine and to keep his constitution regular, even in the gourmet city of the world, he insisted on taking his own brown plastic "begging bowl" and a box of *Bran Buds* for his breakfast.

In payment for his hours of work, he could have taken cash, but instead, Wendy arranged for him to receive a new personal computer and monitor, which arrived in two enormous, heavy boxes. Fred had attained his "heaven".

Simple computing software was available, text databases and a few spreadsheets, but in those days, all code-driven, with no multicolour or graphics. Fred, a maths expert, relished learning a new programming language and developed a database to hold his astrology data, used for calculating our annual horoscopes.

Computing was time-consuming back in the late 1980s, with broadband not yet installed in domestic homes, we listened to the modem's annoying whistling as it connected. With slow transfer speeds, Fred often got up in the night to download software from the American servers. We paid for modem time by the minute, so he calculated 3:00 a.m. as the fastest hour. I remember the groans when the DOS operating system failed, and reinstallation entailed inserting in order, the pile of a dozen 5.25-inch floppy disks. Fred and Wendy were enthralled with this innovative computer wizardry and made time to learn its intricacies and cultivated bags of patience for this painstaking hobby.

Our three children married later in life. Darius at 29 was the first. In 1991, he married Paula Reeve, who arrived in Guernsey from the UK as a dental nurse. She transferred to work in the finance sector and stayed on the island. They met at a local nightclub where she sometimes served behind the bar. They were both sporty, and Paula's expertise was archery. She started young, taught by her father, a champion archer. She won medals and cups for Guernsey at the Island Games and fostered an interest in the sport until she left with Darius to reside in the UK.

Paula's parents live in England, and so Darius and Paula's wedding invitation arrived for a Romsey Abbey ceremony in Hampshire on 28th September 1991, followed by the reception in an English country hotel. Paula's mother needed to know attendee numbers from our side of the family, so I rang her with an offer to help with arrangements, but everything was under control. The vital ingredients for me were church flowers and buttonholes. She agreed for this to be my contribution, but I could leave it with her to arrange it with a local florist.

A visit to Wendy in the UK allowed me to trawl around a variety of department stores to buy a 'mother of the groom' outfit. I chose a floral two-piece in crepe, Italian pink and French blue, easy to accessorise with my blue shoes, handbag, and a hat.

Fred and I stayed with Wendy and Dave, who hosted our other close relatives for two days before the wedding. I looked forward to the scenic road trip from Reading to Romsey in Hampshire, an area I hadn't visited.

I forgot about the climate difference between Guernsey and the UK. In September, Guernsey enjoys a settled and sunny environment, a hint of chill in the air as late summer fades into autumn, but England can be unpredictable. So, in the pouring rain, the convoy of two cars set out. A miserable trip ensued, stuffed with relatives unable to see out of steamed-up windows and not the fun journey I had envisaged.

Paula's two good-looking brothers officiated as ushers at the impeccable, well-planned event. She looked elegant in her long white lace dress with a high neckline, her dark blonde hair curled and pinned up, creamy skin, and slim athletic body. To complete the stylish ensemble, Darius and his ushers hired traditional grey morning suits. Even in inclement weather, the ancient, historic Abbey made a fitting backdrop for the service and photographs.

Apart from standing outside for the official pictures, I wore a long beige mackintosh most of the day over my summery crepe dress. Everyone else had packed an alternative outfit for the day; even Nan had a second choice predicting an unsettled forecast. The mother of the bride wore a plain navy suit. I felt uncomfortable in my light-coloured pastel ensemble, as if "I hadn't received the memo", and arrived in fancy dress, but mollified when it photographed so well.

After a splendid meal at the country club hotel, we left early evening for our long drive back in the soggy conditions, and dropped my friend, Jill, at her home in Salisbury. My brother Alan and Betty stayed on with Wendy in Reading, where we continued the celebrations.

Our schedule for the following day was significant and exciting; Fred and I were meeting another new family member. 'Mum's already replaced me with a poodle,' Darius joked.

Sunshine was forecast for our drive to Broadway in the Cotswolds, to collect Coco, our chocolate standard poodle puppy. Wendy had chosen her from the large litter six weeks earlier. Fred had initially considered it unfair to take on another dog at his advanced age, but Wendy persuaded us to have one and promised she would home it if anything happened to us.

The airline did not take puppies in the hold from Gatwick after a specific date that month, and we missed it by a week. So, Betty took my ticket and accompanied Fred from Gatwick back to Guernsey and visited her relatives and friends.

I flew from Southampton, via Alderney, a nearby Channel Island, with the tiny, dark chocolate brown, curly-furred puppy in a cardboard box on my lap. She howled most of the way, unsure of her surroundings, upset and frightened at the intense noise from the small trislander aircraft engines. In Alderney, during the fifteen-minute stopover, they suggested I take the puppy onto the

298

field for a break. From Alderney to Guernsey, she had got used to the movement and noise and slept soundly. Welcome to Guernsey, Coco.

Paula, Darius's wife, asked me to make an evening dress for a special occasion. I should have known better. They chose the design and material, a glowing, heavy, leaf-green satin. I was proud they were confident enough in my dressmaking skills. I glanced at the elegant fashion model on the cover of the expensive *Vogue* pattern. It appeared to be a simple, long strapless, elegant evening dress and easy to accessorise. I unpacked the large parcel which contained, material, zip, hooks, eyelets, bodice bones and tapes. To support the heavy skirt; it required stiff petersham ribbon sewn in to hug the waist. The last bail of fabric was light satin to make another dress, laughingly called the lining.

Mr Top Line designer was ready to give me my first lesson in haute couture. I opened the paper pattern instructions and completed it precisely step-by-step and presented them with the simple, elegant, strapless evening dress. Paula loved it so much she wore it often.

Let's fast forward two years to 21st June 1993. Stephanie was engaged to Bryan, an Irish banker who moved to Guernsey from Switzerland. Besides speaking fluent German, he also spoke French with an Irish brogue. His mother, Pauline, lived in Cork,

Ireland, and his father, Harry, relocated from Manchester to work in textiles. A heart attack caused Harry's untimely death, leaving Pauline to raise their two sons. They were academically gifted. Bryan's brother, Paul, became a rocket scientist at NASA in California, which involved developing the artificial intelligence of the rover on Mars.

When Pauline and Paul came over on holiday, Bryan and Steph organised a family lunch. A glorious sunny day called for Sunday best. The two-piece dress from Darius's wedding came out of the wardrobe for the second time.

As Fred and I walked to their front door, I said, 'I feel euphoric, as though I'm floating.'

Bryan greeted us, and we noticed Pauline and Paul in discussion with an official-looking man in a suit. Bryan asked Fred to pop upstairs to let Steph know we had arrived.

After a few minutes, Fred trotted downstairs and gestured, 'You'd better go up now.'

I climbed the stairs on wobbly legs; wondering what might have happened to Steph. Nothing could have prepared me for the sight; she stood, tall and elegant, in full magnificent bridal regalia. I touched her billowing long white dress and stroked the headdress of shimmering pearls which formed a peak on her forehead and secured the train.

I welled up with tears and tremulously asked, 'Is this real?'

She nodded, we hugged, and she beamed. 'I'll explain later.' The unknown man in the suit was the Greffier who officiated at civil marriages, and Wendy, the surprised bridesmaid, straight from the office.

It was a joyful wedding, where we wept at such an intimate service held in their house; even the Greffier became teary-eyed.

After the ceremony, we lunched at La Grande Mare, a golf resort hotel on the west coast. Bryan and Steph took the opportunity of stepping onto the beach opposite to have their wedding photographs taken while paddling at the sea edge.

Steph later explained it was such a hassle to get married in a church, Bryan being a Catholic divorcé. They both had large circles of colleagues and friends, and it became impossible to sort out who to invite for the civil ceremony or reception. In the island's business circles, they were well-known, so it became a real cloak-and-dagger game for them, trying to keep their wedding plans secret.

A few days later, the announcement appeared in the *Guernsey Press*, 'To our surprise and delight, our daughter, Stephanie, married William Bryan Morris on 21st June 1993...' They honeymooned in Ireland and later held a reception at their house to celebrate with their friends, which allowed her to wear her wedding finery again and cut the cake.

Steph soon settled into married life, and at home, studied with the Open University and achieved not one, but two, Bachelor of Arts (Honour) Degrees. She also joined Fred in cat worship and chose a white Chinchilla-Persian mix. Misty needed grooming every day, an ornamental but fierce warrior, a match for any large

301

dog. When confronted, she puffed out her fur to double its size and turned into a worthy, white adversary. Misty tolerated birds drinking from the birdbath on the patio, on condition she drank there first. This beautiful cat lived a secure and pampered life up to a magnificent age of 22.

Wendy returned to the island to live with Fred and me and joined the finance industry. She met John Woodcock, a tall, sporty, fair-haired, diligent banker who had just turned 40. They soon became engaged and bought a Victorian villa to renovate. Like her sister, she applied to the Open University and had her sights set on a Bachelor of Science (Honours) Degree. As she worked during the day, she fitted in her studies at night and passed a module per year until she graduated. It took nine years and then flushed with success and to keep up the momentum, gained a Life Coach Practitioner Diploma and various other compliance qualifications.

I wasn't involved in the previous two wedding arrangements, as Darius's took place overseas, and Stephanie's a surprise. It was a pleasure to join in with the preparations for Wendy and John's wedding in Guernsey, scheduled for 29th April 1995.

They held the religious ceremony at the Vale Parish church, St. Michel du Valle. The site of the old 16th-century church made it a seafarer's landmark, glimpsed from many points in the north of the Island. They chose the St Pierre Park Hotel for the wedding reception.

I accompanied Wendy to take a look at a second-hand wedding dress advertised in the newspaper. She bought it there and then; a perfect fit, made from heavy, cream Italian silk, with long sleeves, a low neckline with a row of pink silk roses, and a full skirt.

A gifted florist, Mary Kirkpatrick, lived two doors away from them, always in demand as top establishments requested her exotic and modern flower arrangements for their lobbies. With her, we enjoyed designing the wedding table decorations, sprays, and buttonholes. On the day, Wendy displayed a stunning bridal bouquet; a trail of deep-pink stargazer lilies intertwined with ivy and roses.

Their photographer was Steph's friend, Fiona Adams. In the Sixties, when Fiona worked in London, John Lennon used her picture as the cover photo for the Beatles 1964 *Twist and Shout* album; it shows them leaping into the air. This "Beatles jumping shot" found its way around the world.

Steph, the only bridesmaid, could not imagine herself in a puffball, off-the-shoulder creation, so Wendy asked her to find a suitable dress. She chose a distinct soft-yellow top and pleated floral skirt, ideal for wearing at other times.

For Wendy, apart from the groom, the star of the show was her 91-year-old grandad, my Dad, Billy.

Dad, who now lived in Canberra, Australia, received a wedding invitation, and my sister Grace said, 'As time got nearer, the card gradually moved into the centre of his mantlepiece where it took pride of place'. She asked him if he wanted to go, even though it involved long-haul travel from Sydney to London and onto Guernsey. He didn't hesitate, and as a good traveller, his doctor certified him fit enough.

The doctor gave sound advice to Grace, 'Don't worry about him. If he dies on the way to the wedding, he'll be thrilled he's on his way. If he dies after the wedding, everyone will rejoice that he made it.'

He travelled from Australia, unaccompanied, to attend his granddaughter's wedding. He enjoyed his flight in Club and relayed in his still-strong Mancunian accent that he had gone 'Pub Class.' When he reached Guernsey, my internal brief was to keep him alive long enough to attend the special day. One morning, when late getting up, Fred and I put our ears to the door for any sound. I crept into his bedroom to ensure he was still breathing. Of course, he was. Dad never missed a party.

It rained on the wedding morning and dull when we left for the church. John's father, Rowland, diagnosed with multiple sclerosis, found walking a struggle but was determined to walk unaided down the aisle for his son's wedding.

What could possibly go wrong? Nan was involved!

During the ceremony, the sun came out on cue, ready for the official photographs outside the church.

'All the relatives for this one,' the photographer Fiona called out. I said, 'Nan can stand next to me. Does anyone know where she is?'

No-one had seen her, or Alan. In the excitement of the preparations, I had overlooked their transport to the church. Nan's reputation for anything going wrong was renowned, so when I announced my sister was missing, everyone laughed, and Fiona got a super photograph.

In the search for Nan and Alan, Betty stepped in and drove to their hotel, where Alan told her, 'Nan's left in a huff for a long walk across the beach.'

On her return, Nan dressed again in her finery, and Betty drove them to the reception. At the hotel, a bumper glass of bubbly restored Nan's usual good humour. She was not religious and unconcerned at missing the ceremony.

Darius was the current drummer with a popular local band, City Limits, versatile enough to cater for most events. The group entertained us for the evening dance, and Darius joined them for a few numbers.

Before going on their honeymoon, Wendy asked, 'You will be here when I get back, won't you, Grandad?' 'Of course, he will,' I replied, and linked my arm with his.

He made the journey to the wedding, stayed for a month, and returned to Australia, where he lived for many more years.

The next big event in the calendar was our Golden Wedding on 26th April 1999. Fred and I were delighted to celebrate a glorious and eventful 60 years together with our grown-up children, who were also happily married and living nearby.

John's parents, Rowland and Hilda, travelled from the UK to join us for the milestone luncheon at La Fregate, near the Le Mont Bleu. We marvelled at the same views that Fred and I experienced when we came to Guernsey, 40 years earlier.

Chapter 28 - I Will Always Love You

(Whitney Houston)

Sometimes it's advantageous not to know what the future holds. Everyone I held dear, like a strike in skittles, was knocked down, one by one.

We celebrated the new millennium at Wendy and John's house, and Fred turned 79 a few days later on the 4th of January. Later that month, unwell, he was admitted to the hospital for tests. Wendy and John were not happy to return from holiday to find Fred in there, his lungs drained of fluid, and his skin had developed a yellow tinge. Yet again, Wendy had returned from holiday to bad news.

She privately asked the oncologist for his initial opinion. He confided Fred's diagnosis was terminal lung cancer. Until they confirmed the hospital tests, she couldn't divulge the gravity of the results. She sat on her hands for the longest week in her life.

While in hospital, and Fred undergoing tests, our Siamese cat, Fifi Le Bon Bon, died of old age. Fred was mad about Fifi, and we dreaded telling him his beloved cat had died, so we waited until they discharged him. When we broke the news, he did not react; no tears, no sadness, or at least he didn't show it. With little strength, he was no doubt preoccupied with his failing health.

We attended the oncologist's meeting to discuss his test results. Fred was in complete denial of his impending demise. During the summer and autumn of 2000, he battled through rounds of chemotherapy. It was a frightening ordeal, vomiting to survive.

Fred never talked about his illness, but just before Christmas 2000, he said to us, 'I don't want to go through chemo again.'

Our response was, 'You know what this means?'

He nodded, and it was never referred to again.

Silent, I agreed and tried to be resilient for Fred, even when crumbling inside.

Over the phone to Betty, I'd said, 'The longer illness must give you a chance to come to terms with their death before they go?'

'Oh, Win, you poor thing,' she replied, 'Nothing prepares you for the death of a loved one.'

The Macmillan nurses arranged for an adjustable bed at home. They came in two shifts, the morning "skylarks" and evening "night owls".

' I moved into the spare room; a monumental moment as I had never slept on my own, unless on holiday, and I missed his physical presence.

Through the grim reality of a terminal illness, there were light-hearted, humorous moments around his sickbed. We shared the vigil and gathered in his bedroom over the four weeks he was in decline. As we giggled at the shared stories and memories, we hoped he could hear us.

I cleared out his many drawers of claptrap, amassed at the local Saturday car-boot sales and we rolled about in laughter as we tried on at least two dozen sunglasses of varying colours and styles. I must have also discarded half a dozen coffee makers and electrical radios.

Fred and I were never soppy, coming from staunch, no-nonsense north of England stock. We covered up our feelings and never expressed sentiments of "I love you". We were not demonstrative, a by-product of our hardscrabble upbringing. It was unusual for us to show our emotions, and we never needed to. We knew we were the loves of each other's lives.

After settling him off in his sickbed, I turned at the door and said, 'You know I have always loved you.'

'It's a good job you did,' he replied, 'as I'd be in a fine state now if you didn't.'

The night owls came around ten o'clock and attended to Fred. Darius entered the bedroom after they left.

When I took over the vigil, he told me they said, 'We nearly lost your father, but he's rallied, and he's got his colour back.'

We looked over at Fred, whose skin had turned bright yellow, jaundiced with liver failure, and we saw the funny side at what they'd said. I smiled, let out a little chuckle and Darius joined in. We both gave out great bursts of laughter and clung to each other as tears rolled down our faces.

Our next-door neighbour, Angela, trained in palliative care, was so helpful and reassuring during the weeks of Fred's illness. She checked in on him the next morning, entered the kitchen, and said quietly, 'He has gone.'

'No, he can't be,' I said, 'I was only just vacuuming and tidying up and heard him take a big sigh. I told him, "It won't take long, I'm just doing this while the others aren't here," and I left him in peace.'

'That wasn't a sigh,' Angela said, 'It was his last breath, and you were there.'

On 13th February 2001, six weeks after he stopped treatment, Fred died, at home, in his bed, as he wished.

The phone rang - it was Grace in Canberra. She must have been on the wavelength. Her soothing voice said, 'I know we don't usually phone, but I was thinking about you and Fred.'

'He passed away a few minutes ago.' I said. 'I'll call you back later; someone's at the door.' I was relieved she would relay the news to the relatives in Australia.

My next-door neighbour, Julie, stood on the doorstep with a timely tribute, a bunch of tulips, 'I don't want to disturb you, but I thought you'd like these.'

'He's just died,' I said bleakly.

'Let me know if I can be of help,' she replied. I nodded, and after hugs, tears and condolences, she left, and I placed the vase on Fred's bedside table.

The neighbour opposite came over next. 'I was shopping and saw these daffs; they are so early.' That was just too much; we wept together on the doorstep, clutching the wicker basket arrangement between us.

310

The immediate family gathered at the house. They were amazed to find Fred already laid out, the room clean, empty of medical equipment and spring blooms arranged on either side of his bed.

Someone asked, 'Where on earth did you get the flowers? That was quick.'

'Not as quick as Grace, who had called within five minutes,' I said.

'What kept her!' they chorused.

We stood in a semi-circle around Fred's bed, said our farewells and noted Fred's spirit had gone; there was just a shell left. I wanted his body removed that day, if possible, and as Wendy and John knew the funeral director, she made the telephone call.

I listened in, 'Hi Peggy, my Dad passed away this morning at home. Mum wondered if it was possible to collect him today?'

Wendy covered the mouthpiece, 'Yes, they can do that, but the hearse is already in service. They have a van which could pick him up within the hour, as they are collecting another person. Do you think he would mind sharing?'

It was so ludicrous that it broke the air of sadness for us, and we heartily agreed, no fuss, a white van and company on his onward journey is precisely what Fred would have wanted.

The transit van reversed into the drive, and two men brought in a simple pine coffin. Within minutes, Fred was on his way. We didn't go to the funeral parlour; we had already said our goodbyes.

I heard later; the neighbours were waiting for a black hearse to arrive so they could stand outside and pay their respects. They laughed when we told them about the white van. One of them said, 'Typical of Fred not to stand on ceremony and do it his way.'

I wanted to be able to say, 'Fred never had a day's illness in his life. At 80, he got lung cancer, ill for a year, and died.' Now that wasn't bad at all? But it was bad. Fred's death was nearly 20 years ago, so I now feel comfortable writing about him.

After the cremation at the Foulon Cemetary, I couldn't bear to destroy the impressive white flowers which stretched the length of his long coffin. They delivered the wreath to my house at my request, where someone erected a makeshift trestle table from garden furniture outside the patio window. The incongruous arrangement produced a strange display.

For two days, I stared at it and smelt the heady white lilies. I was at a loss; everything seemed unreal. The flower arrangement subsumed me, but I resisted the urge to tear it to shreds. Instead, I shook my fist at the sky and shouted, 'You've beggared off and left me.'

With difficulty, I trailed the long wreath inside and found it comprised four separate oblong pieces. These sections of foliage and blooms surrounded me, and for a long time, I sat, fingered

312

them and tried to get back to reality. I felt numb when my nearest and dearest visited and carried off their portion of white flowers.

Wendy completed the administration after Fred's death, writing endless letters and form-filling on my behalf. After I signed letters stating, 'my late husband,' so many times, that I believed it.

Steph was a power of strength too. As she lived nearby, we walked with Coco on the beach. It allowed other dog walkers to speak to me and re-establish a relationship on a lighter level, not to cause upset.

One day, on our daily walk, we met the local Hospice director. She said, 'It must've been gratifying to nurse your husband to the end.'

Stunned, we both agreed when I said, 'It was terrible. If he'd been our dog, we would have put him down a month ago.' Saying this to a Catholic seemed a heresy, and she hurried away, horrified.

For weeks after, I felt emotionally fragile, skating on a pond of thin ice. I raked over every painful detail of the last year. I couldn't believe that throughout our married life, we had never discussed his impending death and our beliefs.

After meeting people anxious to contact their dead loved ones via a medium, trying to be dispassionate and scientific in our search for evidence on their behalf, we never spoke together of our feelings on the subject.

We acted out the nurse and patient scenario. Why had it been so challenging to say the words, 'I love you'? Years of "stiff-upper-lip" stoicism had robbed us of our last chance to bond. I deplore that it is spoken these days automatically, without feeling when finishing so many phone calls. Most times, it's lost its impact and meaning.

Chapter 29 - Bridge Over Troubled Water

(Simon and Garfunkle)

A year before Fred became ill, Steph came hurtling in for her usual afternoon visit, waving a leaflet. The ad read, 'With the English Bridge Union the EBU, Mr B. Noakes will teach bridge classes every Tuesday afternoon in term time for two years.'

'You will love it, Mum,' she enthused. 'You've been playing cards all your life.'

At 72, I was Alice entering Wonderland. Mad hatters, March hares, and imperious queens populated my dimension at the bridge table.

In the classroom, we slouched in our seats or looked elsewhere to avoid questions from the teacher. Apart from cryptic crosswords, our brains had lain dormant for years. The student numbers soon dwindled to around 36.

One day in class, I declared, 'I thought I was intelligent until I came here.' The elderly students greeted these words with nods and sighs of relief. We were all in the same boat and concluded, Bridge, pets, and babies are great levellers.

To defeat the supercilious Mr Noakes, we banded together. We met on various afternoons at each other's houses to play specimen games. We turned into silver-haired swots completing homework. Mr Noakes became Brian, our friend, who wanted us to have fun and enjoy our old age. After our first year of tuition, long-suffering people volunteered to play with us to give us a glimpse into the actual world of Bridge.

I didn't complete the second year of my tuition because of Fred's illness. Weeks passed, and Steph talked me into a special Bridge event for a favourite charity. I was petrified, wondered if I would remember how to play. With different standards of players, I needn't have worried, and I didn't feel out of place. Steph was my partner, and we muddled through. The warm, welcoming faces of my ex-classmates encouraged me. Our standard of play was faulty, but the afternoon tea was superb.

Steph admitted later, she gazed opposite at this miserable gibbering wreck and thought, *Why am I putting my poor mother through this?* Far from it, she helped me take a giant step back into life, for which I will be forever grateful. Steph has since encouraged another widow to return to this social hub.

At the Bridge event, I gave out my phone number several times. With trepidation, I took the first call, and confirmed my availability to play that day, but warned I hadn't finished the course or practised.

'Sod that,' she said, 'We want you, and you'll soon pick it up.'

I wish I had learned to play Bridge earlier and not left it until my seventies. It has secured my friends and social life over the past 20 years. They welcomed me, being Steph's mother, she's decades younger than most of us, but an expert player, greeted everywhere.

I met funny, intelligent, and talented people there and one of these was Gwynneth, who in her late 80s was still a musically gifted pianist. In her youth, with a beautiful voice, she sang in choirs and even at the Eisteddfod in Wales.

After several years of partnering her in hilarious Bridge and a joint Mediterranean cruise holiday, I was distraught to lose another female, when a severe stroke left her in a care home.

Steph and I visited her in her suite, and when she called us by name, we were relieved that she recognised us. We thought she was recovering until, with an excited, imperious voice, she said, 'You're the first to hear my news. Prince Charles and I are engaged!'

One of our Bridge ladies, whose husband was celebrating a milestone birthday, had reserved a luxurious lunch for a party of eight; food served with flamboyance at St Pierre Park. We drank sparingly to keep clear heads for playing cards later that afternoon at their seafront home, with easterly views over the other islands.

They had arranged two tables, one in the lounge, the other in the kitchen/diner. We were ready for battle, and the players were individuals, not paired. It was a dance where we chopped and changed places. After two or three hours, everyone had played everyone, and the highest scorer won the prize. Following an afternoon tea, we watched the high tide lap the shore and caught the last rays of sunshine setting on the islands.

To thank them, I sent an elaborate 3D card Wendy had created with a playing card theme. A grand day out deserved a grand card, one they treasured and had framed.

A fortnight later, he was dead from cancer. He had sworn his wife to silence, not wanting to spoil our day out. I was so glad he got his perfect birthday celebration.

That wasn't all; her deceased husband had booked and paid for her grieving programme for a full year ahead. It entailed a Bridge cruise and several visits to relatives. It was a busy year, and following his arrangements, she returned to a real grieving period. She told us the travel had exhausted her, and she now just wanted to relax with her family overseas.

A few months later, Wendy and John invited me on a Caribbean cruise which was a complete break, and I was startled when I heard myself laughing. It seemed ages since I felt so carefree; we danced the samba, took catamaran rides, and got merry on rum punch. Then it hit me: I can't spend the rest of my life as the grieving widow, I'd survived the searing heartache and many other sorrows and deserved to enjoy the rest of my life.

That summer brought more unsettling news; In Canberra, they had admitted Dad into a hospital. The relatives gathered to visit him and celebrate the Melbourne Cup. It was during this holiday period he died, aged 97, according to his great-grandsons, he had just given up. His remaining eyesight had failed, and unable to read, he just got bored, it wasn't a life worth living anymore, and he was ready to leave.

Darryl, Linda's husband, who arrived from Sydney, was unprepared to attend a cremation and had to buy long trousers and suitable shoes; his usual attire was flip-flops and shorts. The Australian relatives scattered Dad's ashes at the beautiful Tidbinbilla Nature Reserve, which he loved.

I was not unduly sad at Dad's passing as he had left his bleak, grey Manchester life for a bright, colourful twenty years in the sun. His extended, close family rallied around him, and he relished the Australian warmth and style, which and gave him a new lease of life. I visited him there while he was still strong and enjoyed with him the local clubs and, where I discovered to my surprise, he resurrected a superb baritone singing voice. The smooth relocation to modern accommodation, with constant exciting things around him, and loving family companionship prolonged his enjoyment of life.

Chapter 30 - Back To Life

(Soul II Soul)

When an extraordinary event occurs, we need the witness to be credible, reliable, and unbiased. Nan and I had planned to attend a wedding in Sydney. As a treat for her, we opted to travel via the States. As befitting Nan's luck, the 9/11 disasters happened, and we abandoned the trip. I rang our sister, Grace, in Canberra, to advise her of the cancellation.

Grace's husband, George, was keen to relay to me in person, an extraordinary happening, but with my visit cancelled, he told me over the telephone.

Sheer delight came through as George recounted this story to me: Grace was on holiday at the coast, so alone when he woke and saw a small figure suspended in the air at the end of the bed. The apparition, surrounded by light, appeared three-dimensional. He recognised Fred, his brother-in-law, who had died a month before. George squeezed his eyes closed and blinked, expecting the image to disappear; it didn't. They exchanged no words, and he watched, mesmerised until it gradually faded away.

Shocked, he couldn't sleep. It was unmistakably Fred and forever imprinted on his mind. George, a Government patent inspector, was not given to flights of fancy.

When he told Grace about the ghostly visit, he described the dark-green, floor-length garment Fred was wearing; similar to a monk's habit, tied with a girdle.

'It might be a religious robe,' Grace suggested.

I was thrilled to hear this, as Fred had cocooned himself for years in this thick woollen, blanket-like, dressing gown with a plaited cord.

Betty's jumble sale collection produced unusual items such as this, which he loved so much, he never replaced it for a lighter, modern one.

Fred had staged an ingenious visit to Australia; his incorruptible, closest buddy and in-law, George, could not have known about Fred's favourite dressing gown, which he never wore outside the house or in front of visitors.

What puzzled me is that Fred appeared small. Much later, I saw a reference to ghosts, which reported they were often diminutive. Films brainwash us to imagine they are life-sized, or spookily huge.

After hearing about George's supernatural sighting, I wasn't surprised when strange things happened at home. I had heard that spirits try to reconnect with loved ones through electrical sound-waves. However, Steph and I were still amazed when the radio turned itself on to play music.

Whenever she visited, we walked the dog along the beach and returned for afternoon tea. With no set pattern to the timing, the stereo switched itself on, and the first tune played, ironically, was a Simon & Garfunkel song, *Homeward Bound*. We accepted this inexplicable phenomenon until it happened when I was alone.

One afternoon, the radio switched itself on, which made me jump. I snapped it off and sat in my little yellow leather chair and sobbed. Everyone was at work; I had no-one to contact. Without warning, the front door opened and in breezed Steph with her friend, Iris.

'Hi Mum,' she said, 'We were shopping in St Sampson's and I had an urge to call in on you.' On the other side of the island, she felt compelled to hurry back to me and forgot to drop Iris at her home nearby and brought her along.

Seeing my tear-stained face, I explained, 'The music came on again, and I shouted to him, "Go away, you're upsetting me. You're not here. You're not real. Leave me alone to live my life." Steph, I don't want this to happen anymore.'

She comforted me but regretted losing this tangible, psychic contact, with whom she believed was her father. We never had another radio episode, but once they ended, we enjoyed reminiscing about them.

Darkness had always spooked me, but when Fred died, my fear of the dark disappeared. I now feel safe to wander alone into unlit rooms and stroll around the garden at night. This remarkable transition is enjoyable and not to be over-analysed.

After Fred's passing and following the 9/11 tragedy later in 2001, Nan and I were still keen to attend our nephew, Neil's, Australian wedding celebrations. We renewed our travel plans, avoided America, in case of any further cancellations, and flew east to Sydney via Singapore.

It was a memorable holiday for everyone, as all our relatives and friends gathered from various parts of eastern Australia. Linda rented two bungalows overlooking Lake Narrabeen, along Sydney's wilder northern beaches, to accommodate out-of-town wedding visitors. As the ocean surf crashed beyond the sandbar, Nan said, 'This is my dream, I want to live here forever.'

After weeks of talking and being pampered by our siblings, Grace and Linda, and melding into the lives of our extended relatives, we boarded the flight for the long trip home. Thankfully, my positive Saturn aspect overrode Nan's travel blight, and there were no hiccups on the return trip. With plenty of room onboard, we slept most of the way to London Heathrow.

We waited to board our respective buses, she was to continue onto Wales, and I was heading for Gatwick airport. My coach arrived first, and the helpful driver got out, took my bright-red case and escorted me onto the steps, but Nan pulled me off, 'A quick hug,' she insisted.

We had been strong until that moment, and it was this heartfelt gesture which brought our streams of tears, a fitting token of thanks for taking her to the other side of the world to visit our younger sisters. That wholehearted embrace felt so genuine. Sometimes less is very much more.

Chapter 31 - Brand New Day

(Sting)

In February 2002, Wendy and John sold their renovated house in the island's centre and bought a 1950s bungalow, with a separate wing, on an acre plot. They knew the West coast area well and could see the potential. The house needed a complete overhaul, and the field transformed into a garden. They were up for the challenge.

I'd had a year on my own, and Wendy didn't want me to be a widow struggling with a small pension and loneliness. So, there were two options, either they moved in with me, or I moved to their house. It was desirable to sell either property with renovation plans already approved. We discussed both ideas and architectural plans drawn up for my house to have a conservatory room, and the top floor extended above. In the meantime, they outlined plans to enlarge and renovate their property to accommodate me.

The prospect of starting a new garden appealed to me. So, I planned to leave Port Soif and my old life, and John fenced in the acre field to keep Coco from straying.

In hindsight, it was not such a smart idea to present my house for sale with approved renovation plans. There was a lot of interest, but when buyers saw the proposed design, they wanted to start the project, but most didn't have extra funds and left dejected.

My house was still for sale in the autumn of 2002, and after such an emotional and tumultuous year, Wendy and John suggested we take another bargain Caribbean cruise to lift our spirits. Two neighbouring young boys offered to babysit my dog, who was now 11 years old.

The day before the cruise, I watched Coco swerve around the kitchen. Worried, I rang Steph, who rushed over and made an emergency appointment with the vet. But before we left, some prospective buyers phoned for a second viewing of my house.

I was so preoccupied with Coco, I said, 'Sure, come along, but I'm packing for my holiday, and I leave tomorrow. I'm taking the dog to the vet now, so you will have to show yourselves around.'

We left her at the vets to undergo tests, and the couple came for the second viewing, while I waited for news. The woman wandered around the property while her husband sat and poured over the renovation plans.

After they left, the vet phoned. He had diagnosed my gorgeous, furry companion with an inoperable brain tumour. His advice was to put her to sleep. I didn't want her to suffer, so agreed and finished packing for my holiday in floods of tears.

After losing my cherished constant companion so suddenly, I desperately needed an escape, but, of course, an overwhelming air of sadness pervaded the trip.

It was a bargain multi-location cruise, a well-organised voyage and a stylish but older ship. On this last-minute temptation, the cruise company assigned our cabins when we boarded the liner.

With a budget price, it reflected in our accommodation. We were allocated two porthole cabins at the bow, to peep out of onto the waterline.

Every morning as we docked at 6.00 am, the ancient anchor woke us with a start, as it clanged against the hull when it dropped to secure the liner.

One night, during a windy crossing, the giant waves boomed against the side of the metallic hull. Wendy couldn't stand the intermittent, thumping vibrations against her head, so she changed her sleeping position and moved the sheets and pillows around, so her feet absorbed the pounding on the cabin wall.

There was one consolation having cabins in the bowels of the earth; we passed walls crammed with artwork for sale. Each night, we admired a serigraph called "Poker Pimps" by Michael Godard; a card-playing saloon scene with players depicted as olives and strawberries. We called it "Strawberry Buttocks", and we stroked it each time we passed.

We enjoyed the shore visits and its facilities, much more than we expected. One evening, a trio joined us at dinner. An older man in his wheelchair, his male nurse/companion, and his daughter. They were elegant, entertaining fellow cruisers, and I enjoyed the stimulating assortment of different characters and generations.

After dinner, we decided on an early night, and I left Wendy and John to go to their cabin. I took a detour to mine past the ballroom where music was playing.

326

'You're surely not going to bed yet?' a voice called from the bar. 'Come and join us for a drink.' It was the trio from the dinner table.

The male companion, an expert dancer, taught us the samba. The daughter and I improvised, taking it in turns to dance with him. It surprised me when his charge climbed out of his wheelchair, to claim me for a dance. We tottered a few steps. He clutched me too tight for the samba; we held each other upright while the others cheered and clapped.

My new dance partner whispered in my ear, 'Are you sexually active, Win?'

Too tipsy to think straight, I whispered back, 'I don't know. My husband just died a few months ago.'

'Oh, so sorry.' He let me go so abruptly that I almost fell onto the floor. He staggered over and slumped into his wheelchair; the only time I saw him on his feet.

The dance teacher grabbed me, and we proceeded with staggering and balletic dance steps. What a temptingly handsome young man, I thought, as he flung me around the floor. So strong and muscular. The music stopped, and with the effect of several cocktails, we stumbled to our various cabins.

At breakfast, the trio ventured over to join us. The daughter said, with a wry smile, to Wendy and John, 'What a pity you didn't join us in the ballroom. Win and I danced until midnight.'

The surprise on their faces was comical. The last they saw of me; I was heading to my cabin for an early night.

327

On this fun cruise, in my mid-70s, I had been drunk, danced like a whirling dervish, got propositioned, which gave me a light-hearted, much-needed respite from the real world.

But every night, alone in my cabin, I cried over another loss. How much more did I have to endure? In one year, I had lost my cat, my husband, my father, my dog, and now fate had decided to take my home.

Towards the end of the cruise, Wendy showed me an email; my house had sold. As I was still grieving for my dog, the sale implications did not register. I didn't care whether it sold and became defensive at any more significant changes in my life. Within two weeks, I had packed and moved, as the buyers had a Christmas deadline.

I had been the longest resident in Port Soif Lane, 43 years, and saw families come and go, their children raised, schooled, and in gainful employment. Many dog walkers knew me as the lady with the big poodle and called me Mrs Polly, Mrs Goggles, or Mrs Coco, depending on the year. Many predicted, 'You'll never move from Port Soif, where would you go that's nicer than here?'

There was no real sadness at packing up and leaving my house and garden at Port Soif, but in the last few minutes, I sat on the empty floor in the sun lounge and pressed my back against the wall. I thought, *I'm leaving my home. We're both now desolate and drained.*

In my head, I heard the resonant Lancashire tones of my father saying, 'Buck up, lass! Wash your face and go'. The melancholy mood didn't last long, and ensconced in my new home, with Wendy and John, amidst my packing boxes, I could see walls for painting and a garden full of brambles which needed clearing.

The bungalow's name was Dawnington, and they wanted to change it. One day at work, the name Samarkand had insinuated itself into Wendy's brain, and on the Internet, she found it was a place in Uzbekistan.

She asked me if I knew anything about it. 'Yes,' I said, 'There's a poem about it, a trading town for silk and spices.' It amazed her when I added, 'Your cat-mad father called our first Siamese, Sammy, but his pedigree name - Samarkand Sabu.'

As far as I knew, no-one else knew this name. Wendy was delighted to have such a continuous psychic connection with her late father, and Samarkand it became.

I moved to a scenic area surrounded by agricultural fields, and from the top of the sloping terrain, there is a distant sea view of Vazon Bay and its red granite Martello tower. The island has a long interesting history with remnants of loophole towers, gun batteries and bunkers scattered around the coast's headlands.

In the plot behind the bungalow, a weed-filled, 100-foot derelict greenhouse stood out on the landscape, an overbearing skeleton, strewn with broken, jagged panes of glass, so it was a priority for us to remove it.

John was adept at the structural side, paths, edging, erecting arches, and a gazebo. Between us, we created a typical English garden. Exotica crept into our planting, as it became mainly a frost-free zone.

We were foolish not to expect any problems when we applied for permission to build a modest loft conversion. They allowed one plan, which did not give enough room height to accommodate John's head.

Instead, we suggested adding rooms to the ground floor rear of the property. A new kitchen/diner, a master bedroom and the largest heated conservatory we could get away with, harmonised with the present structure and provided an all-year living and dining space with garden views on three sides.

One winter, I attended astrology classes with Steph at the teacher's home. At the end of the first year, the students wanted to continue learning, but the venue became unsuitable for the teacher's family, so I offered to hold further sessions in our conservatory. Going to these classes reignited my passion for astrology. When they finished, it buoyed me to decipher Fred's hand-drawn, natal charts and use the pertinent ephemeris to calculate and write out the annual family horoscopes. Nowadays, with such technological advances, anyone can download and print out their natal chart and individual horoscopes.

Chapter 32 - Little Lies
(Fleetwood Mac)

Grace and George's Golden Wedding Anniversary was in January 2004, and I missed the family connection. So, I put out tentative feelers about taking an early trip to Canberra. Kaye, their daughter, emailed back immediately, "Mum and Dad are not expecting you to come over in our hot weather, so why not surprise them?"

There are very few secrets in that close-knit family, and any snippets of gossip soon made the rounds. I arrived a few weeks later at Canberra airport, shocked, but thrilled to be met by a posse of relatives. It was a few days before the party, and everyone knew about the surprise, apart from Grace and George.

Kaye said, 'You'll stay with me, and the others will keep an eye on Mum's movements, so she doesn't spot you.'

Jill, their other daughter, added, 'I've booked a hair appointment for you tomorrow, and on the off-chance she might pop into the mall, the hairdresser will throw a towel over your head and fend her off.'

Kaye's husband, Alex, as my chauffeur, drove us to the Golding Wedding reception. In the carpark, Alex nipped around to open the car door for me. I walked in front of him towards the building when he grabbed me from behind and hissed, 'Duck, it's Dennis!'

He pushed me down as he'd seen a friend who was a late arrival. I looked over and saw Dennis, who knew me well. Alex signalled me to stay crouched between the two cars as he crept forward to check if the coast was clear. I had the tingling sensation I was being watched and looked sideways and my eyes locked onto those of a man sitting in the car, his arm rested out of the open window. Our faces were level, inches apart. He put his head on one side, nodded and winked, and I wondered what he could have construed?

Alex said, 'Quick, we can make a dash for it now!' I kept bent and stumbled with Alex across the path into the central porch. We stood up, adjusted our clothing and looked at each other, laughed and linked arms. We were ready for the grand entrance.

Inside, everyone stood, holding their glasses ready for a toast. Darryl whispered to Linda, 'I'm sure I've just seen Win through the window.'

She dismissed it, 'You must be seeing things. She's on the other side of the world.'

He muttered, indignant, 'I know Win when I see her.'

Alex opened the door, and we walked in. Someone shouted, 'Here they are!' Heads turned to see who had arrived; it was only a surprise for Grace, George and Linda.

Darryl gloated to her, 'I told you I saw her.'

Linda looked at him and shook her head, 'I would never have believed it.'

Later, when Grace got the chance, she pulled me to one side, 'Where've you been hiding? How did you get here?' She kept touching me on the arm to ensure I was really there and not a figment of her imagination and repeated in sheer amazement. 'Where did you come from?' She made me feel as if I had descended like an unexpected angel from the clouds.

After the party, the family returned to Kaye and Alex's bungalow. The beautiful balmy day had brilliant blue skies, but Kaye was right; it was searingly hot. Alex had reserved my seat in their house, positioned near the full force of the air conditioner. I could never get used to it being sunny outside, but everyone sitting indoors in the refreshing cool air.

Canberra is a few hours from the coast, up winding mountain roads through forests of blue gum trees and evergreens. Surrounded by wildlife-filled bushland and serene lakes, the Australian capital is stunning with wide Victorian avenues and sharp modernist architecture. Individual lakes provide beauty and outdoor adventures with a surprising backdrop of mountains, the Brindabella range.

Grace and George lived in this lovely garden city. All the family worked in the medical facilities, and they offered Grace a position in the Canberra teaching hospital, which fulfilled her childhood ambition of being a nurse. After they retired, they wanted to be secure and within easy reach of a medical facility in their old age. They sold their detached bungalow in a Canberra suburb and moved into a new housing complex with manicured gardens. The arrangement was well-planned and was a forerunner for this type of flexible, inclusive accommodation.

There were several types of homes available, depending on the resident's status and requirements. It was convenient for declining health needs and included panic buttons connected to the central building, an alert for instant medical help. Community activities, trips in coaches to places of interests, or shopping malls became a lifeline for non-drivers and people with no close friends or family backup.

Free from household chores, maintenance and gardening, George was unrestricted and cycled to the library and took up playing the organ. Grace had worked in social care as a therapist, and so impressed with the innovative set-up she kept her name on the list for years, ready to move at the appropriate time. With long-established clubs and interests, her social life seemed secure. After George died, her ongoing dementia made it necessary to move from a bungalow into a room in the complex's Alzheimer's section. She wanted to control her life, her surroundings, and her medical provision, on which her family wholly agreed.

I stayed with her for one week in 2017, when Jill and Kaye customised her room with her belongings. Grace's photograph, in a frame on the door, acted as a signpost. The central dining room resembled a restaurant, with organised tables of four. I returned home, happy she was receiving complete medical and social care she had wanted, until her death, two years later.

The strange, difficulty about living an exceptionally long life is facing constant loss. Your heart is always a little broken, your mind always a little clouded with grief.

I then lost my significant long-standing friend whom I loved dearly. Betty, in her late-80s, died of a heart attack, and her funeral took place in her retirement town of Weston-Super-Mare. On a surreal, stormy day, Guernsey, shrouded in filthy mid-winter weather, curtailed complicated travel arrangements. I didn't feel the need to confirm her demise by attending the interment. I'd made the most of her when she was alive and had no regrets.

Darius, now a pilot living near London Gatwick, had expressed keen interest to represent the family and prepared to drive there. But on the morning of the funeral, they summoned him to fly to Ireland as an emergency substitution.

Once in the air, stormy weather caused a slight diversion. Darius heard the Captain laugh, 'I have never flown to Dublin before via Weston-Super-Mare.'

With a bird's eye view and his loving heart beating in remembrance, Darius looked down on the tiny town from the cockpit. Jubilant, he whispered to himself, 'Goodbye, Betty. I made it. Have a good flight.'

He couldn't wait for the end of his shift to call me. Betty was a rare, colourful character, and we had celebrated her life in our unique way.

Chapter 33 - Year Of The Cat

(Al Stewart)

Years before I moved in with them, Wendy and John had bought a brown Burmese kitten they named Suki. Her mother, the 5-year-old, Valentina, had been an indoor cat used for breeding, and this was her last litter. The breeders asked if Valentina could join Suki in her new home?

Of course, they took both. Suki became an adventurer and wandered amongst the nearby greenhouses until one day, only two years old, she disappeared. A frantic search and publicity brought nothing, not even a dead body. We theorised; a heartbreaking mystery, but Valentina was on-hand to console them.

But she was no consolation prize, without Suki, she came into her own and became a charming extrovert. Her only demand, a daily portion of freshly cooked cod. As an indoor breeding cat, she hadn't been outside and didn't know how to hunt. It amused us to watch her chattering back to the birds, which stalked her across the lawn.

In 2008, Wendy and John booked another cruise and asked if I would look after an elderly Valentina? I practised giving her the diabetes injections by using old jeans, the same resistance as skin, ready to take over administration of her daily insulin. I needn't have worried, she was used to needles, always calm, and the process took seconds.

One afternoon she appeared unusually lethargic, and I monitored her. After dinner, I became frantic as she hadn't moved, and I called the vet to our home: the prognosis - kidney failure. I wasn't the registered legal owner, so the vet suggested she took Valentina to the surgery where she could act in the cat's best interests, and, treated like a medical emergency, would euthanise her. Heartbroken and zombie-like, I followed the vet to the door where Valentina opened her gorgeous green eyes for a second and gave me a last look.

I couldn't bear to accompany the vet. *Not again*, I thought, *I can't stand another loss. I must now gather my strength, be brave and inform people I love; their beloved cat will not be here when they return.*

It was a heart-breaking time, and I worried about how Wendy and John had taken the news while still on holiday. Steph and I collected Valentina's ashes, to ensure nothing more for them to face on their arrival home.

'Do you want an urn?' the Animal Shelter asked and was taken aback by my vehement refusal. A mud-brown, plastic urn had been the receptacle for Fred's ashes. It was so hideous; I hid it until we scattered the ashes on the headland at Port Soif.

We didn't want to house our beautiful Valentina in an ugly urn. Amongst the precious bits and pieces in our display cabinet, we found a delicate china pot with a lid, dainty enough for our purpose. Steph and I smiled again. Mission accomplished.

The tradition continues where we plant a tree or shrub for an anniversary or in memory of our loved ones when they die. Where possible, we choose something with the same name. As we walk around the garden, when it flowers, it reminds us of them. John buried the cat's ashes after he found a pink rose, Valentine, and he planted it near the house where we can see the yearlong blooms. The garden is now full to brimming with memorial shrubs and roses and pebbles will be brightly painted with their name and placed next to them.

In 2010, nearing Easter, Wendy saw a young black cat slink across the patio. It sat on the step for a while, and she offered it some ham from the fridge. That was a fatal move; the cat never wanted to leave us. He had very thick black fur and green eyes and strolled across to us at 6.00 a.m. and tapped with a claw on their bedroom window for admission and stayed with us all day until we went to bed. We called him Smokey-Joe, and Wendy followed him home one day, a few doors up the road. She alerted the owners that he stayed with us most of the day, and they were happy to know this and thought he revelled in the individual attention, as he was just one amongst other cats, including his mother.

One day, Smokey-Joe didn't come to visit, and Wendy walked up the road to investigate. The owners hadn't noticed he was missing, as their cats lived outside in a shed and just came and went as they pleased. She found out two cats had run straight into the road the night before and killed outright by a taxi. Wendy

339

offered to go to the animal shelter where she saw a photo of deceased Smokey-Joe, but mercifully, without a nasty mark on him.

We missed having him around and wanted to fill the void. To justify having another pet, Wendy and John agreed they would be at home more because they had already done a fair amount of travelling. As John was nearing retirement, he would be home to look after any animals. Wendy fancied another large poodle and set her heart on a cream one, as a colour change from the others we had owned.

Fate intervened again; that weekend, an apricot standard bitch puppy suddenly became available for immediate collection from Hampshire in the UK. Excited, we kitted out the car and took the fast ferry to Poole to meet the breeders. They introduced us to their two adult poodles, the white mother, the black father, and their litter of twelve puppies. Some had black fur, some white and only one cream one with traces of apricot, the colour descending from a grandparent.

A buyer had pulled out, and the breeders were desperate to find this cream puppy a home. They couldn't believe it when Wendy enquired on the off chance. We loved Maloolooba Crema on sight. John shortened the name to Melba, which suited her apricot/peach overtones.

At home, a few days later, John commented that now we have a dog, he might like to have another Burmese cat.

A grey Burmese kitten was due to be born in the UK, but Steph noticed a breeders card in a local flower stall, so we made an appointment to view the latest litter. Rosettes and certificates for her show cats festooned the hall which sealed the decision to get a pedigree kitten from her.

We earmarked one sturdy female, and we could visit anytime to see how she was progressing. We also saw a tiny grey kitten, not as strongly developed, but on our second viewing, she marched straight over to us, so affectionate and playful, we changed our minds and asked the breeder if we could swap kittens.

The evening sunrays shone across the hallway as this slim-line fur ball streaked across, and Wendy said, as she saw the silvery movement, 'We could call her Silvie'. She was born on 11ᵗʰ August 2010, the night Wendy saw a Perseid's shooting star from her bedroom window. This sighting sealed her pedigree name as "Perseid's Silver Star", and who, at home, is Silvie.

Although small for the breed, she makes up for it with a sharp, penetrating voice, which she uses to control the household. She's a dedicated hunter of mice and shrews and enjoys swiping at passing butterflies and bees. Baby rabbits, if they're unlucky to cross her path, don't stand a chance. After she has wrung the last vestige of fun out of them, she walks down the garden, straddle-legged, because they are her size, and presents them to us as gifts. Some gifts?

As an adventurous kitten, she slithered across the glass conservatory roof, stuck her head through the open skylight and gazed down at us. The drizzle started, and the rain sensor closed the vent, which gripped her neck like a vice. She lay quietly moaning, with her head inside with her tiny body occasionally writhing outside across the glass as she tried to free herself.

Wendy grabbed a chair to stand on and a long-handled brush. From outside, she wedged the broom next to Silvie's neck to stop the skylight from closing and to relieve the pressure. She screamed, 'Get the fire brigade.'

Melba's frantic barking alerted our neighbour who, when she saw the predicament, ran outside to flag the fire engine down. A fireman, dressed in black leathers, stomped into the conservatory, noted the wedged kitten and the frantic female with a broom outside. He scouted around for something to open the skylight and grabbed a spare wooden garden post and thumped the vent open from the inside. It released Silvie, who tumbled down the glass roof and was caught by Wendy.

'I must leave,' he said, 'I'm not supposed to be here, I've got a fire to go to.'

Mystified, we subsequently found out, the crew sent to rescue our cat, had seen a fire engine already outside our house, and so they swapped emergencies and extinguished the hedge fire on the main road. It must have been the only time two fire engines had come within minutes along our narrow lane.

Silvie was checked over at the vets but had come to no harm. However, this incident left Melba so traumatised that whenever the cat or any workmen climb on the conservatory roof, it sets her off barking, and she trembles and whimpers until they get down. It's dangerous up there!

Chapter 34 - I'm Still Standing
(Elton John)

The subtle aches and jags of pain are the downside of a grand age. Wendy suggested I had an x-ray when she saw me staggering up the garden path, holding my lower back. The x-ray confirmed I required a new hip. Within days, a cancellation suddenly manifested, and my hip replacement surgery scheduled for two weeks ahead.

A complete success, and on the second day after the operation, my ordeal ended, and I swept around the ward with the aid of two crutches. The nurse said I could go home when I could manage the stairs. With this as an incentive, I returned home the following day with lists of exercises and schedules.

When Wendy wondered if I was over-doing it, I showed her the list, 'Look, it says, second week - empty the dishwasher bending your knees.' This invaluable list of chores was an excellent incentive to get back to normal mobility.

Wendy and John were my rocks and had dealt with declining movement through John's father, who at first required walking sticks, then crutches and eventually, a wheelchair. John made me a comfortable place to watch television, and I soon recovered.

They knew what equipment was available at St John's medical aid centre, so they hired anything to make me more comfortable. My bathroom was already a wet room with grab bars. Rowland used it when he came on holiday from the UK, and I decamped to the spare bedroom.

Before my operation, the nurse said, 'You'll sail through this. You have a strong heart, the right attitude, and a sense of humour.' She was right. Bless the shiny new tin hip, a few weeks later the garden beckoned, so I wielded my trowel and dibber again. The surgeon inserted a lightweight, titanium joint, which has been a life-changer and alleviated discomfort for the past ten years. With an unknown lifetime, to date, it is still going strong, and thankfully my other hip hasn't required an operation.

Years later, the next operation was not so disabling, but a more psychological trial. I found a ridge near my left nipple. *Perfect present for Christmas*, I thought. I kept it to myself, but after the festivities, I had the abnormal tissue checked out.

Two weeks later, I underwent a single mastectomy. At my age, late 80s, they decided not to deal with lumpectomies or partials. They operated, confident of success because of my continuing good health. Once again, I sailed through the ordeal. I was lucky I found the ridge early enough to warrant immediate surgery with no chemotherapy. Unlike the other two ladies in my ward, who had lumpectomies, of which I was envious, mine turned out to have the most successful outcome. The others had complications, resulting in chemotherapy, eventual mastectomies and trips to the UK for radiation treatment. I didn't opt for reconstruction, so a dense foam breast fills the space in my bra.

In gratitude, Wendy and her colleagues, each, somehow touched by breast cancer in their families, decorated bras, raised money for charity, entered the *Moon Walk*, and marched 26 miles overnight around London completing *Walk The Walk*.

She didn't expect to finish the walk, as she hadn't taken her training seriously. However, on that evening, spurred on by spectators, she completed each mental milestone without difficulty. Many dropped out, weeping by the wayside, nursing blisters and bloodied feet. She credited her stamina and hardened feet to the five years she had walked Melba which had strengthened her leg muscles enough to undertake the challenge.

After a day enjoying sights in London, Wendy arrived at Gatwick airport where she heard her ticket was incorrect. In haste, she had typed in Guernsey to Gatwick twice, so had no return in the system. When she told them, she had been over to do the charity Moon Walk and proudly displayed her medal, the girl phoned Aurigny Airlines in Guernsey to explain the mix-up. The wonderful gentleman on the other end said his mother had just recovered from breast cancer and gladly sanctioned the change of ticket with no charge.

Like a visiting pop star, the family met her off the plane later that evening, with armfuls of flowers. Friends who hadn't sponsored her and heard of the achievement, dropped through the letterbox envelopes of cash for the charity.

I must mention here the excellent, caring organisation, *Guernsey's Pink Ladies Breast Cancer Support Group*. After surgery, I received a box with a prosthetic breast, vouchers for swimwear and suitable bras, and a catalogue for other requirements. A lovely surprise tastefully presented and made me feel part of a unique sisterhood, with contact details if I ever needed advice.

I am now a cancer survivor, and since my operation, have had no problems and received the all-clear in my annual check-ups. Every year, on breast cancer collection days, Wendy stands, rain or shine, shaking a bucket outside a supermarket. One time, she stood outside a butcher's shop on a very windy site on the west coast. By lunchtime, the bucket was full to overflowing with cash. Suddenly, a gust of wind caught the plastic lid, ripped it off the bucket, and a cascade of light banknotes flew out across the road into oncoming cars. Of course, the surprised motorists screeched to a stop, jumped out and helped retrieve the runaway currency. When she mentioned the charity, she even managed to cajole a few extra quid from those kind drivers too - all in a good cause!

The holiday sections in the Sunday newspapers tend to become more interesting, the colder and darker it is outside! A sure sign I am getting fed up of our winter. Always up for a challenge to find me a good deal, Wendy got on the case and booked me through Las Vegas down to Hawaii and onto Sydney.

Las Vegas is another, mad, compact place to stay, and again I would recommend it for a few days stopover. Transport is easy, frequent, and affordable. The selection of hotels I have stayed at has never failed to impress me because of their size, tropical gardens, and swimming pools. Their choice of food is incomparable, whatever you would like, whenever. Their buffets are so magnificent and appealing that I often wonder how people can eat the amount they pile on their plates.

Las Vegas puts on stage shows in grandiose scale and style, and the staff do not look down on single, aged travellers. On the contrary, often I would walk into a restaurant, a singleton without a reservation, and be warmly welcomed, and seated somewhere suitable where I could survey the restaurant and its diners and the best view of any attraction. I recommend a trip there to enjoy yourself but not take anything too seriously.

After my last visit with Fred, I promised myself, if I ever stopped over again in Honolulu, the place to stay is in a luxurious hotel on the beach. Where, in early 2016, I stood in line at the bustling reception desk at the Hilton Hawaiian Village Waikiki. It has a striking landmark, a colourful red, blue and yellow abstract sail painted on the side of one the tall tower buildings. Set among a magical 22-acre tropical landscape, it has the broadest and most spectacular white sand beach and a saltwater lagoon.

It was too early to check-in, my room wouldn't have been ready, so I wandered outside to find coffee and a place to relax. A dwarf wall divided the pool area from the sandy beach where people watched the surfing. Three levels of activity took place, belly boarders and paddlers, beyond those, swimmers, and in the distance were serious longboard surfers, who rode in the swells and curls of the massive breakers.

I returned along the open, palm-fringed walkway to the desk and handed my passport and itinerary to the receptionist. She said, 'Gee, Ma'am. You're amazing. All this long-haul travel at your age and on your own?'

I smiled and retrieved my itinerary. If anyone questioned the arrangements, I produced Wendy's magic spreadsheet and the sight of such a detailed schedule of venues, contact names, and references always elicited a positive response. 'If it's on the schedule, it must be right.'

'You're in luck,' she said, smiling, 'Room Number One is free for two nights. You deserve it for waiting so long. Have a nice stay.'

Bemused, I followed the porter into the lift, and he wheeled my case to the end of a long corridor. He opened the door with a theatrical flourish and stood back and watched my face as I walked in. My mouth dropped open at the enormous triangular room centred around two, floor-to-ceiling picture windows. On the right, was an array of coloured sails in the marina and to the left showed the crescent of the white sandy beach and obligatory turquoise sea, backed by Diamond Head mountain. The dark, heavy wooden furniture suited the spacious, magnificent room.

In both windows were large writing desks with business-like leather chairs, and trays, complete with complimentary stationery, brochures, and pens. I pointed to the beach and said, 'I wouldn't get any work done with that view, there's too much going on down there.'

The panorama from the colossal plush bed was breath-taking. I had hoped to stay at a hotel on the beach, but I never dreamt I would get the best suite in the complex.

Without thinking, I telephoned Wendy to share this moment of euphoria, and she drowsily said, 'Hi Mum. Take photos - it's two o'clock in the morning here!'

Chapter 35 - Sentimental Journey

(The Andrews Sisters)

My niece, Chris, Nan's daughter, kindly took me on a sentimental journey. We stopped for lunch in Buxton on the edge of the Peak District, and I mentioned to her it was where I had spent my honeymoon.

In 1947, Fred and I had taken the train to a village outside Buxton. They cancelled the last leg of the journey, but the stationmaster said, 'Don't worry about accommodation, there is a nice hotel next door.'

Outside the station, in the evening light, we saw a stately home, The Palace Hotel. We could only afford one night, so we made the most of it, and the following morning, after breakfast, we walked around the five-acre landscaped grounds. Before we left, we took coffee in the grandiose morning room, filled with well-heeled old ladies, feet on footstools, holding their Pekingese dogs. I was afraid Fred would catch one of his enormous feet in an ottoman, so we grabbed the nearest armchairs and waited for our coffee, like characters in a Victorian film set.

To them, seeing a vibrant, young couple, it must have been obvious we were newlyweds. I looked around, greeted by benevolent, indulgent smiles. After coffee, I glanced back, gave a little wave and smiled at their envious looks and sighs.

Continuing my sentimental journey, I mentioned to Chris, that during the war, Nan and I evacuated to Macclesfield. Chris pinpointed Sutton Village on the map, and we set off to find it.

The school and the divine church on the hill were unchanged. We hurried to the crossroads and found the lane, but alas, a row of modern homes replaced the Curphey's doll-like house. We strolled along past the houses and leaned over a gate leading to a field, and I stared, lost in memories, at the same rolling meadows, which led to the forest in the distance.

I said, 'I wish Nan were here.' She had died a few months earlier.

Chris replied, 'Perhaps she is.' We hugged and wept at that lovely thought.

Chapter 36 – Changes

(David Bowie)

Rowland, John's father, had been a remarkable businessman and accountant, travelled extensively, and moved with his wife, Hilda, to live and work for a few years in Johannesburg, South Africa. On their return to the UK, he continued to work from home until ill health with MS forced him to retire.

In 2011, John floated the idea of sharing our home with his ageing parents. The disrupted status quo felt like an uneasy arrangement for me. I didn't know how we would get on, having spent only a few hours here and there with them. I could see the practicality and comfort of keeping them together as a couple.

John contacted an architect to draw up provisional plans and established a budget with Rowland for an extension. Several possibilities were explored and laid dormant for a few years until it was time.

They were both in their early eighties when Hilda became too fragile to manhandle and tend to Rowland who, with advanced MS, was now a full-time wheelchair user. He'd noticed, after 20 years supervising his needs, Hilda was not coping, becoming frail and had started to forget items on the weekly shopping list. So, in November 2013, he contacted John to say it was time for them to come to live with us in Guernsey.

It was a compassionate and sensible arrangement to make their final years comfortable and ease their isolation. Rowland and

Hilda were legally eligible to reside in Guernsey, *en famille*, (with members of immediate family).

They sold their house in the UK within a month, so fate must have thought it the right thing to do. The family helped to pack up their furniture and belongings into a container, and they flew across to us in January 2014.

On arrival at Guernsey Airport, Hilda scraped her leg on the steep taxi step. Taking Warfarin tablets, with blood oozing down her shin, and not clotting, Wendy rushed her to the hospital.

Hilda was in a sorry state. Over many years, she had been so attentive to Rowland, and she had neglected herself, was exhausted and full of infection. After tests, they admitted her for three weeks to get her well, rehydrate her, and ensure her daily medication was under control.

John and his father discussed the provision of creating separate living arrangements, and an architect engaged again to formalise our bungalow's extension, but once again, put on hold.

Rowland, who knew he was in declining health before he came to Guernsey, became bed-bound after seven months, and carers came in twice each day to attend to him. After a few falls and only nine months with us, they admitted him to hospital, and in October 2014, died aged 86. It would not be a cliché to say he battled his illness with all his might and avidly studied any new medical papers or diets on the subject. It was a testament to his determination that he lived a full, social life for over 20 years despite the MS.

354

Hilda after her initial hospital respite was still unsteady on her feet but able to potter around the garden. At first, I was content with her snipping off the spent bloom heads and planting up the front borders and patio pots. However, I admit I became anxious when, in the wrong seasons, she vigorously cut back shrubs dotted around the flowerbeds.

We certainly had differing gardening methods. Hilda was obsessed with rounding the plants using the cloud pruning technique with plenty of soil seen in the beds. Bare soil to me was a magnet for weeds, and I cultivated larger natural shaped shrubs and plenty of ground cover. I had found through years of experience, with an acre garden, you need to have established trees and plenty of creeping, spreading plants. This ensures victory against lily beetles, bindweed and couch grass.

Furthermore, I had been nurturing and cultivating some unique plants for years on the seaboard, and she didn't know how to prune these. After a couple of years of plants with no buds and the absence of summer flowers, John diplomatically suggested apportioning the garden. We tended to the borders where we were most comfortable and knowledgeable. With firm demarcation lines, this worked well, and the garden has continued to thrive - as long as John does her work!

Now the borders are mature; we can stand back in wonderment and admire the years of hard work where those tiny cuttings have finally blossomed into huge specimens. We marvel at the surprise combinations of plants, some happy accidents, some contrived.

From the Spanish-tile landscaping, up the offset terraced steps, you can walk across the lawns and browse the beds. If you get weary or just want to sit and enjoy the scenery, there are seats dotted around as you meander along the mottled, Alderney gravel pathways. To mark the various sections in the garden, to describe where I have been planting, or weeding, we have given them such evocative names as, "the woodland walk", "South Fork" and "rhododendron way". It's helpful because if I have lost my border fork, trowel or Dutch hoe, or there is something magnificent in flower, I can easily reference the place.

Hilda's health has improved exponentially, with congenial company, nourishing homemade food, and regular doctor visits. She became settled and happier, but sadly, the insidious creep of dementia took hold.

She was used to watching different television programmes to us, and she became a little twitchy whenever swearing took place or something risqué came on. After tutting and denigrating the programmes we liked, we gave up our evening lounge for her.

For a few years, Wendy, John, and I used our bedrooms as evening bedsits and watched what we wanted on individual televisions. My hearing was in decline, and the tv volume became loud and intrusive, so they supplied me with wireless headphones. They are perfect, I can hear every word, and music is sensational; I never looked back.

We agreed we needed more space in the house as we needed another lounge and somewhere for guests to stay. So, we resurrected and amended the building plans to build a second floor on the bungalow. The renovated house sits in harmony with the landscaped garden. We now have roomy, high-ceiling living areas and a guest suite to accommodate visitors who we lodged in nearby local hotels. I can hold Bridge sessions in splendour on the first-floor lounge, as we break for afternoon tea and daydream out of the new apex picture window at the colourful garden and rising adjacent fields.

With more space, Hilda was delighted to get more of her furniture from the storage facilities into the house and loves her large bedroom suite on the ground floor. It opens onto the patio with picturesque views up the garden, and she is happy and settled and can escape to rest and read or complete her adult colouring books in peace.

I wished to remain in my en-suite bedroom with its patio doors onto the secret front garden bordered by camelias and hydrangeas. I love to sit there in the evenings as I play Bridge on my i-pad or write and watch the oranges and pinks of our glorious sunsets.

From the conservatory, we enjoy the upward sweep of the garden and can catch glimpses of grazing and galloping horses in the neighbour's fields.

The bungalow and garden were adapted to be wheelchair-friendly, and for the new storey, I asked, as a joke, 'Where's the lift?'

Wendy and John agreed it was an excellent suggestion and incorporated one to cater for any mobility problems and to future-proof for access in old age. The lift has been a splendid success, with heavy guest luggage transported and my less agile Bridge friends able to access and play cards in the upstairs lounge.

Melba, our standard poodle, not used to steps, is terrified of the staircase's steep slope, even though carpeted, and prefers to use the lift. She patiently stands outside the doors and soon lets us know when she wants to move between floors.

Chapter 37 - Who Are You?

(The Who)

The magic words jumped out at me from my monthly Bridge magazine: 'Athens to Venice - Ten Day Bridge Cruise. No single supplement. Affordable price.'

I called to enquire. 'There are a few places left; I'll reserve one for you,' a cultured voice said on the other end of the phone. 'It'll be a pity to miss such a holiday. I can hold it for a week.'

I mentioned it to Wendy, who pounced on the magazine. 'What an itinerary, fine dining with wine and bridge evenings. Why are you waiting? Book it!'

After a moment, she added, 'I've had an idea. Why don't I join you in Venice for a few days at the end of your cruise?'

We had visited Venice as a family in 1980 when the girls lived in Italy, and as I hadn't been back, I viewed this as a sentimental journey. I could turn a page on the past and start a new chapter.

Due to a delay in my London to Athens flight, the scheduled hotel car had left. I rang the hotel and told them I would be arriving by taxi. They said, 'Don't pay. We'll take care of it. Just come straight in when you arrive. Their driver should have waited.'

It was late when I arrived at the hotel reception. I leaned against the counter and yawned. They acknowledged my weariness and apologised, 'Wait until you see your room. Lucky for you, it's vacant just for tonight, and you deserve it.'

Intrigued, about my overnight accommodation, I thought, *It couldn't be a sea view from this section of the city.* When we booked the luxury King George hotel, I knew there would be no spare time to visit the Acropolis, but the website said I would get a view of it from the veranda.

The porter took my two key cards, and the lift rose a few floors. We stepped out into a sumptuous cream and white penthouse apartment with three deep settees and comfortable chairs which surrounded a long low table. Fresh flowers and tasteful artefacts covered the dark wooden sideboards. Ornate gold mirrors reflected this elegant room. The dining table had seating for a dozen, situated by French windows. The porter led me through these onto a palatial terrace, lined with long white boxes to resemble flowerbeds, filled with tumbling red geraniums. He escorted me around the private swimming pool, that echoed its uninhibited backdrop of the illuminated Acropolis.

The twinkling city lights and the magnificent edifice with its highlighted columns were mesmerising. In all this splendour, even alone, I still appreciated the stunning panorama sank into a chair and rang the reception for a pot of tea. The receptionist sounded surprised, but a few minutes later, tea, biscuits, and cakes arrived. I tore myself away from the view and retired to bed.

When I couldn't find my suitcase in the bedroom, panic set in. While viewing the suite, the luggage turned up in an identical second bedroom. Relieved, I moved in and unpacked a few overnight items.

The following morning, I explored the rest of the apartment to reassure myself it was not a dream. Behind a heavy door was an immaculate, full-sized kitchen, stocked with everything possible, including polished wooden boxes filled with an exotic assortment of teas - no wonder the receptionist was surprised when I ordered a pot of tea the night before.

After breakfast in the hotel's sunny, stylish dining room, with another perfect vista of the Acropolis, I popped into the hotel lobby. I noticed a colourful banner which displayed my cruise, *Voyage of Antiquity*.

Guests who opted to add days onto the start of their cruise filed out to the waiting buses. The staff had allocated me a space on a bus, but I politely declined as I had booked private transportation.

I returned to my room using the lift and inserted the unique key card. A floor number, not on the list, displayed by magic, and disappeared when it reached my penthouse suite. As the porter wheeled my luggage, I took a last glance from the panoramic window to impress the city scene in my mind and left.

When I reached the cruise ship, two guests who stayed at my hotel, boasted of their room upgrade with a window facing the Acropolis. They said, 'It was so magnificent, we were reluctant to sleep.'

'What a memorable start to your holiday,' I said, unwilling to spoil their moment by gloating about my incredible upgrade to the penthouse with a private swimming pool!

The Bridge cruise was hectic, every day filled with visits to historical buildings or ruins. In the evenings, our party had an early dinner and then retired to another room to play bridge. Positions for play and dining were random, so it surprised an elderly widower and me that we got seated together and partnered with each other most of the time. An expert player, he balanced out my play, and we had a stimulating time. To our amusement, we recognised the other players were matchmaking.

As he was usually seated next to me, I hadn't noticed he had a limp. One day as he hobbled towards me, I realised he too was old. That instant it became clear I couldn't stand the agony of losing another elderly companion.

As we disembarked the cruise ship, we exchanged farewell pecks and handshakes. My friend whispered, 'I have booked to go on the next Antiquity cruise to Norway in the autumn.'

I just smiled. The chill of Norway didn't appeal to me. When I left the UK for Guernsey, I vowed never to venture further north than Manchester, but he didn't know that.

This fabulous, fun-filled Bridge and educational Antiquities cruise started in Athens, cruised the Adriatic, and we disembarked in Venice. After embarkation, I sat on a stone bench at a prominent part of the quay, unaware of how Wendy would arrive to join me.

She had completed a 24-hour obstacle race to get to Venice. Her evening flight from Gatwick diverted to Verona because of lightning strikes in the Venetian area. A coach eventually dropped her at midnight at a hotel near Venice airport. She caught the first local bus in the morning to the maritime port where the cruise liners docked, but when she arrived, my ship was not there. A port official checked his schedule and located it on the opposite side of the port area. Wendy dragged her case behind her and zigzagged over the various bridges in the general direction. Not wanting to be late meeting me, she spied a speedboat and, in her best Italian, dredged up from 35 years ago, persuaded the water taxi captain to take a canal shortcut.

At 10.00 am on the dot, I heard her shrill football-match whistle and saw her waving from a bright-red speedboat racing towards me, her windswept blonde hair blowing behind, in true cinema fashion. They scooped me up, and we zoomed over the waterway to the Hilton Molino Stucky on Giudecca island, one of the large islands along the Venetian lagoon. Once a flourishing flour mill, the imposing brick building has been beautifully restored, with a bijoux rooftop bar next to a welcoming pool with a view.

Venice was a whirlwind. I adored this dream city, with its grand, jaw-dropping architecture, the maze of stately palazzi, and gondola-packed canals.

In the daytime, we visited art galleries, bought inexpensive but chic Venetian jewellery and clothes. We delighted in every trip on the free Vaporetto to and from our hotel to St Mark's Square.

At night, we dined and drank, and people watched. Wendy, who thought this might be a one-off trip, had reserved the best hotel restaurants. On the first night, we took the private motor launch and dined at the Belmond Cipriani. The eye-wateringly expensive hotel, a legendary 1950s getaway, is perfect in every way, flanked by 15th-century palazzos, with rambling gardens. We dined on a floating raft on the canal and watched the sunset over the Basilica di Santa Maria della Salute.

The following evening, we had a table reserved at the Gritti Palace Hotel, which had a bijou floating restaurant on the Grand Canal. Wendy suggested going earlier to sip cocktails at their outdoor Riva Bar, designed in wood and white leather to resemble the iconic motor launches.

It was expensive to get a direct private water taxi from the Hilton to the Gritti Palace and too far to walk from St Mark's Square. We saved money by taking the hotel's Vaporetto to the Square and hailed a water taxi around the corner to the restaurant and planned to do the same on the return.

We enjoyed a luxurious start to our evening and on arrival at the Gritti Palace landing stage, the staff rushed to escort me up the broad sweep of steps. The hotel porch took centre stage, and the left held musicians who played quiet music on the pre-dinner decking.

Wendy explained to the maître d' the reason why we were early for our dinner reservation. She held my arm and escorted me up and down the steps between the two decked areas to the outdoor terrace whose tables were already full of Bellini-sipping guests.

The waiter said, '*Mi dispiace, Signora*, - I'm sorry, it's Saturday, all the tables outside are already reserved.'

'*Niente problema*,' Wendy said, 'We'll have a drink inside at the bar.' We stood and marvelled at the compact, plush palace interior, adorned with significant artefacts and paintings. Before we reached the counter, the waiter sidled over and ushered us outside to a free table overlooking the canal. Over cocktails, we watched the bobbing gondoliers as they ferried sightseers along the choppy waterway.

After half an hour, Wendy took my arm and carefully manoeuvred me again, up and down the decking steps to the adjoining exterior dining area. A waiter bustled over and with arms outstretched, proudly showed us our table. We expected one towards the back of the restaurant, but we were seated in pride of place, front line on the canal. Opposite us was the white, glistening Basilica di Santa Maria della Salute we had admired from afar, the previous evening.

Wendy chatted about the menu with the waiters and practised her Italian. They advised us on the best choices for each course and suggested accompanying wines.

With such a perfect, balmy evening, we took our time dissecting the menu. We came to the same conclusion: 'Sod the expense, let's have every course, drink all the recommended wines, and enjoy every minute of this unique experience.'

While savouring our gourmet feast, the full moon appeared, reflected in the canal - utter bliss. We lingered over coffee and petit fours until we were the last to leave.

Wendy asked the headwaiter for the bill. I heard her ask the maître d' if her husband, John, had organised the surprise for us, but he shook his head.

Incredulous, she turned to me and said, 'You'll never believe this. A gentleman in the bar has settled our bill. He's paid for everything tonight.'

She asked him, 'Has he ever paid for someone's evening before?'

'Occasionally,' he replied, 'but never on my watch.'

'At least let me thank him for his generosity,'

'No, no, it's not necessary, he doesn't wish to be thanked,' and scuttled off to find our wraps.

She whispered to me, 'We can now justify taking a water taxi directly back to our hotel.'

Not wanting our perfect evening to end, back at our hotel, we took the lift to the rooftop bar and listened to a live group playing sophisticated music. The moonlight danced on the Giudecca canal and splayed out over the lagoon to St Mark's Square.

We were intrigued and amazed a stranger had secretly paid for the most expensive meal we'd ever had. Over our Bellinis, we speculated who it might be; perhaps an older man who missed his wife or mother?

Our mysterious benefactor was only ever referred to as "he", and that's all we'll ever know.

If by some chance, "he" ever reads this book, we would like to say, 'Grazie per una serata generosa e memorabile'.

Chapter 38 - Reelin' In The Years
(Steely Dan)

Turning 90 was no big deal for me, as I had ignored time, enjoyed excellent health, but everyone else suggested I should celebrate the milestone. My overriding emotion was gratitude that I had sailed through two major operations.

The iconic arch logo, which depicts the Sydney Opera House or Qantas's flying kangaroo reminds me of my Australian jaunts and relatives. I flipped through a travel magazine and thought it would be an ideal time to go there for my 90th birthday, on 11th March 2017, and celebrate with my sisters. I would get rid of February, avoid the dull island winter and the dormancy of the garden.

Wendy had recently stayed at the over-the-top six-star Madinat Jumeirah in Dubai, with its spectacular view of the Burj Al Arab, a white glass sail of a building on the beach. She said it would be fun and company if she joined me in Dubai on the inward and outward legs of my celebratory trip.

She booked us a room at the Jumeirah Dar Al Masyaf within the Madinat Resort, where the architect sprinkled ornate villas amongst the canals leading to the sea. They reminded us of latter-day Arabian Nights.

We caught a ride on a magic carpet when upgraded to a magnificent villa suite, with water on three sides and luscious foliage which engulfed our private terrace. The only sound was the swish of open-air barges that glided by ferrying guests. The private reception lounge had a complimentary open bar, where, in late afternoons, cocktails and canapes were available. Sipping our champagne, we fought the temptation to skip dinner and stay there all evening.

Apart from the cultural differences, I was dazzled by the colours and scope of the hotels and their amenities. Even though it's evident someone has paid a ton of money for huge buildings and statues, lavish carpets, gold leaf and mosaics, I especially enjoyed the opulence of fabrics and decor of golds, reds, greens and turquoise.

It is so well planned as a city by the sea and is architecturally and artistically splendid. I would always recommend someone to go there once, and a three-day break will give you the flavour of the cuisine, the sandy beaches, and the high-end shopping malls.

If it were to your taste, your second visit could be a little longer for lounging and pampering in the spectacular, luxury spas. It's not a cheap place to stopover, but you will definitely remember it.

After Dubai, I met Jill, my niece, for an interesting few days catch up and sightseeing in the city of Perth. On my return there, I discovered a whole new side, panoramic mountains, sea views and shops!

I also caught up with my sister, Linda, who met me in bustling Melbourne. It was the first time in the city for both of us, and we found they were experienced and ready for visitors. The people

369

were helpful, happy and charming, and we thoroughly enjoyed exploring the river rides down to the coast.

The luxury of both stopovers was to have one-to-one experiences with my close relatives and not have to share them with our lovely gaggle.

After a few days, Linda and I checked out of the hotel and took a short walk where I caught my sandal on a raised flagstone and catapulted forward. As I fell, my shoulder and hip took the weight. I thought I had got away with the tumble but had forgotten how heavy heads were, as my cheek and the corner of my specs hit the pavement with a crunch, and the arm of my glasses snapped.

I walked back inside the hotel, in shock. The staff were attentive and sat me down with water, relieved they were not culpable as it happened on the street and not in their establishment.

My only concern was for Linda and me to reach the airport in time to catch the small weekly plane directly to her home in Port Macquarie.

When we landed, I was stone deaf. I flung myself into Darryl, my brother-in-law's, arms and sobbed. As he helped me into the car, Linda explained, 'She's had a fall and lost her hearing.'

At Linda's, I felt safe and at home. The following day, her family and neighbours gave me a warm welcome. They stared at the black-and-blue bruises which covered half my face, but two weeks later, the rainbow colouring had disappeared.

One of the most appealing things about Australia is its strange and colourful animals. Port Macquarie, a seaside town in New South Wales is famous for its year-round sunshine and is a bird lover's paradise. Surrounded by long sandy beaches and vivid-green rainforests, birds and wildlife flourish on this sub-tropical coast.

Darryl is as colourful as the birds he fussed over and cared for in his backyard. The cuddly, fuzzy-headed kookaburras perched along the patio rails and fed from his hands. Laughing kookaburras, the largest of the kingfishers, live in the eucalyptus forests and are known as "kings of the bush". It's mesmerising to watch them but hearing the kookaburras laugh is one of the most cheerful and comical sounds.

Sulphur-crested cockatoos and magpie larks hung around Darryl and Linda's garden for a snack. With a scoop of his plastic leaf collector, Darryl rescued any birds who miscalculated their dives across the pool and landed on the cool water. His favourite circus act was to throw titbits into the air to be caught by a mother as easy food for her young brood.

We embarked on a three-day coastal tour to relatives in Canberra, with Sophie, known as Bird, their comical pet parakeet. They chose motel rooms that allowed the car to be parked in front of the door so Linda could attend to the caged Bird.

My 90th birthday in Canberra arrived with sunshine. I didn't expect anything fussy or fancy, just a quiet and mellow lunch

371

with a handful of close family members in a favourite restaurant overlooking Lake Birley Griffin.

I was the last to arrive at the venue with its sweeping views of colourful boats and serene wooded scenery beyond. As I stood in the foyer, I heard everyone inside, shout, 'Surprise! Surprise!' A Chinese family got the 'surprise' as I had waved them in ahead of me.

I didn't realise this greeting was intended for me and hadn't noticed the coloured balloons and banners as I slipped along the side of the hall to Kaye and Jill, who waited for me at the far table.

When I reached my nieces, all the diners rose and sang 'Happy Birthday.' I turned around and gradually noticed over 40 familiar faces of relatives and friends whom I had met over my many visits.

It was heart-warming to watch my sister, Grace, with advanced dementia, singing along. With memory lapses, patients can sing songs from their past, note and word perfect. For once, I was speechless. What a coup and thank-you Jill and Kaye for organising a memorable birthday.

In Guernsey, noting the time difference, Wendy, John and Hilda slipped down to our local bay the evening before, and on the beach, to the amazement of onlookers, had created a huge heart out of pebbles with the number 90 inside. They had just enough time to photograph and email it to me before the rising tide swept over it.

When I returned home, that's when it hit me; I was now ancient. The fall in Perth had shaken my confidence. I'd taken for granted my robust constitution and hadn't recognised the fragility of age, so now when I move about quickly, I'm more aware and cautious.

Chapter 39 - Free Bird

(Lynryd Skynyrd)

We delude ourselves when we think our minds control our bodies. Without my permission, my ear holes have shrunk. Inexplicable incidences disrupt my days. For instance, Wendy rushed to help the bird she heard tweeting, trapped in my bedroom.

John assisted by moving furniture. 'Where can it be?' he asked. It wasn't a cavity wall, just stud with insulation and plastered so the bird couldn't be behind there.

'Tweet, tweet, tweet,' it continued in distress. Wendy considered calling the RSPCA or their builder to make a hole in the plasterboard to rescue the bird. Mystified, John patrolled the outside and roofline, which formed my room. The recent building project left no exterior holes, so how the bird found its way in was a mystery.

After our futile search, we reluctantly agreed to sacrifice the bird and hoped if it had got in, it might find a way out.

The tweeting persisted, and after late night tv viewing using my headphones, I switched my hearing aid to complete silence and prepared to sleep. I pulled my earplugs out again and listened – the bird should be dead by now, or at least asleep. It was agony waiting for the final cheep. At nearly midnight, I emailed Wendy upstairs. 'Still tweeting! It isn't a bird. Birds sleep!'

Wendy trotted downstairs, followed by the cat who inspected the bedroom and sauntered out. She said, 'If it's a bird, Silvie would be rushing all over the room investigating.'

'The aerial, perhaps?' I suggested.

'No, we have satellite dishes, Mum. By the way, where's your hearing aid?'

I opened my hand, 'Here.'

She placed her ear next to the bedside table, nearer the sound.

'What's that?' she said and pointed to a black matchbox-sized box which contained my spare hearing aids.

She pounced on it. The noise stopped. I had not removed the batteries, and when the earpieces touched each other, it caused an intermittent tweeting sound. The diligent cleaners must have disturbed the box while dusting.

Wendy sighed with relief and stared at this tiny gadget. 'What a good job we didn't knock the wall down!'

Hilda, John's mother, has been living with us for six years, and a daily routine has evolved. We make our breakfasts, and light lunches then gather formally around the dining table for a cooked evening meal and a glass of wine; it resembles fine-dining most evenings. We catch up and reminisce on what we've been up to during the day. In summer, if we expect a dazzling sunset, we stroll, with clinking glasses, to the top of the garden, and sit around the fire pit for a "happy hour" sherry or gin and tonic. We are truly blessed to enjoy all of this.

Hilda is tall, slim, and elegant, not a coiffured hair out of place. With her matching pearls or diamonds, she's always dressed ready for an invitation to afternoon tea in the Home Counties around London. A living tribute to her drive and rise from humble beginnings in the North of England countryside, to a luxurious life as a wife of a successful managing director.

Sometimes life takes an unfortunate turn. Recent tests confirmed the severity of Hilda's Alzheimer's. Her memory is patchy, and her conversation full of holes and pauses, but she invents her version of the past, with perfect pets and smart people. We try to accept this and over dinner, with raised eyebrows and smiles, are entertained by "her ideal life" and "exotic travels". We find it alarming how her short-term memory over the last few months has deteriorated at speed.

Wendy and John have accompanied her on lovely holidays and recently organised her 90th birthday party in the UK. Friends and relatives gathered for a weekend in the country. *South Lodge* is a magnificent, former family country house, the perfect place to relax, unwind and enjoy the finer things in life. She enjoyed it immensely, and family and friends could re-establish contact.

Hilda loves nothing more than a country walk, afternoon tea and dinners out. As the grand old ladies of the house, we make a point of dressing up and wearing our finery when we visit restaurants, and she is always first, ready and waiting. We've pencilled in this regime for the foreseeable future, but the worrying Coronavirus has put it on the backburner.

I'm thankful for each day and consciously try to enjoy any beauty around me. I've always thought the secret to a long, joyful life is staying active and having a positive attitude.

My children have kept me up to date with a changing world, and, like them, I have never stopped learning. Is it my fault that I raised three independent offspring, who instead of raising families, preferred to qualify in higher education?

After the enjoyment of collaborating with Wendy on this autobiography, we are developing a war-time romance fiction novel, The Golden Dog Tag, loosely based on that event that happened to my grandmother.

Chapter 40 - Life's Been Good
(Joe Walsh)

It's now March 2020, and at the point of publishing my book, I find myself plunged into a disaster, greater than the First World War, where our young men in the trenches were slaughtered. Greater than the Second World War where we looked to the heavens and prayed we wouldn't catch the bomb's full force and blasted into smithereens.

This time, just to be a human being is the target. The world is experiencing the Coronavirus pandemic where many people have died of complications resulting from a deadly lung infection.

The aged and physically weakest people are most at risk. At 93, I'm one of our society's oldest, and what is usually a privileged age to boast about, is now a cruel joke.

Just like my childhood during the war, food rationing and stockpiling are taking place. We eke out provisions to defer another foray to the supermarket. Guernsey has announced the first virus-related death which brings home the reality of the problem. We had hoped the contagion would have less impact on an island relatively detached, but through travellers, the virus has still invaded our shores.

Islanders are permitted two hours outdoors in which to do their shopping and exercise. What used to be a charming, friendly walk across our horseshoe bay, has now been tainted by social distancing, where initially dogs had to be on leads, unable to roam free to play or be patted. Walkers who stopped to talk and while away a few minutes, now hurriedly pass by self-consciously, adhering to the two-metre space regulation.

They cancelled large social events for the foreseeable future; pubs, clubs and some hotels have closed indefinitely. There are bound to be financial repercussions and mental problems stemming from weeks or months of continued isolation.

Hilda and I are fortunate, having large living areas with a spacious garden to walk about and tend. We are mindful of those who don't have such luxury as the freedom to grab fresh air and sit in the sunshine.

Again, as fate would decree, we are the lucky ones, as even in lock-down, or home isolating, through Wendy and John, we have security, constant company, moral support, so our daily lives are almost unchanged. We continue our fine dining each evening, and the blossoming garden continues to require attention.

Our only deprivation is not being able to see Steph and hug her through her ordeal while she guards Bryan, who is a possible candidate for infection. We long for this lengthy enforced separation to be over, and some normality returned.

In the UK, for two months they have grounded the airline Darius works for, and our island flights are for medical or essential passengers only. Anyone entering the island must go into immediate14 days self-isolation.

Communication with my family and friends is easier than in the 1940s blitz. We have Netflix, satellite television programmes, the internet, social media, and a home telephone. However, technology isn't a substitute for the personal touch or the vibrancy and fun of a social gathering with its repartee.

I had no idea that to aspire to play Bridge and deal a round of cards would mean so much. Authorities advised the elderly to stop socialising with people outside their immediate household, so we have postponed our kitchen Bridge.

While still reeling from this global horror, I heard my dear brother, Alan, had unexpectedly dropped dead of a heart attack, unrelated to this virus. He had collected his daily newspaper from the shop and on the way back, collapsed on the pathway.

He popped in and out of my life, but sadly this time, will not return. Even more poignant was that at 76, he was much younger -17 years my junior. Linda, in Australia, reminded me we are the only surviving siblings, she, the youngest, and me, the eldest.

During this time of uncertainty, I will trot out the mantras learned from the past, as I know they work. High morale and discipline are the most potent weapons in our armoury. We should "Keep Smiling and Carry On". The islanders are banding together, and it's heartening to see the towers of pebbles, some rainbow coloured, popping up all over our beach walls to show solidarity – "Guernsey Together".

Over the weeks, the lockdown news has been of continuing success and gradually lifted. I know if we do not become complacent, we can inch our way back.

On a recent glorious, calm, Sunday morning, Wendy and I paused at the top of the wooden steps which led to Port Soif beach, while Melba rushed on ahead around the sand dunes to greet the children who created sandcastles and frolicked on the water's edge.

I dropped my gaze from the blue, cloudless sky and followed the rim of the unspoilt crescent of shimmering sand. A dozen or so hardy swimmers up to their necks dipped up and down and cheerfully chatted, while they kept a perfect two-metre distance. The bobbing head symmetry reminded me of those early children's activity books, "connect the dots", and with an imaginary pencil, I mentally joined them.

It was a heartening moment to see such fun and frivolity, and my thoughts wandered fleetingly to those loved ones I have brought here, over my incredibly fortunate life, to enjoy this, "my horseshoe bay".

The End

Illustrations

My hardworking father, William (Billy) Briggs,
wearing WW2 army uniform in 1942.

My loving, strong, and determined mother, Betsy Rowlands.

The only official photograph we had taken. Manchester, circa 1932.
Grace (Age 3), Me (Age 6) & Annie (Nan) (Age 5).

I was born in the poor, dingy backstreets of Red Bank,
Manchester, 1927.

After our move to Forber Crescent, Manchester, 1936.
Me (Age 9), Nan (Age 7) and Grace (Age 5).

Fred and me on our Wedding Day in Gorton, Manchester,
26 April 1947.

Levenshulme Palais, Manchester, circa 1950.
Back: John (Jack) Stafford, Ken Thorpe, Fred Bone, Roy Robb,
Jean Thorpe.
Front: Grace Stafford, Me, Nan Robb, A Friend, Bet Manley.

Felicitous Rowlands (Granny) and me. Lyon Street,
Ardwick, Manchester, 1948.

Fred, a maths teacher at Gorton Mount Junior School,
Manchester, 1956.

Fred's mother, Lily Bone - Gorton, Manchester, 1947.

My sister, Linda, her friend, my brother, Alan, Mum, Dad
and Roy Robb.

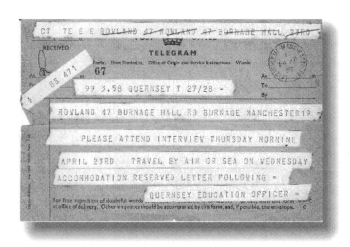

The unexpected telegram which changed our lives.
A request for Fred to attend a teaching post interview in
Guernsey, April 1959.

Fred holding Darius, Stephanie, Me and Wendy, Guernsey, 1962.

Wearing the traditional island sweater called a Guernsey.

Fred, Me, Wendy, Stephanie and Darius, Guernsey, 1965.

One of my favourite photographs. My father, Billy, with Fred
who often came straight to the beach from school.

My sisters, Linda, Nan and Grace

On Port Soif beach (Horseshoe Bay), Guernsey, 1964,
wearing my birthday present – a playsuit.

Fred on Port Soif beach (Horseshoe Bay), Guernsey, 1964.
Bizarrely, someone's cat and dog were already there.

My two long-standing best friends, Jill Vaudin and Betty Denoual.

Fred on saxophone in the Dave Lynsey Five, Guernsey, 1970s.

My attempt at grooming Polly of Minikena, our first standard poodle.

Golly (Goggles) our grey sub-standard, standard poodle, whom we adopted and loved.

Melba, our apricot/cream standard poodle.

Silvie our adventurous Burmese cat, walking on the
conservatory roof.

My son, Darius, and his new bride, Paula, at their wedding held at
Romsey Abbey, England, 28 September 1991.
L-R: Fred Rowland, Me, Darius Rowland, Paula Reeve,
Michael Reeve, Elizabeth Reeve.

Bryan Morris and my daughter, Stephanie, who gave us a
wonderful surprise with their wedding in Guernsey, 21 June 1993.

My eldest daughter, Wendy, and John Woodcock on their
wedding day in Guernsey, 29 April 1995.

Fred and me celebrating our Golden Wedding Anniversary,
in Guernsey, 26 April 1997.

Rowland and Hilda Woodcock, parents of my son-in-law, John,
who came to live with us in Guernsey in 2014.

A Port Soif Sunset – "Horseshoe Bay".

I hope this small choice of photographs has brought some of the characters alive for you.

If you think others would like to read my autobiography, it would be appreciated if you could spare a few moments to write a review on the website from where you bought it.

Don't miss out on further new book releases or newsletters, please leave a message via Wendy's website: https://www.wendyjwoodcock.com

Let the conversation begin by following or posting comments on any of these social media links. We'd love to hear from you:

https://www.facebook.com/WoodcockWj

https://twitter.com/WoodcockWj

https://www.linkedin.com/in/wendyjwoodcock

https://www.instagram.com/wendyjwoodcock

https://www.pinterest.com/WoodcockWj

Chapter Song Title References

Song Title   ## Artist

	Song Title	Artist
1	Living for the City	Stevie Wonder
2	In The Ghetto	Elvis Presley
3	We Are Family	Sister Sledge
4	School's Out	Alice Cooper
5	What A Wonderful World	Louis Armstrong
6	Work To Do	Average White Band
7	Call Me Irresponsible	Frank Sinatra
8	What Are You Doing The Rest Of Your Life?	Frank Sinatra
9	Spooky	Peter Grant
10	Electric Avenue	Eddie Grant
11	What's New Pussycat	Tom Jones
12	Saving Grace	Everlast
13	Daughters Of The Sea	Doobie Brothers
14	Boys Of Summer	Don Henley
15	You're My Best Friend	Queen
16	The Heat Is On	Glen Frey
17	Tragedy	Bee Gees
18	On The Beach	Chris Rea
19	Witchy Woman	Eagles
20	Highly Strung	Spandau Ballet
21	Who Says You Can't Go Home?	Bon Jovi/Jennifer Nettles

22	Lily Was Here	Candy Dulfer/Dave Stewart
23	Riders On The Storm	The Doors
24	Mambo Italiano	Rosemary Clooney
25	Come Fly With Me	Frank Sinatra
26	Another Day In Paradise	Phil Collins
27	Golden Years	David Bowie
28	I Will Always Love You	Whitney Houston
29	Bridge Over Troubled Water	Simon & Garfunkle
30	Back To Life	Soul II Soul
31	Brand New Day	Sting
32	Little Lies	Fleetwood Mac
33	Year Of The Cat	Al Stewart
34	I'm Still Standing	Elton John
35	Sentimental Journey	The Andrews Sisters
36	Changes	David Bowie
37	Who Are You?	The Who
38	Reelin' In The Years	Steely Dan
39	Free Bird	Lynyrd Skynyrd
40	Life's Been Good	Joe Walsh